The Acquisitions Budget

Forthcoming topics in *The Acquisitions Librarian* series:

Note: The order of the series is subject to change

The Acquisitions Budget

Edited by
Bill Katz

School of Information Science and Policy
State University of New York at Albany

The Haworth Press
New York • London

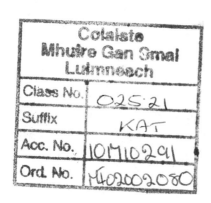
The Acquisitions Budget has also been published as *The Acquisitions Librarian*, Number 2 1989.

The Haworth Press, Inc., 10 Alice Street, Binghamton, NY 13904-1580
EUROSPAN/Haworth, 3 Henrietta Street, London WC2E 8LU England

Library of Congress Cataloging-in-Publication Data

The Acquisitions budget / edited by Bill Katz.
    p. cm.
"Has also been published as the Acquisitions librarian, number 2, 1989" – T.p. verso.
Includes bibliographies.
ISBN 0-86656-930-8
    1. Acquisitions (Libraries) 2. Library materials – Prices. 3. Library finance. 4. Budget. I. Katz, William A., 1924-
Z689.A273   1989   89-33790
                                    CIP

The Acquisitions Budget

CONTENTS

ABOUT THE EDITOR

Bill Katz, editor of *The Aquisitions Librarian*, is internationally known as one of the leading specialists in reference work today. In addition to the two-volume *Introduction to Reference Work*, he is the author of *Magazines for Libraries* and *Reference and on-line Services: A Handbook*. Past editor of *RQ*, the journal of the Reference and Adult Services Division of the American Library Association, Bill Katz currently edits a magazine column in *Library Journal*. He is also the editor of the Haworth journal, *The Reference Librarian*.

Introduction

Bill Katz

The purpose of this volume is to address the problem of the acquisitions budget. There are numerous paths, pitfalls, and solutions, but most of the papers share common points.

If there is one problem in acquisitions today it is a familiar one — money. But this time around the familiar has become downright sinister, literally threatening many collections. What's happening?

The shrinking dollar means a book in an English bookstore now sells for about what it did only a few years ago and, if it can be done, the same book may be purchased in America for at least one-quarter less. The price of British periodicals has reached for the sky, too.

Unfortunately, the falling dollar is not only equated in fewer pounds and more expensive materials in England. The same sad story is heard the world around. Possibly an exception: third world countries, but this is a condition hardly to be desired.

At the same time publishers, both here and abroad, are plagued by rising costs. Postal rates, wages, paper, binding, and even the cost of desktop publishing have gone up. Seeking to make a modest profit, or in the case of scholarly journals and books, just to break even, the publishers literally are forced to raise their prices. Librarians may and should complain. The publisher looks anguished and disappointed in the librarian's failure to appreciate the dollars and cents problem from the point of view of the seller.

There are, of course, unconscionable desires to not only make a modest return on investment, but to get downright rich by raising prices under the disguise of equally increased costs. An example is almost any journal publisher who seems to think librarians are a captive audience, who not only can stand an average of 10 to 20% (or even more) increase each year, but can willingly appreciate why

xiii

the same slim journal costs the library, say $75, while an individual may buy it for one half or less the price.

Equally unreasonable administrations, city councils and boards seem to think the way to govern without raising taxes is simply to cut budgets off all services. At the top of the list, too many times, is the intellectual underclass, i.e., the library. The squeeze between publishers, uncompromising rulers of library funding, and a faithful staff which still asks to be paid is to rework, rethink, and revise a requiem for the traditional acquisitions budget. Whatever is less reassuring is the economic resistance to a solution, particular or general.

Representatives of the besieged rear guard are here. Many have discovered intellectual and working methods of marking time. None are that sure that the future won't catch up with the best formed approaches to a shrinking budget. All agree that more money is needed. While compromise and review is an engaging, necessary notion to acquisitions, it is hardly a long term solution to what has become increased suffering.

So, let's applaud all for intellectual analysis, stopgap solutions, and even observations which point to ways out of the dollar slavery. And there are many practical, working, even decisive points of view represented in these outstanding papers.

Acquisitions Budgets:
Planning and Control for Success

Robert C. Miller

SUMMARY. Planning and controlling are the essence of sound management of acquisitions funding. The goals are obtaining the desired funding and using whatever is received in the most effective manner. Success requires varying parts of science and art, inspiration and perspiration, at all stages, whether it be establishing a structure, determining needs, making a presentation or controlling the final budget. There is no one right way at any stage. Much depends on the institutional environment. The successful manager, at any level, will be sensitive to that environment and flexible enough to work effectively within it.

The academic library has frequently been called a bottomless pit in financial terms. Nowhere is this more true than with the acquisitions budget. Yet the reality is that for any academic library the funding sources are not bottomless and the library needs to operate within very real, indeed sometimes even grossly inadequate, financial constraints. The challenge to the library manager is to get the highest possible level of funding, and then make the best possible use of those necessarily limited resources. It requires both advance planning and ongoing control. This needs to be done with the full realization that not everyone (if anyone) will ever be totally happy. On the other hand, if everyone is unhappy, either the level of funding is grossly inadequate or the allocations are misdone.

The players concerned with the acquisitions budget are many and varied and bring to any discussion widely divergent values and priorities. The university administration wants to spend as little as nec-

Robert C. Miller is Director of Libraries, Theodore M. Hesburgh Library, University of Notre Dame, Notre Dame, IN 46556.

essary to do as good a job as possible with the resources available. The faculty are usually concerned mainly with getting material they need, though at times more territorial interests surface and sometimes dominate: how much of the pie are we getting and how much are others getting. Bibliographers and other fund managers typically seek to maximize the size of the funds they control and the flexibility they have in the use of those funds. Acquisitions and fiscal personnel tend to be most interested in routinization and control of fund use. It is the library director who must ultimately pull all these differing viewpoints together into a budget and a relatively smoothly functioning operation that maximizes from an institutional perspective the resources available. With a view to broadening the understanding of all the players, the issues in this area will be considered here in four categories, budget structure, needs determination, budget presentation and budget management.

BUDGET STRUCTURE

Considerations of the nature and structure of the budget ultimately depend on the extent to which the budget is perceived as a mechanism to control expenditures, as an organizational expression of the library's resource access goals or some mix of the two. Any budget is essentially the financial institutionalization of priorities, expressed or assumed. The first step in effective use of funds — and that is one of the purposes of budgets — is to understand and articulate those priorities, lest by default unintended results occur; for example, research level material may be acquired at the expense of essential undergraduate level resources. Can, should, must new programs be supported, even in a limited fashion, at the expense of existing ones? Are some areas important for collecting, even if not currently in vogue locally?

On a very practical level, decisions need to begin with what is included within the acquisitions budget. Should it cover book and journal purchases only or include nonprint materials such as video, audio and machine readable resources as well? Since obtaining resources for teaching and research depend on resource sharing programs such as interlibrary loan and the Center for Research Libraries, should their costs also be financed by the acquisitions budget? Similarly, access to remote databases serves as a substitute for local resources, suggesting that these costs should appropriately be paid from the acquisitions budget. A convincing case can be made for including all of these costs within the acquisitions budget. Indeed, expenditures in the last three areas may obviate the need for certain local acquisition. On the other hand, it may be politically very difficult to obtain support for inclusion if it must be at the expense of current spending for print materials. Institutional regulations may largely determine these decisions for some libraries. Elsewhere, the answers may depend on considerations such as the overall institutional budgeting approach (line/incremental, zero-base, PPBS), current adequacy or future funding prospects for different budget categories, the type and degree of control available in these other budgets, the desirability of making certain types of expenditures more or less visible to the administration and the university community and the flexibility to accommodate future change.

As for the overall structure of the budget, there are two basic approaches: by academic unit or by type of material (books, journals, microforms, a-v etc.). The approach chosen, if not institutionally mandated, can assist the library in achieving its broad goals. Is the focus to be on supporting academic units, or on overall resource development? In the former case, budgeting by academic department makes great sense, as it tends to heighten faculty interest and involvement in the development of collections and gives them a greater stake in the overall budget. However, that approach can also lead to serious distortions if other goals have higher priority for the library. For example, it makes much more problematic successful operation of a broad approval program. A separate budget line can greatly assist in this. Similarly, if continuity of serial collections is a high priority, a separate, non-allocated serials budget can help reduce the tendency of this area to become a political football. Again the task of the budgeter is a balancing act. There are or should be both discipline specific goals—strengthen holdings of pre-1800 French poetry—and broader resource goals that overlap needs of individual academic units—improve library coverage of non-American research level monographs. At the same time one must recognize that there are very real differences among disciplines in the types of resources most needed. The conventional wisdom is that the sciences require journals and the humanities monographic literature. This may be true in some settings, but that will depend very much on local circumstances, including the state of both monographic and serial collections and the type of research currently underway. Sometimes a change in structure can assist in the implementation of a shift in priorities, as was the case with one institution where the library sought to improve support for the teaching program by insuring the acquisition of a broad base of current English language monographs. This would have been difficult and time consuming to introduce in an environment where most funds were tightly controlled by individual academic units. By changing to a type of materials structure with a separate line item for approval programs this change was able to be accomplished relatively painlessly.

The sources of acquisitions funding can play a critical role in the library's budget structure. For many libraries, particularly publicly supported ones, institutionally allocated funds account for the great preponderance of monies. In other cases, grants and endowment income, both general and subject restricted, may provide a large proportion of acquisitions funding. This creates a whole new set of issues, the most important of which is the extent to which the institution takes these other sources into account in local budgeting. There are also issues within the library. Should ongoing commitments be made on the basis of soft money? This can be very dangerous since the institution may be unable to support the commitments when the soft money is exhausted. To what extent does such "outside" funding replace or supplement institutional funds?

An important distinction here is between restricted and unrestricted funds. Special problems exist in the case of restricted endowments. How can they best be utilized to meet overall institutional and library objectives? Several alternatives are possible. If, for example, endowment income becomes available for French literature, can/should it be used to underwrite existing expenditure levels so that institutional funds can be freed up for more "important" uses? Should the total available new money be put to increasing the level of purchase for French literature? Would some mix be appropriate or even possible? Answers appropriate to the case of French literature might be very different for an endowment for

Transylvanian history. Decisions can be made only after careful consideration of donor desires (and presence), the amount involved, the subject and its place at the institution, the state and current collecting activity in the area and the political power of faculty covered by the endowment. Important as it is, restricted funding can easily skew acquisitions expenditures, sometimes without intention.

Even relatively dependable endowment income is a risky source of funding for commitments such as serials, since historically the increases in income have not kept pace with rises in prices. Thus, endowments that thirty years ago adequately supported 100 specific subscriptions today may well be unable to support half that number. Institutional funds are left holding the bag, requiring the hard choice between cancelling subscriptions or cutting back in other areas.

In some institutions, the budget process is such that the library receives specific allocations for each line of the budget, and the process is largely completed. In others a total dollar amount is allocated for acquisitions and the division of those funds is a further step of the process, but completely within the library. This is, of course, a simplification, for most budget processes of either type involve a significant number of "what if" iterations. In most cases, what is involved is an overall statement of needs, followed by a process of allocating those funds likely to be received.

A few comments are in order here on formula budgeting. This can exist at two levels: to determine the overall budget, or to distribute funds among academic units. The former is usually mandated by legislative bodies that need to provide funding for a number of competing institutions. There are two broad problems with this approach. The formulas themselves, no matter how complicated, tend to be necessarily arbitrary and are unable to take into account the inevitable institutional and programmatic differences. Commonly, more emphasis is placed on relatively simple quantitative institutional data such as enrollment, numbers of faculty and courses, rather than on real library cost factors such as the state of the collection, materials cost differentials and relative intensity of library use. In addition, even if one were to grant that this approach had some overall validity, unfortunately full funding as called for by the formula is frequently not provided, and the resulting equally proportional underfunding of all institutions across the board is not an effective way to use funds. Realistically, all need is not really equal: the needs of traditionally underfunded institutions is usually far more pressing than the established, well funded ones – there really are such places. These two circumstances tend to make the approach merely bureaucratic papershuffling.

On the institutional level, there have been many attempts to allocate available funding by a more or less complicated formula, involving factors such as enrollment by level or course, number of faculty, costs of material, circulation levels, research activity (Sellen). Those who have utilized this approach realize that formulas can be grossly misleading. More significantly, perhaps, it can be manipulated to produce whatever results are desired. There are environments where this approach is politically expedient, but all involved must be aware of these shortcomings. In addition, formulas can be useful to test various allocation alternatives, but only when they are recognized for what they are, aids not answers.

ESTABLISHING NEED

Need is, or should be, the foundation of any budget process. Perhaps the most serious shortcoming of the formula approach is its simplistic approach to this. Establishing the needs is less easy than it might appear. How can one judge whether undergraduate English courses are well supported? Is the full scope of local faculty research really known to the library, and especially to those in the library attempting to build the case for a budget? The subjective element in evaluating needs is very great and will always reflect to some degree both the proclivities of the budgeter and a necessarily limited knowledge base.

The determination and statement of needs is a complex process and at its core requires prioritization. In most but not all cases the highest priority is the maintenance of current effort, in other words, how much will be needed next year to do just what was done this year. Two factors are involved in this determination, inflation and changes in publishing. For the former, in most cases libraries will use gross figures, obtained from monographic and serial vendors and various published sources such as *Library Journal, Publishers'*

Weekly and *Library Resources and Technical Services*. Yet great care needs to be exercised in utilizing such data, to be sure that the local mix of purchases is reflected in terms of monographic and serial acquisitions, foreign and domestic publications, trade and scholarly monographs, print and nonprint media. It is especially important to avoid the tendency to err on the high side, for that can seriously affect long-term credibility. The other element — publishing trends — is far more uncertain and depends ultimately on vendor projections, since they are almost always in a far better position to stay close to publishers.

Once maintenance of effort is provided for, the next level of need is continued growth of support for existing programs, in terms of adding new journal subscriptions, correcting shortcomings in current monographic acquisitions, the addition of new electronic media and retrospective buying to fill monographic and serial gaps. These all need to be considered, costed and requested.

Finally, there are programmatic changes. If a new degree program is being added, funds for both current collecting needs and required or desirable retrospective collection building must be accounted for. In fact, such needs are frequently ignored, with the result that support for new programs is at the expense of existing programs. Nonetheless, the case must be made. Similarly, changes in faculty through replacement or addition of positions can have major impact on the need for resources. For example, replacing a specialist on the French Revolution with one focusing on twentieth century French social history can bring many new demands and result in a major shift in library collecting.

Yet considering these three factors, maintenance, growth and new programs is not a simple one, two, three process. Honest approximations (guesses?) of costs should be obtained to the extent possible. Moreover, realism dictates that not all "needs" should be presented. Asking for too much may be as counterproductive as asking for too little is shortsighted. To help ensure a reasonable balance of satisfaction among the library's diverse clientele, the final realities of the budget will inevitably require compromises both within the library and with budget officials. Those compromises will be governed by both the existing collection situation and the political forces currently at work.

BUDGET PRESENTATION

If the determination of needs is complex and fraught with uncertainties, that is even more true of the budget process itself, which is always a highly personal and political one. Arguments that are persuasive in one institutional setting may be meaningless or even counterproductive in another. Hidden agendas are frequently involved, regardless of the degree of bureaucratization and paperwork involved. Indeed these can be good covers for highly personal and subjective processes. The successful library manager will be one who understands the processes and the personalities of the actors involved.

Presentation is usually a key element of success. The best methods for presenting needs will vary considerably from institution to institution, and indeed from year to year. In some instances, detailed documentation, sometimes with appropriate graphics and near professional presentation is essential. In others, such an effort in terms of the actual presentation would be a waste of time. Yet the preparation is essential, even if not immediately used, for there is nothing more damaging to the success of a budget session, however informal, than the inability to answer reasonable questions. Shooting from the hip in this environment can be disastrous, both short-term and longer-term, for credibility can easily be lost.

It is extremely important that the library manager be sensitive to the process and participate effectively in it. Few things are ultimately more important to the success of the library — and the individual. This will require knowing those involved in the process and the nature of their involvement. Are there committees utilized? Are they meaningful, or largely for show? What are the backgrounds, biases of the members? Are their feelings about the library, its services, staff, manager known? Have they a track record with regard to library support generally or within the budget process? What other units have been particularly successful in the budget process in the past and why?

What kinds of questions are likely to be raised and how can they be handled in an effective manner? The regularly compiled annual report type information? The costs of specific operations? The use of various materials by different segments of the population? The cost and potential use of desired new acquisitions programs?

It is also important to develop a sense of institutional priorities, even the unarticulated ones, and to develop ways to relate library needs to them. To do this, the library manager must get to know the people personally and professionally and follow the institution in many different ways.

In a larger sense, the real job of selling the library in the budget process is one of selling the library to the university, administration, faculty and students generally. A library held in little or low esteem is unlikely to get support at budget time. This selling must be a year around task. Public relations is very important. The public must know about the library and its needs, but PR can never substitute for the product. Quality service is the key to a positive image of the library.

MANAGING THE BUDGET

Once an overall budget is finalized, the challenge to the manager is twofold: to make the final allocations to lines and units, if, as is hopefully the case, those allocations are not part of the official budget, and to stay within the overall budget throughout the year. In setting the final unit allocations, two observations are in order. First, fairness to individual units is a phrase that is sometimes used here. It should not be, for "service to both present and future generations," not fairness—whatever that means in this context—is the goal of library collection building, and hence budgeting (Osburn 142). Secondly, to offset that theory to some extent, it is worth noting that there are seldom major shifts in allocation patterns (Cline and Sinnott 79). At most there are modest changes and movements, this probably to start a change process without undue upset.

To aid in the actual goal of the budget, it is critical to maximize the use of available dollars. Concern with vendor discounts is an important element of this, while at the same time balancing discount against service. Libraries doing a significant volume of foreign purchases need to recognize the real cost advantage in ordering from country of origin. Those with especially large business in individual countries should consider the possible advantage of buying foreign currencies. While this may not actually save money, it does provide a means of knowing how much purchasing can be done, regardless of currently fluctuations.

A key question in budgetary control is the role of individual fund managers, whether these be within the library or in some cases in the teaching faculty. The flexibility they have in utilizing their funds—viz. monographs versus serials—can have major impact on both overall budget control and consistent development of the collections.

A critical element in successful budget control, with or without individual fund managers, is the development of techniques for accurately monitoring and reporting the state of the budget both overall and by individual fund. An especially difficult aspect of this is getting a handle on what is "in the pipeline," where orders have been submitted but not yet fully processed. Continuation orders, especially for foreign publications, are another very difficult area as both cost and publication cycle are frequently totally unpredictable. The overall control becomes especially critical late in the fiscal year when relatively small unexpected expenditures can be disastrous. It is also important to be able to act on the results of that monitoring, as for example, requiring the maintenance of decreasing minimum balances in individual funds during the year. This prevents individual selectors from making their case for increases by using up all their funds early in the fiscal year. However, some tightly controlled flexibility is essential to enable the selector and/or the library to deal effectively with special opportunities that might arise. In the past much time and paper shuffling was required to obtain the kinds of controls necessary. Fortunately the advent of automated acquisitions systems, if carefully specified, should make this task far easier and less painful for all involved.

In smaller organizations the desired fiscal control can be reasonably easily maintained. However, where many individuals and funds are involved, the situation is far more difficult, and the organization must be prepared to deal with potential deficits. Depending on circumstances, a number of specific actions are possible. These include the use of discretionary funds to cover deficits; stopping or suspending activities, whether these be binding or individual or blanket orders; allowing activity to continue but carrying forward to the next fiscal year invoices for the deficit activity; or paying and carrying forward the deficits involved. Each of these actions essentially merely carried the problems into the next year and compounds any inadequacies in that year's budget. In some instances in academic institutions, deficits may be covered and cleared out by the institution, though this can never be presumed, especially more than once. Thus it is far preferable to plan and control expenditures throughout the year than to deal later with the uncertainties and perhaps the disasters.

CONCLUSION

Planning and controlling are the essence of sound management of acquisitions budgets. The goals are obtaining the desired funding and using whatever is received in the most effective manner. Success requires science and art, in varying parts, and inspiration and perspiration, at all stages, whether it be establishing a structure, determining needs, making a presentation or controlling the final budget. There is no one right way at any stage. Much depends on the institutional environment. The successful manager, at any level, will be sensitive to that environment and flexible enough to work effectively within it.

REFERENCES

Cline, Hugh F. and Loraine T. Sinnott, *Building Library Collections: Policies and Practices in Academic Libraries*, Lexington Books, 1981.

Osburn, Charles B., *Academic Research and Library Resources*, Greenwood Press, 1979.

Sellen, Mary, "Book Budget Formula Allocations: a Review Essay," *Collection Management*, 9(4) Winter, 1987, 13-24.

Vasi, John, "How Academic Library Budgets are Really Determined," ACRL Third National Conference, 1984, *Proceedings*, 343-345.

Werking, Richard Hume, "Allocating the Academic Library's Book Budget: Historical Perspectives and Current Reflections," *Journal of Academic Librarianship*, 14(3) July, 1988, 140-144.

Managing the Reduced Purchasing Power of the Acquisitions Budget

Sharon Bonk
Heather Miller

SUMMARY. The recent rapid escalation of journal prices and the decline in purchasing power of the acquisitions dollar have required academic librarians to put into practice drastic short term measures to balance budgets and pay invoices. One library's experience is cited to give examples of short term measures which can be put into effect quickly to handle shortfalls or overencumbrances. Budget balancing reductions must be monitored and integrated into long term financial plans and revised collection development strategies. The acquisitions librarian must be prepared to make operational modifications and develop the ability to forecast the effects of external and internal changes on the library's resources budget and its services while the collection development librarian must change the criteria and course of acquisitions strategy.

Managing a library's materials budget requires much planning and forward thinking, but it is, in essence, a reactive process. Most acquisitions budget managers come to realize that despite the use of past and current year's cost information and publication rates with a projection of inflation or the rise in the Consumer Price Index, the actual expenditure of funds during a specific fiscal year is very reactive to external forces.

The parent institution may have a financial setback and cut library funds at the beginning of a fiscal year, or, worse yet, midway through the year. A number of factors in the book trade such as

---

Sharon Bonk is Assistant Director for Technical Services and Heather Miller is Head, Acquisitions Department, University Libraries, University at Albany, State University of New York, Albany, NY 12222.

13

increased production by publishers or changes in discounting arrangements between publishers and specific booksellers may cause the price of library materials to rise. Forces in the national and world economy may also affect the acquisitions budget. Currency fluctuations may create sudden unanticipated increases in the price of library materials. A decrease in the value of institutional investments or endowments can also decrease library acquisitions funds. Separately, or in combination, external factors regularly affect the expenditure plans for the acquisitions budget.

A dramatic and recent example of this is the escalation of foreign journal prices in combination with a decline in the value of the dollar on international currency markets. These two separate yet related phenomena hit academic and special libraries during 1987. Most acquisitions librarians who have been involved in purchasing foreign publications over the last six to seven years are aware that the *rise* in the value of the dollar was financially advantageous to libraries for several years in the early eighties. They are now aware that the strength of the dollar contributed to the increased dollar prices of foreign journals.[1,2] They also knew then that any fall in the value of the dollar would have an adverse effect on the library's acquisitions budget. They assumed or hoped that there would be ample warning to modify expenditure plans as the dollar fell in value.

Publishers, especially foreign scientific and technical publishers, did more than hope. They built in protection against the potential fall of the dollar by establishing dollar prices at higher than current market exchange rates.[3,4] Thus, the prices of foreign publications rose steadily, even while the dollar was strong. When the dollar began its dramatic drop in value in 1986, it increased the cost of foreign subscriptions. This has resulted in drastic short term measures being taken by libraries to balance current year (1987/88) budgets.

A review of the literature indicates little recorded awareness on the part of acquisitions librarians and collection development officers for the need to plan for a reversal in journal expenditures or to plan contingency budgets. The now famous article by Hamaker and

Astle alerted librarians that there was much more involved in journal pricing by publishers than the costs of paper, printing and postage.

The 1985 College of Charleston Acquisitions Conference dealt with the fiscal realities acquisitions librarians face, including discussions of projecting materials budgets, fiscal aspects of bookselling, vendor-publisher price negotiations, and publishers' journal pricing policies. Bonk outlined options for balancing a budget when major changes in funding or prices occur within a fiscal year.[5] The 1987 College of Charleston Acquisitions Conference continued explorations into the effects of net pricing, exchange rates, publishers' pricing policies, and publisher discounts and vendor prices.[6]

A new journal, *The Bottom Line: A Financial Magazine for Librarians*, appeared in 1986. The existence of the journal is a recognition of the eroding fiscal bases of many libraries and the myriad of complex financial decisions required of library managers. Little attention has been given in its pages to the management of acquisitions budgets although articles have been published on ways to save or stretch acquisitions dollars.[7] Budget reduction within a public library system demonstrated the effects of external economic events on library budgets.[8]

The Hamaker and Astle article spawned many other studies and caused librarians to confront publishers.[9-12] Librarians also began a publicity campaign that resulted in national publications recognizing the problem.[13-16]

It appears, however, that acquisitions and collection development librarians did not move into a defensive budget position despite their increasing awareness of the continual escalation in prices of a major portion of their acquisitions. Instead, they were caught short in 1987 when renewals for 1988 reflected both the publishers' price increases and the decreasing value of the dollar. The publications of many libraries record the recognition of the problem and the few immediate alternatives librarians have for staying within budgets.[17-20] Unfortunately, problem recognition does not always mean problem resolution, and numerous libraries are left to cope with the problem in their own context.

THE IMMEDIATE PROBLEM

The University at Albany Library is not a newcomer to coping with budgetary shortfalls nor has it been without experience in collecting and analyzing financial data and making budget predictions from it. Nevertheless, this library too has found this year's money disappearing at an accelerated rate. This is not to say that it was a total surprise. At its commencement, the current fiscal year was expected to be a difficult one and as a consequence discretionary allocations were reduced by 25% from the year before.

A library can be poised to act, but action cannot be taken until evidence accumulates that belies, corroborates or goes beyond original projections. In the business of library acquisitions no amount of data analysis can do more than produce "ball park" estimates of future costs because there are too many unknowns such as the actual cost of renewals and the actual numbers and cost of items supplied by approval plans. Not until invoices arrive does one know the truth and then there is little to be done but pay the bills and put the brakes on. These brakes will be slow to take effect because of the length of time it can take to put changes into effect and because of the additional time for these changes to have discernible results. Knowing all this, this library has, nevertheless, been ready since the start of the current fiscal year to take action should on-going data analysis so indicate.

This library's experience with fiscal data collection and analysis goes back a number of years. Subject based fund codes have been used for over twenty years and an automated fund accounting system since 1983. The original automated system, Sperry's report writer MAPPER, was capable of manipulating data in order to produce reports of expenditures by vendor as well as by material type, permitting considerable flexibility in data manipulation. In 1986 this system was replaced by the Geac Automated Acquisitions system. The previous system of subject based fund codes was retained, but reformulated to make the numbers compatible with the new system. Numeric material type codes were replaced by alphabetic order types in the new system. Gained was more detailed analysis of purchases by subject as well as on-line availability of data on each fund's and the total budget's expenditures and balances at any time. Numerous off-line reports are analyzed by the head of collection development and used to produce a monthly balance for a variety of categories. When necessary, such as when nearing the end of a fiscal year, these reports are produced more frequently. Thus it has been possible to provide monthly or on-demand the amount of funds expended in program areas across all types of materials.

The availability of such data and experience in using it have been useful in previous crises. For example, during the 1984/85 fiscal year, a budget deficit was expected from the first. This was determined by analysis of data on expenditures during the previous fiscal year and such published data as figures on the numbers of books expected to be published, inflation rates, and foreign buying power. At the beginning of the 1984/85 fiscal year, periodical and standing order cancellation projects were in place with an aim of a 5% reduction in expenditures for each group. At the same time, more rigorous scrutiny of approval books was enforced and discretionary funds were drastically reduced. Nevertheless, by mid-year the two major approval plans were running ahead of estimates with a projected total overrun of nearly 25% of allocation. Both plans were changed from books to forms entirely during the fall, a change that the vendors were able to put into effect quickly. Book shipments did not resume until the next fiscal year. This permitted a reduction in expenditures sufficient to avoid extensive cost overruns during that fiscal year, albeit with significant implications for the collection as well as for internal processing procedures.

Because this library purchases a significant amount of foreign materials, the acquisitions staff long ago began watching the condition of the dollar. In June 1985, when the dollar was strong, and after extensive study, Oxford and Pergamon publications were moved from the North American to the British approval plan. In January 1987, a study of the West German mark including a comparison of rates published in the *Wall Street Journal* with those used by this library's primary supplier of German material showed that between June 13, 1985 and January 27, 1987 the dollar had lost 68% of its buying power against the mark.

Because published data are not always pertinent to specific situations, this library continues to do its own calculations. This kind of constant examination of data, regular budget review and expenditure prediction have proven increasingly useful as the fiscal situation of this library, along with that of others, continues to decline. It has been necessary to be particularly alert during the present fiscal year as all indicators pointed to increasing serial costs coupled with a continually weakening dollar. Moreover, the acquisitions budget increased only 6% over that of the previous year, clearly insufficient even to maintain the status quo.

Thus, the opening of the current fiscal year was not accompanied by a flurry of discretionary ordering, even though a sum had been allocated for this purpose. Orders were placed cautiously and on a monthly basis. At the end of each month, off-line reports were produced by the system and carefully analyzed by the head of collection development. At the end of the first quarter it was clear that expenditures prorated on a monthly basis were ahead of allocations. Approval expenditures were identified then as an area to cause great difficulty, with other areas highlighted to be watched in future months. By the end of the second quarter all but 26% of the acquisitions budget had been spent whereas at the same time during the previous year, 47% remained. At this point periodicals also appeared to present a great threat.

Although selections from the two major approval plans had been reduced, further action was taken. The number of publishers treated by both plans was reduced significantly. One small foreign plan was cancelled. Periodical and standing order cancellation projects were begun. All renewal invoices showing price increases exceeding 25% of the previous charge were reviewed. Bibliographer review of such titles was actively sought, resulting in a number of cancellations. Discretionary orders that were billed at prices more than $20.00 beyond our estimated price were also reviewed by bibliographers, resulting in some returns. At the end of the third quarter the library's periodicals vendor was asked to cease multiple year renewals with the expectation that this would save over $65,000 in 1988/89 and roughly $21,000 the following year. Eventually, such savings will cease, of course, as previously paid multiple year subscriptions expire. Nevertheless, analyses of data from the vendor shows a decreasing advantage to multiple year renewals and it is felt that the flexibility to be gained from single year renewals more than outweighs the eventual slightly increased cost.

During the third quarter a detailed analysis was made of the budget with projections for both the current and next fiscal years. Problem categories (approvals, periodicals and standing orders) were discussed. Current and future options were put forth and evaluated. In sum, it was seen that cost cutting measures in place at that time were not having sufficient effect. Options varied from outright cancellation of major approval plans to holding invoices in various categories. It was decided to further restrict the major approval plans, especially the British plan because data indicated a 24% increase in the price of British imprints received in the previous 6 months.

This means that despite constant detailed analysis of data and continuous attempts to reposition strategies during the current fiscal year and despite considerable experience in doing so, this library could not claim complete success in avoiding the budget crunch threatening it and many other academic libraries. Some benefit was felt but, at the end of the fiscal year, invoices remained on hand ready to take the first bite of over 8% from next year's allocation.

Approaches to the immediate problem in this library may have not been entirely successful, but they have certainly decreased the amount of overexpenditure, set a course for further reduction and provided considerable data to work with. The situation would be considerably worse had the course outlined here not been followed. These short term strategies will continue while longer term strategies are developed. These include more cancellations and closer scrutiny and evaluation of serial commitments as well as reliance on new technologies and increased sharing of resources.

A major periodical review program was initiated in September 1987 when teaching faculty were sent a memo explaining the need for reducing costs, a strategy for evaluating individual titles and a plea for their cooperation in the project. Significant restrictions of approval plans continue including a complete rewriting of at least one profile. Discretionary purchasing will remain tightly controlled.

Such restrictions can permit a library to live within a limited budget, but simply doing less of what has been done means that quality collection building will fall victim to a balanced budget. In this library there is a recognition that long term, more creative ways must be found to obtain needed information for the collection while balancing the budget. Old patterns are difficult to change, and little progress can be claimed here yet.

FUTURE DIRECTIONS

It is clear that the collection development strategies and selection/ retention criteria that were developed when the national economy and higher education were in a growth cycle are unlikely to remain unchanged. Librarians must develop flexible strategies and the regiment of continually reviewing and revising them if they are to manage acquisitions budgets as well as some publishers seem to manage theirs. Librarians, being buyers rather than sellers, having limited or diminishing budgets, and having sharing rather than market share as a motivation, are limited in their capacity to contend with commercial firms. Nevertheless, librarians can recognize the fact that such results are not due to happenstance and can emulate the kind of forward thinking and firmness that produces profitable results. Although the attempt to gain additional funds cannot be abandoned, it must be recognized that it is unlikely for a parent institution to be able to raise its library's acquisitions budget base significantly upward.

What choices do those responsible for collection development have?

SHORT TERM ACTIONS

Revised Selection Criteria

Restricted purchasing and journal and serials cancellation projects may help reduce spending, but they cannot become the basis of collection development. Renewals, new titles, and cancellations should be based on revised criteria for selection and retention for each discipline or campus program. These criteria should not focus solely on cost but on the value of that title to collection priorities and anticipated or demonstrated use, and availability through other means.

Librarians must be willing to say that the information contained in a specific serial is or is not worth the price and must be sufficiently knowledgeable about the subject, the library's clientele, campus priorities, and alternative means of obtaining the information not purchased to defend both positive and negative decisions.

Selectors may say that this is already the case. Selections and cancellations are based on specific criteria. If that is the case, why are librarians finding it so difficult to rank order the subscriptions and make cancellations? It may be because the selection criteria are few and equally weighted. It may be because selection has been left to the faculty with the librarian managing the funds. It may also be because librarians have been too easily swayed by faculty, unwilling to displease them and unsure of their own judgments. It is also due to selection based on an acquisitions budget that formerly kept pace with publishing. Twigging has created many speciality journals in a number of disciplines especially in the sciences. This increase in the number of publications and concomitant price increases have changed purchasing power before mind set or selection power has been changed.

Houbeck has pointed out that naivete and inattentiveness on the part of librarians has resulted in purchasing behavior that favors the mainstream publishers and publications, considers quality the only criterion, and lacks effective monitoring of both prices and publisher market share strategies.[21] As a result, librarians have subverted a prime collection development goal, that of building a quality collection, into stretching the dollars to purchase as many publications as possible.

Improved Analytical Tools

Monitoring tools are needed to compare local costs with national and international trends in average cost by discipline, in price per page, and price increases by publisher. The Library Materials Price Index Committee of the Resources and Technical Services Division of the American Library Association has been producing historic indexes for an increasing number of types of publications. The committee has been asked to develop price forecasting tools as well. At the July 1988 annual meeting of the American Library Association, a program was given on how to use the existing monitoring tools. More education of this nature is necessary to give librarians insight, skills, and facts for more informed local decision making and more credibility when discussing budgets with faculty or administration.

Librarians should continue to develop local indexes to compare local conditions with national and international trends. Only local data collection and analysis is sufficiently relevant to the campus to become the basis for collection management decisions.

Selection decisions for journals and continuations should be recorded in some standard and retrievable way so that future actions regarding the title may be taken with more information at hand. For example at the point of selection the following should be indicated: program/courses/research being supported; the faculty member requesting the title; a retention plan; a review schedule; and a ranking of importance to the faculty or collection. The ranking should be based on specific criteria. In his study of price differentials and perceived value of journals, Houbeck used local use, citation frequency, inclusion in an evaluative bibliography, and the number of holding libraries in OCLC as value indicators.[22] These are not necessarily the same value indicators that may apply to each discipline on a specific campus, but they indicate the wide variety of information that can contribute toward selection/retention decisions.

At a future date, the current conditions can be compared with those at the time of selection. A new ranking can be assigned if there have been significant changes in any of the criteria. A new review date should be established. Automated acquisitions systems may allow for the storage of this data along with the receiving and financial data. Certainly, inexpensive database management systems provide the indexing and retrieval capabilities to set up a monitoring system.

Faculty Alliances

Informed faculty are perhaps the most important and useful allies in collection development and management. This is not only as a defense strategy to keep them from questioning the effectiveness and ability of the collection development staff or the library administration but also as an offense. Faculty are not only the consumers or readers of the publications. They are the producers as well. They write the monographs and the articles that the librarians purchase. They form the editorial boards and the referees. They are the conduits for the materials that are eventually published and find their way to library shelves. Local faculty are approachable about the specific situations and constraints a library faces. The abstract collective and hallowed "Faculty" are not. It is the latter that librarians often quote as uncompromising and uninformed — "The Faculty don't . . . , won't . . . "

Clearly, building faculty alliances is not a simple matter. It is a long process requiring frequent meaningful contact in which both parties share information about information. It is not sufficient to make infrequent presentations and then expect cooperation and understanding when faculty are "suddenly" confronted by the effects of reduced purchasing power.

LONG TERM STRATEGIES

Resource Sharing

Faculty and university administrators informed about the publishing marketplace should also be informed about the realities of the resource sharing that libraries are involved in or will be required to do as they purchase fewer materials. True reliance on resource sharing and cooperative collection development requires an understanding of methods, time requirements and costs of providing alternatives to purchasing books and serials.

It also requires a commitment to the concept not only by selectors and faculty but also by library staff outside of collection development and acquisitions. This means that interlibrary borrowing and lending has to have a high priority and efficient mechanisms to deliver materials as soon as possible — not in as long as it takes. It may require the use of direct point to point borrowing rather than hierarchical referral systems. It will require the use of more efficient delivery systems, including express courier service and telefacsimile. It will require reciprocal direct access to collections. Many of these operational areas of responsibility will need to be in the purview of collection development if libraries intend to rely on other collections for a growing number of materials.

Richard Dougherty considers the reliance on interlending as a substitute for acquisition of curricular support materials a misapplication of the concept of resource sharing for research libraries.[23] The dramatic increase in volume of interlibrary lending that resulted from national and international online databases has threatened many research libraries' ability to provide the level of service associated with the concept of resource sharing.

However, Dougherty and most librarians realize that self-sufficiency is not possible for most libraries, and interlending among libraries is unlikely to decrease. Thus, careful analysis of the dynamics of a library's current borrowing and loaning activity must be undertaken to determine what is borrowed for whom and from whom — and with what success. For "commonly" held materials in support of student assignments, performance indicators of speed, reliability, and cost per transaction should be the measure of effective support. Volume and nature of borrowing transactions by subject area should be routinely reported to collection development staff for analysis and appropriate action. For research materials, availability to the borrowing institution, number of filled requests, and speed should be the prime factors, not cost per transaction.

Costs of borrowing a publication will always be less than the cost of purchase and processing. However, the reciprocity of the interlending and resource sharing concepts makes the costs of lending also part of the cost of borrowing. In a theoretical world both borrowing and lending would be equal. However, this is rarely the case. Collection strengths, efficiency of service, complete holdings available in a number of bibliographic sources, lending fees or lack thereof, and geographical location all contribute to making some libraries net-lenders. If the difference between loaning and borrowing activity is significant, the cost of the resource sharing has become unbalanced. In these cases, resource sharing agreements need to be developed among several key institutions identified through an analysis of loaning and borrowing activity. These would replace the open-market, unpredictable and quite often unaffordable situation of being a net-lender. Resource sharing agreements might provide subsidies for institutions that by collection size or location will always be net-lenders within a specific group of libraries.

Reduced circumstances may mean maintenance of a well used

core collection (with usage documented) supplemented by online, CDROM, document delivery, and interlending agreements. In this environment, continually evaluated, updated, detailed collection development policies stating what is and is not collected will be critical. Success will also depend on communication between subject specialists in different libraries as well as institutional support of the concept of cooperative collecting. Also essential will be rapid means of communication between cooperating libraries including electronic mail and telefacsimile. An online or CDROM union catalog of libraries in a resource sharing partnership serves patrons as well as selectors by readily showing which of the libraries in the partnership holds a particular title. This information can be used by all members in making purchasing/retention decisions of monographs and serials. Examples of existing resource sharing support systems include: the Triangle Research Network in North Carolina; the TOPCAT online catalog service of SUNY/OCLC; CUNY Plus, the shared NOTIS catalog of the City University of New York; the multitype library CDROM catalog of the Finger Lakes region of New York; and MAINECAT, a statewide database on CDROM.

This kind of collection management, so different from the traditional building of an "ideal" collection, albeit within certain parameters, will require determination, clear understandings among all involved, careful documentation and the faculty alliances previously discussed. It will not be an easy task.

Electronic Formats/Document Delivery

The burden of acquiring information may well shift to means other than purchase of printed materials. This will be accompanied by a shift in the allocation of the acquisitions budget. This cannot be treated as an added cost, but as a reallocation of funds accompanied by decreased spending for printed materials. Data must be collected to show that such a shift is cost effective—that more information can be purchased through new technologies than through traditional methods.

In this library, online access to databases is an integral part of service provided to patrons. As such, it is subsidized to 70% of online costs. CDROM databases are in use on an experimental ba-

sis. The plan is to reduce the outlay for subsidized searches as librarians and patrons use CDROM files for retrospective literature searches. Because of the high initial purchase price of retrospective files and the high annual subscription or licensing costs, savings in acquisitions monies can only come after these costs are amortized. Although the number of databases available in CDROM format is continually increasing, Quint points out a number of deficiencies in CDROM databases that make it highly unlikely that CDROM will provide the cost relief that librarians and vendors have been expounding.[24]

Online searching itself, even at 100% subsidy, may be less expensive than providing certain titles in printed form. Access to full text databases is crucial. The amount and variety of full text material available online increases daily. BRS and Dialog, and other database vendors already provide access to several hundred full text journals. UMI, as a document provider, has access to full text of key scitech journals on CDROM produced under the ADONIS project. OCLC is predicting the existence of full text files of monographs through its EIDOS (Electronic Information Delivery Online System) project.

As the components of the life cycle of information change, libraries must change policies and technical infrastructure to cope with the changes. Toni Carbo Bearman's research on how changes in information life cycle affect the use of scientific and societal information by the government policy makers forecasts, "what is now considered a flood of information is likely only a trickle of what the future holds."[25] Faster, multitasking microcomputers, personal microcomputer workstations for scholars, and extensive data and telecommunications systems will continue to change the origination, manipulation, analysis, retrieval, access, and use of both raw data and the resultant reports and "literature."

Although the idea of a system of online generation of articles, peer review, and electronic publishing has been tested, evaluated, and considered moribund by many, the technical barriers which created human resistance are falling and the methods of accessing information electronically are increasing. Bearman predicts that libraries will need to provide more customized information services to more sophisticated users. This is particularly true for those librarians serving academic and research communities.

This means that there will be a de-emphasis on traditional collection development and acquisition processes. The problem of maintaining sufficient journal subscriptions and bookstock will be complicated by determining policy, budget, and staffing for acquiring information for individuals that will not be cataloged to reside on shelves. For large academic and research libraries, print will not be entirely supplanted because the educational system will not forsake traditional methods, but will supplement them with interactive electronic learning tools. Libraries serving educational institutions will have the difficult task of incorporating and maintaining two systems of information delivery.

It is not the purpose of this article to predict a collection development star wars strategy, but to urge collection policy makers to consider, incorporate and begin planning for a very different set of services for and demands from faculty, students, researchers. The labor intensive work being done on collection analysis via the RLG conspectus is valuable, as it will describe the locus of print collections of national importance, prevent unintentional duplication, and reduce the need for intentional duplication in order to build collections in other areas. The work of conspectus analysis is the underpinning for true cooperative collection development which in turn will make resource sharing a realistically useful approach to collection development. However, resource sharing of printed materials in discrete collections is not the ultimate solution to problems of limited resource budgets. Along with fine tuning of interlibrary lending and borrowing, it will be but one of the many sources/tools in the future options for information "acquisition" and delivery systems.

NOTES

1. Hamaker, Charles and Astle, Deana, "Recent Pricing Patterns in British Journal Publishing" *Library Acquisitions: Practice and Theory* 8(1984):225-232.

2. Tuttle, Marcia, "The Pricing of British Journals for the North American Market" *Library Resources and Technical Services* 30(Jan/Mar 1986):72-78.

3. Page, Gillian, "Journal Pricing Strategies" *Learned Journals Pricing and Buying Round*. Letchworth, England: Epsilon Press, pp. 12-17.

4. Courtney, Keith, "British Journal Pricing: A Publisher's View" *Serials Librarian* 11 No. 3/4(December 1986/January 1987):163-165.

5. Bonk, Sharon C., "Rethinking the Acquisitions Budget: Anticipating and Managing Change" *Library Acquisitions: Practice and Theory* 10(1986):97-106.

6. College of Charleston Acquisition Conference November 1987. *Library Acquisitions: Practice and Theory* 12 No.2(1988) In press.

7. Hayes, Sherman, "Deposit Accounts for Monograph Acquisitions: A Budget-Stretching Technique" *Bottom Line* 1 No.4(1987):28-29.

8. O'Brien, Patrick, "Reduction Budgeting Hits Home: The Dallas Story" *Bottom Line* 1 No.2(1987):4-7.

9. Ruschin, Siegfried, "Why are Foreign Subscription Rates Higher for American Libraries than they are for Subscribers Elsewhere?" *Serials Librarian* 9(Spring 1985):7-18.

10. Astle, Deana and Hamaker, Charles, "Pricing by Geography: British Journal Pricing 1986, Including Developments in Other Countries" *Library Acquisitions: Practice and Theory* 10(1986):165-181.

11. Houbeck, Robert L. Jr., "British Journal Pricing: Enigma Variations, or What will the U.S. Market Bear?" *Library Acquisitions: Practice and Theory* 10(1986):183-197.

12. Okerson, Ann, "Periodical Prices: A History and Discussion" *Advances in Serials Management* Vol.1. Greenwich, Connecticut: Jai Press, 1986, pp. 119-127.

13. Holden, Constance, "Libraries Stunned by Journal Price Increases" *Science* 236(1987):908.

14. Dougherty, Richard, "Scholarly Publishers Who Charge Outrageous Prices for Journals May Get Some Unexpected Competition" *Chronicle of Higher Education* 33 No.38(June 3, 1987):40-41.

15. Mallozzi, Vincent, "Rising Prices Hit Library Shelves" *New York Times* Education/Life, Section 12(November 8, 1987):12, 16.

16. Black, George, "Research Libraries Threatened by Weak U.S. Dollar" *BioScience* 38(January 1988):6.

17. "Current Acquisitions Threatened" *Notabene; News From Yale* 1 No. 2(Fall 1987).

18. Atkinson, Ross, "The Rising Costs of Scholarly Journals" *University of Iowa Libraries Newsletter* 16 No.1(September 1987):3.

19. Allen, N. "Journal Price Increases Cause Budget Problems" *Wayne State University Libraries Newsletter* 19(Fall 1987):3.

20. "Major Problems with Subscription Costs" *A Year of Major Changes; Report of the Director of Libraries University of Pennsylvania 1986-87* pp. 4-5.

21. Houbeck, Robert L. Jr., "If Present Trends Continue: Responding to Journal Price Increases" *Journal of Academic Librarianship* 13 No.4(September 1987):214-220.

22. Houbeck, Robert L. Jr. "British Journal Pricing: Enigma Variations, or What Will the U.S. Market Bear?" *Library Acquisitions: Practice and Theory* 10(1986):183-197.

23. Dougherty, Richard, "Resource Sharing Among Research Libraries: How it Ought to Work" *Collection Management* 9 No.2/3(Summer/Fall 1987):79-88.

24. Quint, Barbara, "How is CD-ROM Disappointing? Let Me Count the Ways" *Wilson Library Bulletin* 62 No.4(December 1987):32-34, 102.

25. Jul, Erik, "Toni Carbo Bearman Speaks at OCLC on Changes in the Life Cycle of Information" *Research Libraries in OCLC* No.23(Summer 1987):8-9.

Forecasting Expenditures
for Library Materials:
Approaches and Techniques

Kathryn Hammell Carpenter

SUMMARY. Forecasting expenditures requires the librarian to develop competencies in a number of areas. These areas include economic conditions, the publishing industry, collection development policies and money management. Developing competencies in these areas involves general reading on economic issues, focused reading on the publishing industry and the use and/or development of national and local price indexes for significant categories of materials collected by the library. Command of various techniques for forecasting payments and managing funds is necessary to fully expend without overexpending the annual materials budget.

INTRODUCTION

Forecasting acquisitions expenditures generally does not involve mediating with crystals or consulting daily horoscopes, though many of us would secretly pursue these guides if we knew them to be prophetic. Accurately predicting expenditures for library materials requires several areas of competency rather than, or perhaps in addition to, an understanding of the occult. These competencies are: an understanding of general economic conditions; knowledge of publishing industry history and trends; an awareness of local collection development policies and practices; and the command of money management techniques. Mastering these competencies will enable the librarian to forecast and manage acquisitions

Kathryn Hammell Carpenter is Bibliographer for the Health Sciences, University of Illinois at Chicago, Box 8198, Chicago, IL 60680. She is also Chair, ALA RTSD Library Materials Price Index Committee, 1988-89.

expenditures with a much greater degree of understanding and opportunity for accuracy than previously was possible.

ECONOMIC FACTORS

Understanding how the U.S. and world economies function and staying current on economic conditions at home and abroad is undoubtedly the most challenging task for the librarian to master. The difficulty of this is due in part to the greater familiarity that librarians have with publishing, collection development and budget administration and in part due to the limited or nonexistent training they have had in economics. Economics seem foreign to most librarians; they actually are foreign if we consider the factors which exert great influences on the price of library materials. The degree to which prices for foreign imprints rise or fall is influenced by the relative strength of the dollar against foreign currencies. Related to the level of foreign trade and balance of payments, the value of the dollar weakens when the demand for it falls in the foreign exchange markets. Under the principles of the International Monetary Fund, the U.S. authorities may act to devalue the dollar to achieve a stability in the dollar value and in the foreign exchange.[1] When the value of the dollar falls, this movement stimulates American exports and reduces the demand for imports in the general market. This may or may not be true in the library market, that is, rising costs for imported library materials may be a problem to be borne rather than resolved by libraries that require foreign imprints to maintain scholarly collections. The U.S. Federal Reserve Bank's posture on the value of the dollar is an element of American economic policy that affects the prices that consumers pay for goods imported from abroad. When the Bank intends to maintain a stable dollar, it may be doing so to avoid more drastic measures to hold the dollar's value such as limitations on imported goods.[2]

The International Monetary Fund codifies the movements of the foreign currency exchange into daily exchange rates. These rates are published on a monthly basis in *International Financial Statistics*. This publication is the source of the authoritative rate of exchange of the dollar against foreign currencies. It provides world summary tables and detailed tables for each country.[3] Exchange rates are also posted in a variety of sources, including local newspapers. Economic analyses directed to the educated layperson can be found in *The Economist*, which includes a table on "Trade, Exchange Rates and Reserves" in each weekly issue, *The Wall Street Journal*, and the *Federal Reserve Bulletin*, which provides a table of rates by month.[4] These publications generally do not target library issues as the focus of economic analyses for the general reader. *Publishers Weekly* discusses economic conditions in terms of library and publishing concerns. A dialogue on the impact of economic factors on libraries has continued for many years in the professional literature of librarianship.[5] More convenient a source of information for busy or overworked librarians are analyses prepared by library wholesalers. Vendors have attempted to synthesize information on the dollar in a clear and explicit manner for their clients in their newsletters and renewal memos. For example, in May/June 1988, the Faxon newsletter reported that

> the U.S. dollar has stabilized more than anticipated, although it is still about 6 percent weaker than it was last June. We expect current values to hold, at least until journal prices are set, which is generally between June and August.[6]

The article goes on to estimate the price increases for European, U.K., Japanese and U.S. subscriptions, to further assist librarians in budgeting. For librarians who rely on one or two vendors, this data helps a great deal in projecting expenditures.

NATIONAL PRICE INDEXES

The inflationary leap and crawl of prices is an economic condition that librarians are as keenly aware of as the movement of currency values and rates of exchange. The Consumer Price Index (CPI) is widely recognized and its meaning understood by anyone who pays personal bills. Again, the economic literature targeted to the educated reader and the professional literature provide evidence of a continuing dialogue on this problem area. Harvey and Spyers-Duran conducted a thorough investigation of the impact of inflation on library budgets. They discovered that the effect of inflation on libraries affected by an increase in publication rates, coupled with a rise in prices and an increase in enrollments and academic course offerings is austerity and retrenchment.[7] Many others, notably White, De Gennaro, Kronenfeld and Thompson, have graphically depicted the how rate of inflationary increases in library materials has exceeded the overall inflation rate of the time. Kronenfeld and Thompson reported a 250.7 point increase in the index of journal costs from 1967-79; during this same period the CPI rose only 116.9 points.[8]

The need for library-specific price indexes was first recognized by William H. Kurth over thirty years ago. Mr. Kurth expressed alarm at the rapid rise in book and periodical prices throughout the world and the lack of substantive data quantifying these movements.[9] His efforts, and those of others interested in gaining control over price inflation were summarized by Frederick C. Lyndon in his useful article on sources of price information. Lyndon pointed out that the first subject indexes compiled by the ALA Costs of Library Materials Committee appeared in 1959, and in 1960, the first complete annual index was published in the *American Library and Book Trade Annual*.[10] The first periodical index appeared in 1960 using methodology developed by Helen M. Welch of the University of Illinois.[11] She selected titles from *Ulrich's International Periodicals Directory* and grouped them into related categories. This work was carried on by Norman B. Brown, with Jane Phillips, until 1984, when it was again undertaken by the ALA Committee, now known as the Library Materials Price Index Committee.[12] In the intervening years, the Committee has modified the methodology to include the full subject database available from Faxon rather than the selected, *Ulrich's*-based list initially used. In 1974, Frank F. Clasquin analyzed periodical price data using a different database, classification system and methodology and other Faxon staff have continued this work to the present.[13]

Nationally produced databases and indexes provide an excellent resource for librarians intent upon forecasting increases in their subject collections and subscription lists. According to Lyndon, in his enormously useful survey on library materials cost studies, the need for detailed information on the costs of library materials is pressing due to factors already noted, i.e., the unprecedented rate of inflation for books and journals, the devaluation of the dollar and the conditions of austerity in higher education. Other concerns cited by Lyndon were the continued high increase in the rate of publications, the appearance of new and costly formats in which information was packaged, the lack of substantive data on prices of foreign imprints, the lack of systematic communication on coping techniques, and little discussion in the literature on the development of local studies. National databases document national bibliographic output and are useful to cite as benchmarks against which price increases for individual libraries can be estimated. Because national databases reveal overall price trends for library materials, they provide comparisons for libraries whose buying patterns, and therefore local price data, may not mirror national trends. They display in a standard manner the movement in prices of published materials.[14] Currently published indexes in *The Bowker Annual of Library and Book Trade Information* include average prices and price indexes for U.S. periodicals, hardcover books, academic books, college books, mass market paperbacks, trade paperbacks, nonprint media, British academic books, German academic books and average cost of Latin American books purchased by selected U.S. libraries. Figures on book exports, imports and international title outputs are reported in the same manner.[15] New areas, such as serials in microform and microform sets, CD-ROMs and foreign serials are currently under investigation by the Library Materials Price Index Committee.[16] Additional data on U.S. title outputs and average prices by broad subject category are compiled annually for *Publishers Weekly* and reprinted in *The Bowker Annual*.[17] Although not a price index per se, this data can be formulated as a price index for purposes of comparison with local data on prices and units added.

LOCAL COST STUDIES

As noted, such aggregate data for U.S. publishing outputs and prices may not accurately mirror the costs of the particular mix of materials which is acquired by an individual library. The American Book Price Indexes were initially criticized by Robert Frase of the American Book Publisher's Council because they omitted backlist books, encyclopedias, textbooks and paperbacks, and did not re-

flect discounts to libraries. Because number of units were not recorded, Frase criticized the index for placing undue emphasis on
high priced books sold in limited quantities.[18] H. William Axford
also questioned the validity of national price indexes as a predictor
of library acquisitions costs. He compared these prices to the average price per title acquired through approval plans maintained by
three academic research libraries during 1966/67 to 1971/72. He
encountered methodological problems in formulating comparable
data, i.e., calendar versus fiscal years, differing subject categories
and U.S. imprints alone compared with U.S., British and Canadian
imprints. He discovered that libraries paid a lower average price per
subject than the prices listed in *The Bowker Annual* for the same
subjects.[19] The selectivity of a purchasing program was cited by
Atkinson as the reason for libraries experiencing prices which were
higher rather than lower than the published indexes.[20] The data provided by local indexes must be accepted cautiously because the selective character of a library's buying patterns means that price data
may be atypical in certain subjects. Local indexes are influenced by
wholesaler discounts, local taxes, and shipping and handling
charges, which affect the prices paid for selected materials. Lyndon
and Birkel attempted to achieve a balance in this controversy by
asserting that there is a place in budgetary planning for local as well
as national data.[21]

Local price indexes have been successfully used by a number of
librarians. Several universities reported on local cost studies in the
ARL *SPEC Kit on Library Materials Cost Studies* in 1980.[22] Dennis
Smith reported on his compilation of a local index for the University of California system.[23] The development, use and effectiveness
of a local index at Harvard College Library was reported by Williams in 1979 and the results updated in 1983.[24] Lyndon summarized efforts to collect local price data at twelve private university
libraries.[25] The librarian interested in establishing a local price index
may be able to use data compiled by a wholesaler on the number
and costs of titles shipped annually to the institution. Wholesaler
data from Baker & Taylor, Coutts Library Services, Blackwell/
North America, Otto Harrassowitz and B. H. Blackwell is the
source of several of the national price indexes published in *The
Bowker Annual* by the Library Materials Price Index Committee.[26]

One advantage of using wholesaler data is that it has been compiled and formatted by the wholesaler and is available for analysis by the librarian. It provides a complete record of prices and subjects acquired from that vendor. Another advantage of data compiled by vendors is that it is often more timely than the *Publishers Weekly* figures for prices and outputs, which lag by nearly one year.

Another approach to developing local cost studies is to compile price data, either manually or by using data from the library's automated system. Lyndon provided a wealth of advice to librarians who wished to attempt a local price index in his survey of cost studies.[27] The American National Standards Institute (ANSI) *Criteria for Price Indexes*, first published in 1974 and revised in 1983 and under consideration for a third revision in 1988, gives specific guidelines for indexes for different types of library materials, i.e., hardcover trade and technical books, periodicals, newspapers and serial services. It defines materials to be included in each category and specifies the method of compilation of data. For example, a periodical is defined as "a publication that constitutes one issue in a continuous series under the same title, published more than once a year over an indefinite period, with individual issues in the series numbered consecutively or with each issue dated." To compile a price index for periodicals, the ANSI Standard states that the index shall be organized by subject categories, preferably based on Dewey, UDC or LC classification systems; each subject category shall include as many titles within the total population that can be identified for which annual subscription prices can be determined on an ongoing basis. Additional titles should be added as they are subscribed to. The annual subscription price, based on the total price divided by the total number of units, is to be divided by the average price of the base year and multiplied by 100.[28]

PUBLISHING INDUSTRY AND PRICING

Price indexes can seem somewhat abstract to the librarian who is not familiar with the publishing industry, its history and the current trends in its development. Taylor Hubbard published a useful introduction to the history of American trade publishing and the transformation from intellectual calling to commercial conglomerate which occurred in the past several decades.[29] Frye and Romanansky have examined the life cycle of the book and how it affects library acquisitions.[30] At least two other accounts, *The Book Industry in Transition*, 1978 and *In Cold Type: Overcoming the Book Crisis*, 1982, analyzed the changes in greater depth.[31] A wealth of statistical data on a number of book and periodical publishers, title, subject, and format outputs, consumer expenditures and sales by subject and format, and prices by format and subject was compiled in *The Mass Media: Aspen Institute Guide to Communication Industry Trends*, much of it compiled from *Publishers Weekly*, the *U.S. Census of Manufactures*, *Ayer Directory of Publications* and Association of American Publishers' publisher surveys and therefore readily updated with current editions of these works.[32] *Publishers Weekly* frequently contains articles which explore changes in the publishing industry, such as Benjamin's important article on the history of book publishing from 1929 to 1979 and an in-depth look at the book industry edited by John P. Dessauer.[33]

Pricing is a particularly sensitive issue for producer and consumer alike. The publishing press contains several accounts which explain or defend pricing strategies. One author posed the question "Why are book prices so high?" and then responded,

> One answer may be that the pricing policies of publishers so mystify the reader that he suspects them. Why else would an otherwise well-informed public question the price of a book when, on the average, it is less than the cost of a normal meal in a medium-priced restaurant, or when a drink in a hotel bar now costs approximately as much as a 300-page mass-market paperback? Which involves the most labor—the meal, the drink or the book?[34]

He reviewed the cost as the sum of payments plus profit margin to those who contribute to the book: author, editor, designer, production planner, printer, binder, salesman, invoice clerk, accountant, shipper, wholesaler and retailer. A similar analysis was targeted for school librarians by Robert J. Verrone and to librarians in general by Dessauer.[35] Other authors have been more critical of pricing policies, i.e., Colin Day evaluated gross margin pricing and found it unsatisfactory.[36]

As might be expected, librarians have not been sympathetic to publishers' defense of price increases. Kent Hendrickson reviewed pricing from the perspectives of the librarian, the wholesaler and the publisher and concluded that prices have risen dramatically, markets have declined and wholesalers have created a profitable niche for themselves by serving both retail outlets (bookstores) and the consumer (libraries).[37] He noted that the time has come when the materials budget can no longer keep pace with the cost of library materials; Edelman and Tatum, Jr. maintained that "at no time in American library history, including the 1960s, was it ever the case that the research libraries of the country could satisfy their appetite for books."[38] In their history of library collection building, they noted that prices for a list of 633 periodicals received by Cornell increased by 181.9% from 1910 to 1925, indicating that rising prices have been an issue for quite some time.

In some ways, librarians have blamed themselves for the predicament they are in regarding obtaining the funds they require to maintain increasingly expensive collections. Practices such as cancelling duplicate titles, even if they are heavily used, shifting funds from monographs to serials, and putting a freeze on the selection of new serial titles permit the publisher to take advantage of libraries in the eyes of some authors. Librarians' justifiable concern with the quality of their collections has at least in some instances contributed to the publishers' perception that because librarians want to maintain runs of costly journals they can charge as much as the market will bear, in fact at times achieving a profit margin as high as 47 percent.[39] Hendrickson cited a publisher of scientific journals whose firm performed a market survey after several years of declining market share. The results indicated that when academic libraries were forced to cancel one of two journals covering the same subject matter, they cancelled the least expensive title. This publisher's response was to raise his firm's prices to equal or surpass those of his competition.[40] Librarians have not succeeded in rousing the outrage of their faculties because they have tried to minimize the impact of budget cuts and loss of purchasing power. This approach has created a constant source of irritation to faculty whose requests are not purchased.[41]

Though many librarians have drawn attention to the high cost of periodicals and recommended combative measures, the battle has recently become more focused. Librarians have investigated which publishers account for the bulk of the price increases and targeted dollar reductions toward those publishers, identified new channels for publication, planned in advance the maximum to spend, participated more fully in resource sharing and in cooperative collection development programs. More recently, the Association of Research Libraries has launched a study of periodical pricing and has announced its intention to work with small publishers and university presses to launch journals which compete against costly titles published by a small number of publishers.[42]

COLLECTION DEVELOPMENT PRACTICES

Collection development policies and practices are a factor in forecasting expenditures both nationally and locally apart from the bitter recognition that they may indeed contribute to higher prices. The percentage of foreign imprints acquired will influence renewal costs by forcing them upward when the dollar is weak relative to other currencies and allowing them to plummet when the dollar is strong. Foreign imprints later published in the United States will be less costly as reprints when the dollar is weak and less costly as original imprints when it is strong. Wholesaler data or price index figures for foreign publications assist the librarian in determining the anticipated rate of increase for foreign imprints.

The mix of formats collected is also a local factor to consider in forecasting expenditures. Certain disciplines, especially in the sciences and health sciences, rely heavily on the periodical literature for the most timely information and vital dialogue among practitioners. Without a cap or ceiling on the percentage of dollars to be allocated to serials, annual price increases would eventually cause the near elimination of other formats in order to fund the subscription list. This is not to say that price increases for monographs do not at times match or exceed annual increases for serials. Apart from the standing order, there are no commitments to purchase newly published monographs, so such expenses can more easily be regulated. Given the smaller print runs of recent years, such parsimony may result in avoidable gaps in retrospective holdings. The Thor Power Tool Decision of 1979 had a direct impact on press runs according to Leonard Shrift, who asserted that the loss of preferential treatment in depreciating inventory would accelerate the decrease in units of a new title produced. He noted that 15 years ago 2,500 copies of a graduate research level psychology monograph might be produced, whereas in 1985, even in a much larger marketplace, only 1,500 to 2,000 copies would be produced.[43] Audiovisuals are more important as teaching aids in certain disciplines and are quite costly to acquire, even if the average price has not risen as rapidly as it has for books and journals.[44] Pressure from public services staff to acquire indexes and databases on CD-ROM puts additional pressure on the materials budget which is usually not relieved by cancelling the same titles in other formats. Knowing the mix of formats to be acquired permits the librarian to assign relative weights to price increase data in order to forecast annual costs.

The presentation of the same information in different formats, or parallel publishing, is an especially troublesome question. In years past, the introduction of electronic bibliographic databases eventually had an impact on the cancellation of the least used or most costly printed counterparts. The introduction of CD-ROM versions of important index files such as Medline do not appear to be having the same impact. Libraries are paying for the same information in three or more formats, which reduces the funds available for unique materials. Producers appear to be entering the marketplace in a haphazard rush with little concern for technical standards. Predicting expenditures for this type of material at present involves little more than skimming funds off the top of the budget and compressing other commitments into the remaining funds.

The percentage of automated acquisitions versus selected acquisitions has an influence on anticipated expenditures. Approval plans, and for the most part, standing orders, assure that the most fundamental materials are being acquired quickly, before they go out of print. Cargill has pointed out that acquiring these materials quickly means that many will be acquired at a lower cost than if they were acquired later.[45] This pattern has been the experience of the author as well. Approval books can be returned if necessary and many wholesalers may put a freeze on distributions if asked to do so. Historical data on approval plan units and expenditures assist the librarian in predicting future expenditures. Fifteen ARL university libraries surveyed maintained local cost data, principally through approval plan figures.[46] Local data on standing order price increases over the years helps predict the annual increase and commitment for those titles.

TECHNIQUES FOR MONEY MANAGEMENT

Understanding and using techniques for money management helps the librarian anticipate and influence expenditures for new acquisitions. Such techniques come into play when the library nears the end of its fiscal year and must close the books on the materials budget. The focus changes from forecasting prices to managing the remaining fund balance and the close of individual accounts. The library's and the institution's philosophies on over- versus under-expending funds are important to know. If carrying funds over to the following fiscal year is an acceptable practice, the librarian need not endeavor to spend every dollar by any means possible, ethical or nearly not, in order to successfully expend the annual budget. Overspending may be acceptable, even proper, especially if the library or institution maintains a contingency fund to cover unexpected deficits. The librarian should determine whether under-spending or over-spending is politically correct and plan his/her approach accordingly.

Many techniques for forecasting future events, both informal and quantitative, are available. The techniques which hold the most promise for library materials cost studies are single and multiple regression analysis and various time series approaches, such as exponential smoothing and moving averages.[47] Williams used single regression to correlate local with national cost indexes and applied the method of least squares to predict the local average price from national prices.[48] Emery investigated four patterns of time series data, the horizontal, linear, quadratic and trigonometric patterns, to examine journal costs and determine trends in pricing. He discovered that predictions generated by the quadratic model most closely approximated historical data for 1965-83.[49]

In the unlikely event that zeroing out is required, the librarian will have to use a number of techniques to assure that fully expending the budget without overspending takes place. The budget must be overencumbered, or overcommitted, to the extent that sufficient invoices are received to expend the remaining funds. Tim Sauer developed a statistical formula for predicting the amount which will be expended at any point in the fiscal year and the amount of orders which must be placed in order to fully expend the remaining funds. This was accomplished by (1) deriving the statistical probability of any order being received, outstanding or cancelled and (2) estimating the portion of the budget expended by subject. The outcome is affected by the institution's choice of vendor in terms of consistent variations in turnaround time. Sauer commented that he developed this model with firm orders in mind and has excluded approvals, standing orders or serials from consideration. It may be possible to develop a statistical model which includes these factors. Sauer recommended that a statistical model using transitional probabilities, a much more complex technique, but one that may be used to check limits of confidence and tests of significance, which in turn provide data on optimum sample size and time intervals best used for the various other groupings.[50] Sampson presented a slightly different approach to forecasting annual expenditures with an algebraic technique for measuring inflation in allocating the materials budget. The value of his model, which requires baseline data on inflationary increases by subject, is the ability to predict the number of units to be acquired as well as the dollar amount necessary to obtain that material. Correlating this figure to publishing outputs in each subject enables the librarian to anticipate how well its collection development practices support its mission. Such data can also be used to estimate the dollar amounts of obtaining the various subjects and formats to be acquired and practical annual limits on these amounts.[51]

Less scientifically, but more pragmatically, the probability of fully expending the materials budget can be judged intuitively by observing a variety of factors related to collection development policies and practices. The percentage of funds to be overencumbered depends largely on the mix of materials acquired by the library. A certain amount of the remaining funds must be set aside to cover standing orders, approval books and any supplemental invoices for serials which the librarian anticipates receiving. This percentage can be derived by observing the payment patterns of previous years and taking into account any recent changes in the amount of automatic and selected acquisitions. The degree to which the library acquires U.S. versus foreign imprints, current versus retrospective titles, and standard versus elusive publishers influences the percentage of orders which must be placed. A large research university which acquires as much as 30 or 40 percent of its materials in foreign imprints may need to overencumber as much as 20 percent of its monographs budget, while a smaller academic institution acquiring primarily current English language titles may need to overcommit as little as 4 percent. A cut-off date for placing domestic and foreign orders helps assure that sufficient selections will have been made early enough to receive and expend the funds for those materials. One disadvantage to this approach is that a rather high level of encumbrance is carried forward into the new fiscal year and must be taken into account when forecasting expenditures for that year.

Another technique for zeroing out the materials budget is to create deposit accounts or make prepayments to wholesalers or publishers when there is a surplus of funds at the very end of the fiscal year. Such funds are essentially carried forward to the coming year but in a manner which doesn't violate the institution's regulations. Deposits can be made to existing deposit accounts to expend a surplus of funds. Another technique is to order and prepay for serials replacement volumes once it becomes evident that the library will have a surplus of funds. Should it appear that the library may overexpend its budget, such a deficit may be avoided by holding invoices until the coming year. This technique has the disadvantage of carrying urgent expenses forward into the new fiscal year which must be covered by funds taken off the top of the materials budget.

The opposite situation may prevail if the library receives an unanticipated allocation of funds or if staff shortages prevent the expenditure of current funds. A contingency fund can be set up and carried forward into the new year if the institution permits this. Funds in bountiful years can intentionally be retained in this manner for use in years where budget increases are low.

Forecasting expenditures requires the librarian to develop competencies in a number of areas. These areas include economic conditions, the publishing industry, local collection development policies and techniques for money management. Developing competencies in these areas involves general reading on economic factors and issues, specialized reading on the book industry and the development and/or use of national and local price indexes for significant categories of materials in the library's collection areas. Developing and using these indexes requires an understanding of the mix of subjects, formats and countries of origin sufficient to create relevant indexes. Finally, command of various techniques for money management is necessary in order to anticipate final expenditures in order to fully expend the annual materials budget.

REFERENCES

1. International Exchange and Payments. In: *Encyclopaedia Britannica*. Chicago: Encyclopaedia Britannica, 1986, p. 842-854.

2. O'Shea, James. Fed Favoring Stable Dollar. *Chicago Tribune*. June 5, 1988, p. C1-2.

3. *International Financial Statistics*. Geneva: International Monetary Fund. Monthly. v.1- 1948-.

4. *The Economist*. London: Economist Newspaper Ltd. Weekly. v.1- 1843-   . See also, *The Wall Street Journal*. New York: Dow Jones and Co. Daily. v.1- 1889-   , and *The Federal Reserve Bulletin*. Washington, D.C.: U.S. Federal Reserve System. Monthly. v.1- 1915-   .

5. Pearson, Lois R. Falling Dollar Imperils Research Collections. *American Libraries*. 18:317-18, May 1987.

6. Lower Price Increases Projected for 1989. *FAXletter*. 4(3):1, May/June 1988.

7. Harvey, John F. and Peter Spyers-Duran. The Effect of Inflation on Academic Libraries. In: *Austerity Management in Academic Libraries*. John F. Harvey and Peter Spyers-Duran, eds., Metuchen, N.J.: Scarecrow, 1984, p. 1-42.

8. White, Herbert S. Publishers, Libraries and Costs of Journal Subscriptions in Times of Funding Retrenchment. *Library Quarterly* 46:359-77, 1976; see also, De Gennaro, Richard. Escalating Journal Prices: Time to Fight Back. *American Libraries* 8:69-74, 1977; and Kronenfeld, Michael R. and James Thompson. The Impact of Inflation on Journal Costs. *Library Journal* 106:714-17, April 1, 1981.

9. Kurth, William H. A Proposed Cost of Books Index and Cost of Periodicals Index. *College and Research Libraries* 16:390-95, October 1955.

10. Lyndon, Frederick C. Sources of Information on the Costs of Library Materials. *Library Acquisitions: Practice and Theory* 1:105-116, 1977.

11. Welch, Helen M. Proposed Procedures for Establishing a Cost of Periodicals Index. *Library Resources and Technical Services* 3:202-08, Summer 1959; See also Welch, Helen M. Cost Indexes for Periodicals: A Progress Report. *Library Resources and Technical Services* 4:150-57, Spring 1960.

12. Articles on price indexes for U.S. periodicals and serial services were published by Norman B. Brown from 1975 to 1978 in the July or August issue of *Library Journal*; from 1979 to 1984 this annual survey was continued by Brown and Jane Phillips. Brown also published separate articles on price indexes for U.S. periodicals in the July issue of *Library Journal* for 1972-74; articles on price indexes for U.S. serial services were published by William H. Huff and Brown in the July issue of *Library Journal* from 1965 to 1974.

13. Clasquin, Frank F. Periodical Prices: A Three Year Comparative Study. *Library Journal* 99:2447-2449, October 1, 1974; see also the October issue of *Library Journal* through 1979; the update for 1980 was in *The Serials Librarian*. Updates for 1981 and 1982 were compiled by Gerald R. Lowell; the 1983-86 updates were compiled by Rebecca T. Lenzini, also in *The Serials Librarian*; the 1987 update was compiled by Leslie R. Knapp and Lenzini and published in *Library Journal*.

14. Lyndon, Frederick C. Library Materials Cost Studies. *Library Resources and Technical Services* 27:156-62, April/June 1983.

15. *The Bowker Annual of Library and Book Trade Information*. Sponsored by The Council of National Library and Information Associations, Inc. 33rd ed. New York: Bowker, 1987.

16. ALA RTSD Library Materials Price Index Committee. Minutes of the July 11, 1988 meeting, New Orleans.

17. Preliminary figures on U.S. book title outputs for the previous year are reported in March and final figures are reported in September; U.S. book exports, imports and international title outputs are reported in September for the year two year's prior to the current year. These figures have been compiled by Chandler B. Grannis since 1973.

18. Lyndon, 1977, p. 107.

19. Axford, H. William. The Validity of Book Price Indexes for Budgetary Projections. *Library Resources and Technical Services* 19(1):5-12, Winter 1975.

20. Lyndon, 1977, p. 107.

21. Lyndon, Frederick C. and Paul E. Birkel. Letter to the Editor. *Library Resources and Technical Services* 20:97-98, Winter 1976.

22. Association of Research Libraries. Systems and Procedures Exchange Center. *Library Materials Cost Studies*. SPEC Kit 60. January 1980.

23. Smith, Dennis. Forecasting Price Increase Needs for Library Materials: The University of California Experience. *Library Resources and Technical Services* 28:136-48, April 1984.

24. Williams, Sally F. Construction and Application of a Periodicals Price Index. *Collection Management* 2:329-44, Winter 1979; see also, Clack, Mary E.

and Sally F. Williams. Using Locally and Nationally Produced Periodical Indexes in Budget Preparation. *Library Resources and Technical Services* 27:345-56, October 1983.

25. Lyndon, Frederick C. Library Materials Budgeting in the Private University Library: Austerity and Action. *Advances in Librarianship*, v. 10, 1980, p. 89-154.

26. *The Bowker Annual*, 1987, p. 424-41.

27. Lyndon, 1983, p. 158-60.

28. *American National Standard for Library and Information Sciences and Related Publishing Practices – Library Materials – Criteria for Price Indexes.* New York: American National Standards Institute, Inc., 1983.

29. Hubbard, Taylor E. From Pride to Profit: One Hundred Years of American Trade Publishing. *Drexel Library Quarterly* 20:4-27, Summer 1985.

30. Frye, Gloria and Marcia Romanansky. The Approval Plan – The Core of an Academic Wholesaler's Business. In: *Issues in Acquisitions: Programs and Evaluation*. Sul H. Lee, ed. Ann Arbor, Mich.: The Pierian Press, p. 111-20, 1984.

31. Compaine, Benjamin M. *The Book Industry in Transition: An Economic Study of Book Distribution and Marketing*. White Plains, N.Y.: Knowledge Industry Publications, 1978; Shatzkin, Leonard. *In Cold Type: Overcoming the Book Crisis*. Boston: Houghton Mifflin Co., 1982.

32. *The Mass Media: Aspen Institute Guide to Communication Industry Trends*. New York: Praeger, 1978.

33. Benjamin, Curtis G. The Weaving of a Tangled Economic Web: Book Publishing 1929-79. *Publishers Weekly* 219:41-45, April 24, 1981; Dessauer, John P. Economic Review of the Book Industry: A Special Publisher's Weekly Feature. *Publishers Weekly* 210:35-58, July 26, 1976.

34. Bohne, Harald. Why are Book Prices So High? *Scholarly Publishing* 7:135-43, January 1976.

35. Verrone, Robert J. Why Books Cost So Much. *School Library Journal* 25:20-22, February 1979; See also, Dessauer, John P. Projecting Profits at the Hypothesis Press: A Mythic Tale with Implications. *Publishers Weekly* 214:48-52, July 24, 1978; and Dessauer, John P. Where the Buyer's Money Goes. *Publishers Weekly* 204:42-44, July 30, 1974.

36. Day, Colin. The Theory of Gross Margin Pricing. *Scholarly Publishing* 14:305-26, July 1983.

37. Hendrickson, Kent. Pricing From Three Perspectives: The Publisher, the Wholesaler, the Library. In: *Pricing and Costs of Monographs and Serials: National and International Issues*. Sul H. Lee, ed. New York: The Haworth Press, Inc., p. 1-12, 1987.

38. Edelman, Hendrick and G. Marvin Tatum, Jr. The Development of Collections in American University Libraries. *College and Research Libraries* 37:222-45, May 1976.

39. Houbeck, Jr., Robert L. If Present Trends Continue: Responding to Journal Price Increases. *Journal of Academic Librarianship* 13:214-20, 1987.

40. Hendrickson, 1987, p. 8.

41. White, Herbert S. Library Materials Prices and Academic Library Practices: Between Scylla and Charybdis. *Journal of Academic Librarianship* 5:20-23, March 1979.

42. Dougherty, Richard M. and Brenda L. Johnson. Periodical Price Escalation: A Library Response. *Library Journal* 113:27-29, May 15, 1988; see also, White, Herbert S. The Journal That Ate the Library. *Library Journal* 113:62-63, May 15, 1988; and Turner, Judith Axler. U.S. Research Libraries Search for Ways to Combat Spiraling Costs of Scholarly Journals. *The Chronicle of Higher Education* 34:A5-A6, June 8, 1988.

43. Schrift, Leonard. After Thor, What's Next: The Thor Power Tool Decision (U.S. Supreme Court) and Its Impact on Scholarly Publishing. *Library Acquisitions: Practice and Theory* 9:61-63, 1985.

44. Walch, David B. Price Index for Non-Print Media. *Library Journal* 106:432-3, February 15, 1981; see also recent years of *The Bowker Annual*.

45. Cargill, Jennifer. The Approval Connection: Pricing the Ordering Alternatives. In: *Pricing and Costs of Monographs and Serials: National and International Issues*. Sul H. Lee, ed. New York: The Haworth Press, Inc., p. 13-25, 1987.

46. Association of Research Libraries, 1980, Intro.

47. Wheelwright, Steven C. and Spyros Makridakis. *Forecasting Methods for Management*. 3rd ed. New York: Wiley, 1980.

48. Williams, 1979, p. 337-40.

49. Emery, Charles D. Forecasting Models and the Prediction of Periodical Subscription Costs. *The Serials Librarian* 9:5-22, Summer 1985.

50. Sauer, Tim. Predicting Book Fund Expenditures: A Statistical Model. *College and Research Libraries* 39:474-8, November 1978.

51. Sampson, Gary S. Allocating the Book Budget: Measuring for Inflation. *College and Research Libraries* 39:381-83, September 1978.

Managing the College Library's Acquisitions Budget

Mickey Moskowitz
Joanne Schmidt

SUMMARY. The day-to-day monitoring of the acquisitions budget in a small to medium-sized college library is examined within the context of the educational and fiscal realities of the parent institution. The acquisitions budget is discussed in terms of the allocation of funds for different types of materials, internal accounts for monitoring the budget within these categories, and recommendations for coping with unexpected changes during the course of the fiscal year. A discussion of the book budget offers advice on controlling encumbrances and expenditures, as well as guidelines for a fiscal timetable and the use of allocation formulas. Special problems associated with monitoring standing orders and approval plans are examined. A section on monitoring the periodicals budget addresses concerns with their escalating costs as well as methods for ordering journals and allocating periodical funds in a college library.

This paper will focus on the acquisitions budget of the small to medium-sized college library. As reported by HEGIS in 1985, the average library collection in four-year academic institutions, excluding universities, was 205,769 volumes.[1] Although college libraries may support a number of graduate and professional programs, their primary emphasis is on the undergraduate student. Unlike larger academic libraries, their mission is not to build research collections but to support the curriculum of the parent institution. With this goal in mind, four kinds of materials are generally

Mickey Moskowitz and Joanne Schmidt are Library Director and Head of College Development, Emerson College Library, 150 Beacon Street, Boston, MA 02116.

49

acquired by the college library: basic collection to meet curricular needs; good reference collection; cultural and recreational materials; after these have been achieved, materials to meet occasional research needs.[2]

College libraries differ widely in ways which will impact their respective budgets. As stated in the *Standards for College Libraries* 1986, these differences include:

1. The scope, nature and level of the college curriculum;
2. Instructional methods used, especially as they relate to independent study;
3. The adequacy of existing collections and the publishing rate in fields pertinent to the curriculum;
4. The size, or anticipated size, of the student body and teaching faculty;
5. The adequacy and availability of other library resources;
6. The range of services offered by the library . . . ;
7. The extent of automation of operations and services . . . ;
8. The extent to which the library already meets the College Library Standards.[3]

The college library's budget is a reflection of the fiscal and political realities of the parent institution. It is molded by the college's strategic plan as it addresses the overall direction of the institution and new academic programs. Most academic library budgets have had to deal with rapid changes in academic programs over the past decade. Many college libraries are also responding to institutional expectations for access to computer software, CD ROM databases, document delivery and telefacsimile services. Their traditional materials budgets are being transformed to meet the costs of new technology.

As part of the college-wide fiscal plan, the library budget must conform to the overall accounting and budgeting regulations of the college. Although the business or accounting office may not understand the unique aspects of library purchasing, it is essential that library staff involved in budgeting keep in touch with personnel in these offices and work closely with them to streamline functions and to comply with overall college procedures.

THE BUDGET PROCESS

Martin refers to the library budget as a "statement which defines in monetary terms the ways in which an institution will seek to achieve its goals during the period for which it is valid."[4] Cargill states that "the budget should be viewed as a planning tool, the map that the library follows for the rest of the fiscal period to attain its mission."[5] Kelly says "budgeting is a managerial tool which facilitates both planning, or deciding how to allocate resources, and control, or monitoring the results to ensure they conform with the plan."[6]

As suggested above, the budget process starts with fiscal planning and concludes with fiscal management or control. The budget process is different things to different people at different times. The book budget being monitored by the collection development librarian today was probably prepared by the library director close to two years ago. The budget starts as a planning document nine to twelve months before the actual fiscal year begins—with as much as nine to twenty-four months often elapsing between the original request and the close of that fiscal year. As a new fiscal year begins, the budget cycle shifts from the planning to the control stage, the process of monitoring to ensure that the budget is spent as appropriated. At some points in the year, these phases overlap: as next year's budget is being prepared, this year's budget is being monitored.

The day-to-day control of the budget, often referred to as budget monitoring, fiscal management or operational budgeting, will be the focal point of this paper. It will be discussed specifically in terms of the library materials, or acquisitions, budget which is traditionally made up of books and periodicals. The acquisitions budget may also include bindery, nonprint materials, computer software, online services, and/or a general contingency fund. Although acquisitions funds may come from endowments or donations, this paper will deal with institutionally derived funds. According to the *Standards*, between thirty-five and forty percent of the library budget is normally allocated for the acquisition of resources.[7]

Who is responsible for the expenditure of the library materials budget? The *Standards* state that "the Library Director shall have sole authority to apportion funds and initiate expenditures within the library budget . . ."[8] Although the library director is accountable for the fiscal soundness of the library, responsibility varies considerably among institutions. In colleges with larger budgets, planning and monitoring the budget may be delegated to the collection development or acquisitions librarian; in smaller libraries, the director may make all budgetary decisions. In all cases, the library director has the fiscal overview and brings together acquisitions requests from serials, collection development, and other separate departments. Individual staff members, on the other hand, seldom think of the budget as a whole, but only how it will affect their respective units.

MONITORING THE OVERALL
ACQUISITIONS BUDGET

This phase of the library budget goes into effect after the overall library appropriations have been approved by the college. It is a game of balance played throughout the fiscal year. On the one hand, one does not want to encumber all funds too early in the year; on the other, one does not want leftovers at the end of the year. The challenge is to close the fiscal year with all accounts balanced and reconciled with the college's administrative records. What is the penalty for not doing so? As Trumpeter so aptly states, "To underspend suggests miscalculations in your projections and implies that your requested budget was high so that future requests may be disregarded; to overspend is not only bad management, but illegal."[9]

The first step in monitoring the budget is to allocate funds to different line-items and to designate who is responsible for spending these funds by the end of the fiscal year. The materials budget may be assigned to relatively few categories; e.g., subscriptions, standing orders, books, binding, with the remainder often in a general fund from which all other acquisitions will be made. College libraries also allocate by subject or academic division, often using highly structured formulas. Allocation formulas are discussed under "Monitoring the Book Budget" below.

Whether the library allocates by subject or within broad categories of materials, the most significant issue for college libraries concerns the distribution of funds between serials and monographs. The big question is: what proportion of the library's total acquisition expenditure is for subscriptions and standing orders? In an academic library, it is recommended that the expenditure for serials not exceed sixty to seventy percent of the total materials budget.[10] When serials expenditures go beyond that percentage, the library loses the flexibility to purchase other materials as needed. Methods of monitoring standing orders and periodicals are discussed further under "Monitoring Standing Orders and Approval Plans" and "Monitoring the Periodicals Budget" below.

Within the library materials budget, a distinction can be made between types of expenditures that are independent of subjects or programs.[11] Bonk calls the first type "continuing obligations"; these include periodicals, serials, standing orders, approval plans, etc. These items automatically arrive by predetermined arrangements and aré billed in advance on a regular basis. She labels the second category "discretionary purchases," which include monographs and other similar materials ordered on a title-by-title basis, as well as new serials and subscriptions, backfiles, microform sets and replacements. After continuing obligations are expended, discretionary purchases are divided among the college's curriculum areas, traditional subjects, or college departments. In addition, some budgets may have a contingency fund for library materials to allow for special purchases.

One record of materials expenditures is provided in most college libraries by monthly accounting reports generated by their business offices. However, these printouts are often not available until weeks after the actual invoices are paid; the information is therefore of little value in determining an accurate and up-to-date account for the library. The *Standards* recommended that the "Library shall maintain internal accounts for approving its invoices for payment, monitoring its encumbrances, and evaluating the flow of its expenditures."[12] It is essential to check these in-house records carefully against the college's monthly accounting sheets to verify that library expenditures and encumbrances were authorized and have been received. The library must set up an internal accounting system that will update financial records and encumber funds needed to pay for materials at a later time. Many library administrative offices use microcomputer-based database management or spreadsheet programs to track overall encumbrances and expenditures. The budget is divided into the subaccounts that have been assigned to it. When the cost of an item is entered into a subaccount, the amount is also encumbered against the total budget. When the item is received it is disencumbered and included in both general and subaccount expenditures. Examples of both manual and online accounting systems used by libraries have been presented by Clark, Cargill, and Smith.[13,14,15]

An encumbrance places a hold on funds needed to pay for materials so the library does not receive more items than it can finance. However, an encumbrance is nothing more than an educated guess. If the actual cost of the item is greater than the amount encumbered, the library will have less in its budget than anticipated. On the other hand, overencumbering is equally dangerous since it can prevent the use of funds for materials until late in the budget year when it is difficult to spend the money quickly.

Even the most carefully monitored budget is subject to chance and change, as illustrated by the following cases:

Case I. Sometime in May the library receives a windfall of surplus institutional funds to spend in a matter of weeks. Avoid the temptation to spend these funds on a few high-cost items that are outside the collection development objectives of the library. Consult the desiderata file, consider additions to deposit accounts, and look seriously at the gaps in the library's microform collection.

Case II. The big ticket orders expected to come in on time don't. This is when ongoing dialogue and accumulated goodwill with budget office personnel come in handy. Know what the college's actual timetable is for closing the books at the end of the year; there is often a week or so grace period before the books are finally closed. Know also under what circumstances the college will pay for invoices dated after the close of the fiscal year. To cover unexpected situations like this, some libraries arrange with their jobber to send undated invoices for materials received in June. If the budget is underexpended, these can be paid in the current fiscal year; if overexpended, in the next.

Case III. A sharp increase in the cost of periodical subscriptions has forced a retrenchment and reallocation of funds within the library's operational budget. Resist the urge to make across-the-board cuts in spending. Consider what must be acquired now, what later, what not at all. Allocate for different materials and for different academic departments on a cost-benefit basis. Let faculty and students know the reason why purchases have been cut back.

A college with a "use it or lose it" budget is always vulnerable to unexpected changes. These could come in the form of an institutional setback such as a sharp drop in enrollment or the loss of state funds. It could be the effect of the overall economy—i.e., the impact of inflation or a weakening dollar in the price of library materials. It could be the result of a sharp increase in the output of the book or journal trade. Or it could be the impact of new technology and the expectation that the expensive products of this technology will be another item to be expended from the acquisitions budget.

MONITORING THE BOOK BUDGET

Monitoring the monograph budget is the most difficult fiscal task for libraries because of the detail involved in tracking diverse expenditures. Money is encumbered and then spent for thousands of individual titles with low per unit cost. An effective acquisitions accounting system prevents the library from overspending or underspending. Other benefits of such management systems include access to information on the status of funds; ability to compile and produce statistical and financial reports on demand and in the format desired; and access to a detailed picture of acquisitions spending patterns.[16]

Encumbering

The act of preparing formal commitments to expend funds (encumbering) eliminates the need to cancel orders due to lack of funds. The cost of books may be encumbered two ways. In the vendor method purchase orders are issued to one vendor for several titles. In the single title method one purchase order is prepared for each title. The advantage of the single-title-per-purchase order system is that unused funds, from books never received, can be released quickly. The vendor method requires a purchase order being kept open until all titles are received, but saves considerable time by eliminating the need to write individual purchase orders.

Monitoring the book budget is usually done in the acquisitions office. It is a separate and distinct function from the overall budget monitoring done by the library director. Automated bookkeeping systems may be used in college libraries. The principles involved in computer and manual book budget monitoring systems are the same. The goals of an acquisition's encumbering system should be to provide an audit trail and to allow for simple accuracy checks. The system itself should be straightforward and easily maintained. The following ledger book procedures may be useful in setting up or monitoring an encumbering system:

1. Record the purchase order date, vendor name, purchase order number and price from multiple order forms (MOFs) after they have been typed, separated and grouped by fund.

2. Keep a running total of encumbered prices in a separate column. Subtract this total encumbered figure from the original allocation to yield the free balance for each fund.

3. Check for accuracy of ledgering by adding individual prices on MOFs just posted to the free balance. Result should be the previous free balance.[17]

4. Track approval plans, blanket orders and standing orders separately in order to ensure that the amount estimated annually for each is correct.

5. Encumber for the list price of each item. Using a price from a standard source, such as *Books In Print*, ensures that the encumbrance will adequately cover the expenditure. It eliminates the guesswork involved in anticipating discounts and additional charges.

6. Keep the number of staff involved in each purchase order to a minimum. One person whose knowledge of institutional procedures is complete and up-to-date should inspect all orders.

7. Send encumbrance documents to the account clerk as soon as possible, so orders may be mailed with minimum delays.

8. Encumber and spend total allocation, except for a small reserve, in the first nine to ten months of the fiscal year.

9. Overencumber by ten to twenty-five percent. This figure ac-

counts for items not received and items returned during one fiscal year. Use records from previous years to determine the correct percentage of overencumbering.

Expending

Expending is the actual disbursement of funds for materials received. Expenditures are for the actual price of books, including discounts and additional charges. Libraries keeping track of their own expenditures know at all times exactly which funds have not been spent. The following procedures keep expending systems simple:

1. Expend only after books have been received and checked for damage.
2. Verify delivery by stamping invoice.
3. Record actual cost, receipt date and invoice number on MOF to provide audit trail.
4. Post expenditures to the same fund from which money was originally encumbered. Record price, date received, and invoice number opposite encumbered amount.
5. Subtract total encumbered amount (of items being expended) from the total encumbered. Add actual costs and post the result in total expended. Subtracting the new total encumbered plus total expended from original allocation yields free balance.
6. Check postings by subtracting paid amounts from new total expenditure. The results should equal the previous total expenditure.
7. Cancel encumbrances by writing "canceled" and the date in the expended column and on the MOF. Record the total amount being canceled in the encumbered column. It may be helpful to use red ink or record the amount in parentheses to distinguish it from other encumbrances. Subtract this amount from the original total encumbered column. Subtract the new total encumbered and total expended from the original allocation to obtain a new free balance.[18]
8. Check statements by ensuring address and account number are

correct. Check that the library has been billed the correct amount for items received.

Fiscal Timetable

Before the Fiscal Year Starts

Refer to past records to find the average cost per book for your library. Figuring averages by fund may be necessary. Dividing the total allocation by the average cost of a book yields the approximate number of books it will be necessary to buy to spend the budget. If the number of items purchased per year for each department is not of great concern, then an easier approach may be used. Divide the total allocation per fund by the number of weeks purchases will be made during a fiscal year. This determines how much money should be expended from each fund during each week. An even distribution of purchasing activity throughout the year eliminates backlogs in receiving, cataloging and shelving.

Invoice and payment procedures should be simple. Arrange with jobbers what type of invoice is required, how long incomplete purchase orders will be held and other payment procedures. Some suggest holding invoices for incomplete orders no longer than thirty days and, at that time, making partial payment and claiming the missing items.[19] Another procedure is to pay for items as they are received and leave incomplete orders open until near the end of the fiscal year. At that time closeout procedures can be done.

Develop procedures for returns and cancellations with jobbers. Letters for cancellation should include purchase order number and invoice number. Methods for making adjustments to accounts include: holding invoices until correct title is received, paying the invoice and receiving a credit memo, striking from the invoice, self-credit memos, and requesting a corrected invoice.[20]

During the Fiscal Year

Fund allocations should be available as early in the fiscal year as possible and ordering deadlines announced immediately to help selectors plan their purchases. Bookkeeping should be done on a daily basis. This includes encumbering funds for items ordered and expending funds for items received. Prompt encumbering ensures up-to-date account balances. Prompt expending can maintain good relationships with vendors. Bills overdue for longer than sixty days are not only undesirable, but may carry penalty charges.[21]

The library's internal bookkeeping systems should provide regular reports. Monthly is usually appropriate until close to the end of the fiscal year when weekly reports will become necessary. There is no need for the reports to be elaborate, but they must be reliable and understandable. The goal of the reports is to keep those responsible for expending the budget informed as to how and at what rate the budget is being spent, the status of the free balance and obligations still to be paid. Reports, for each fund, should include the initial allocation with last year's outstanding encumbrances subtracted; money spent; money encumbered; and the total remaining. It may also be useful to know the percent of money still uncommitted.[22]

On a monthly basis, the library's internal system should be reconciled with the official statement of the college. As soon as a statement is received from the college it should be checked. List errors with procedures for correction. Keep a copy of this list so that next month's statement can be checked for proper updating of records.

Throughout the year expenditures should be proportionate to the portion of year elapsed. Data should be gathered and spending trends observed throughout the year. At least four times per year balances should be compared to previous years when all of the budget was spent. Compare goal figures to actual expenditures and encumbrances, examine deviations and take corrective action.

Closing Out the Fiscal Year

The first step in closing out the fiscal year is to know the timetable set by the college for closing out books. Several months prior to the end of the fiscal year, check with vendors on outstanding orders. Determine whether or not delivery will be made by the end of the year. At this time decisions can be made about cancellation or balancing encumbrances which might not come in with orders more likely to be expended by the end of the fiscal year.

Towards the end of the year it may be necessary to insist that each shipment from jobbers be invoiced separately. This is also the time to use up credit memos. If the college system is flexible, the end of a fiscal year may also be an appropriate time to transfer money between funds. Overspending in one area can be offset by underspending in another.

Allocation Formulas

Much has been written about how funds should be allocated between academic departments and library staff and how much of the library materials budget should be spent by faculty. Three basic patterns can be observed: (1) total faculty control of the materials budget; (2) partial control by the library with dollars reserved for reference, special collections and general collection development, with faculty controlling the remainder; (3) total control by the library.[23] Gardner points out that faculty know the literature of their own subjects and may be best prepared to select course-related items. Nevertheless, he asserts that in a college setting, where the mission is undergraduate instruction, not research, the faculty cannot be expected to have current knowledge in all fields collected by the library.[24] In a small college library, "faculty responsibility must be clearly defined and understood so that book selection not be haphazard."[25]

Allocation formulas have been used to assure a fair distribution of library materials funds to different academic divisions and disciplines. Formulas are arrived at by assigning numeric values to factors such as: strength of existing collection; growth, development and decline of programs; number and cost of books currently published in the field; number of the college's faculty members teaching in the field; number and level of courses; number of graduate and undergraduate students in each field; circulation counts; number of major and minor fields; interlibrary loan statistics, and inflation rates for materials in the field. In addition, the level of faculty publishing and research may be included. Formulas must be based on local experience; there is no universal pattern for allocation.

Allocation formulas "should be the result of academic and fiscal planning that can express identifiable needs in terms of dollar amounts."[26] Formulas may help equitably distribute available funds when programs are growing rapidly and budgets are growing slowly. They may guard the library against claims of unfairness if faculty, administration and librarians have agreed on guiding principles and the measures by which those principles are applied.[27] However, there are disadvantages to using formulas to allocate money to faculty. The library loses flexibility and control as it turns over the responsibility for building a balanced collection to faculty. In addition, allocation formulas take time to develop, calculate and monitor. Once in place, they should be evaluated annually in terms of fiscal and academic changes.

MONITORING STANDING ORDERS AND APPROVAL PLANS

Standing orders are an automatic means for receiving titles appearing in series or sets. Approval plans are arrangements with professionally operated services to send new books in selected subjects to the library; they are designed to provide comprehensive coverage of new titles in certain subjects, languages, and levels. Libraries can define the scope, set budget allocations for the plans, and exclude certain types of materials (workbooks, texts, pamphlets, etc.).

There are two methods of tracking approval plan and standing order expenditures. One requires titles to be charged against an internal fund. The second tracks each plan without breaking them into separate funds.[28] The second method is recommended because vendors can provide frequent subject analyses and detailed accounting specifics including: number of titles received, list price for all received, net price for all received, average net price, number of returns and percentage of returns.

Budgeting for these plans can be difficult and libraries using them for the first time should start with a relatively small commitment of funds. Vendors can help by providing one-year cost projections based on similar profiles. During the first year of a plan, improve the odds of neither over- nor underspending by adding a ten percent cushion.[29] In succeeding years, base allocations for plans on previous expenditures, then figure in inflation rates, projected return rates, and discounts.

Monitoring requires knowing exactly what has been expended.

Maintain a running check on funds and compare these totals to vendors' projections. Any radical differences in spending patterns must be caught early in the fiscal year. Internally kept statistics should be reviewed monthly. Included should be number of titles and volumes received, total spent and balance remaining.[30] When reviewing account balances remember that publishing tends to be heaviest in fall and spring.

Towards the end of the fiscal year two situations may develop. Either the original allocation is not enough to continue with the plan in its present form or too much money was originally allocated. If the first situation arises with an approval plan, cutbacks can be made in the following ways: further limiting country of origin, lowering upper price limits, accepting only unnumbered series, cutting back the profile to a size which can be supported, or, changing from receiving books to receiving announcement forms to increase flexibility.[31] Canceling plans should be used only as a last resort. In underspending situations, approval plan vendors can help ensure that the full allocation is spent. Since vendors select titles for shipment several weeks in advance of the books' arrival at the library, the vendor can provide an invoice number and cost up to two weeks before a shipment of books arrives.[32]

MONITORING THE PERIODICALS BUDGET

The journal and newspaper holdings of a college library are its prime intellectual and informational resource and a significant financial investment must be made to support them. One of the most difficult problems in budget monitoring is to prevent periodicals costs from taking such a large percentage of acquisitions funds that there is inadequate money left for the purchase of other materials.

Escalating Costs

Why has the periodicals portion of the library budget increased so dramatically? One reason has been the remarkable proliferation of journal titles over the past few decades. Publishers have responded to the expansion of information in various disciplines by producing narrower and more specialized titles; this is reflected in an overall increase of serials from less than 63,000 titles in 1974[33] to almost 200,000 titles in 1988.[34] Increased supply has been accompanied by increased demand; college libraries have added more and more journal titles in response to new programs and to support existing curriculum.

Maintaining current subscriptions and adding new titles is a major challenge when the average cost of journals for academic libraries has gone up well above the annual increment added to most acquisitions budgets. For instance, the average price of a journal in an academic library in 1987-88 was $117.75, an increase of 12% over 1986-87—and an increase of 135% over 1978-79 when the average cost was $50.11.[35]

Over the past few years, the sharp increase in periodical prices has been largely due to the weakening of the U.S. dollar. More journals are published outside the U.S. or owned by firms located outside the U.S. Their titles are priced in foreign currency and their cost has escalated primarily because of the drop in the value of the dollar. Many library materials budgets were planned without anticipation of this precipitous fall in the value of the dollar and, as a result, were caught short when it came to spending and monitoring the budget. They faced a number of unpleasant options, including the following:

1. Sacrifice the book budget—commit a larger proportion of the acquisitions budget to periodicals, resulting in little money available for books or other purchases.
2. Freeze the periodicals budget—avoid any new subscriptions in favor of maintaining existing titles; unacceptable in institutions that teach subjects only covered by new journals.
3. Establish a static growth policy—demand that every order for a new subscription be accommodated by a cancellation of an existing subscription; this disregards both the nature of the disciplines supported by the library and the needs of its users.
4. Cancel subscriptions—cancel only on the basis of low use—not on cost or publication location and realize how impossible it will be to obtain runs of canceled titles at some future dates.

A recent Faxon survey of 264 academic libraries (56 of which represented colleges) indicated that the largest increase in their library materials budget for 1988-89 was for periodicals.[36] Few cases of level funding and almost no planned periodical spending cuts were reported. In fact, about two-thirds of the medium-sized academic libraries expect to increase spending on periodicals by ten percent or more in 1988-89.[37] Although many libraries plan to cancel low-use subscriptions, many also plan to add new titles. The effect of inflation at home and the price control enforced by a dwindling number of journal publishers make it unlikely that the periodicals budget will ever be easy to predict or control.

Ordering Periodicals

College libraries order periodicals directly through publishers or, more commonly, through a vendor such as Faxon or EBSCO. Libraries that order direct from publishers point to the greater and more immediate control they have over starting and stopping subscriptions as well as the savings incurred by publishers' discounts and by eliminating vendor service charges. On the other hand, use of a reliable periodicals agent can facilitate monitoring the budget by providing common expiration dates for all subscriptions, billing via a single printout, summary reports on all claims and publisher responses, and a list of all renewed subscriptions and their costs. Although some journals are not available through subscription agents, the use of an agent for the bulk of journal orders cuts down considerably on the in-house costs of handing, renewals, and payment. The annual publications vendors provide free to their clients—Faxon's *Guide to Serials* and EBSCO's *Librarian's Handbook*—are also invaluable tools for locating current pricing and other relevant information.

Allocation of Periodical Funds

Miller argues that periodicals should not be apportioned by department in a college library and that, for the most part, they should reflect titles covered in the major indexing tools the library receives.[38] From a budget-monitoring perspective it is considerably simpler to draw from one single periodicals account, rather than keeping track of dozens of departmental journal funds. Another advantage of having all subscriptions paid for from one periodicals fund is there is no discrimination between subject areas for which the titles are purchased. Because of the interdisciplinary nature of so many journals, it can be very difficult to apportion periodical funds by subject or department. However, in a college library where book funds are allocated by department, faculty may not feel responsible for holding the line on new subscriptions if they do not consider these part of the departmental allocation.

Long-Term and Other Costs

In college libraries one of the toughest problems in monitoring the library materials budget is distribution of limited funds between monographs and periodicals. The percentage of the budget spent on periodicals takes on special importance because the purchase of a subscription commits the library to a long-term process involving repeated payments over a period of time. Periodicals selection is not a one-time decision — the price of a new title may be low when the library first acquires it but may easily triple in cost over the next few years. To the subscription price itself must be added the cost of acquiring backfiles, replacing missing issues, binding back issues, and/or purchasing microform editions and providing the indexes, abstracts and bibliographic databases that provide access to the journal articles. The periodicals collection also impacts other areas of the library budget; e.g., staff time to receive, check-in, claim and record lost issues, automation costs to perform these functions by computer, and space costs to store the periodicals collection.

CONCLUSION

This paper has examined the overall acquisitions budget and looked specifically at the issues involved in monitoring book and periodical expenditures. In closing, it is important to recognize that a number of other costs are often included in the library acquisitions budget. For example, the following goods and services may be supported and controlled by the college library materials budget.

Nonprint Materials — include a number of expensive items, such as film and video, as well as slides, compact discs, phonograph records and tapes. Although some colleges have a separate audiovisual department that orders its own equipment and media, in many cases the media center is part of the library and responsible for monitoring a nonprint materials budget line allocated from the library acquisitions budget.

Access Fees — these "refer to library expenditures on products or services, including auxiliary costs whose purpose is to provide information on demand to library users."[39] Online searches, interlibrary loan, copy charges, and document delivery may be charged back to the user or supported out of operational or other funds. However, in a number of libraries, these services are fully or partially supported by the library materials budget and must be carefully monitored within that budget throughout the year.

CD-ROM and Microcomputer Software — Although the purchase of CD-ROM databases often results in savings on online search costs, these databases are extremely expensive and often involve annual license fees. If word processing and other microcomputer packages are included in the college's overall collection development goals, they also require a systematic method of allocation and control.

In institutions where all or some of the above are charged to the library materials budget, it is essential to adequately augment that budget so that funding for books and periodicals is not encroached by the costs of these additional services.

REFERENCES

1. U.S. Department of Education, *Higher Education General Information Survey (HEGIS) of College and University Libraries*. 1985. Washington, D.C., U.S. Department of Education; p. 7.

2. Evan Ira Farber, "Limiting College Library Growth: Bane or Boon?" *The Journal of Academic Librarianship*. 1975, 1(5); p. 14.

3. "Standards for College Libraries." *College and Research Libraries News*. March, 1986, *47*(3); p. 199.

4. Murray Martin, *Budgetary Control in Academic Libraries*. Greenwich, CT: JAI Press, 1978. p. 14.

5. Jennifer Cargill, "Bottom Line Blues: Preparing Library Budgets." *Wilson Library Bulletin*. June, 1987, 61(10); p. 31.

6. Lauren Kelly, "Budgeting in Nonprofit Organizations." *Drexel Library Quarterly*. Summer, 1985, 21(3); p. 3.

7. *Standards*. p. 200.

8. *Ibid*.

9. Margo Trumpeter, *Basic Budgeting Practices for Libraries*. Chicago, IL: American Library Association, 1985. p. 118.

10. Martin. p. 123.

11. Sharon C. Bonk, "Rethinking the Acquisitions Budget: Anticipating and Managing Change." *Library Acquisitions Practice and Theory*. 1986, 10(2); pp. 100-101.

12. *Standards*. p. 200.

13. Philip M. Clark, "Accounting as Reporting: The Uses of Online Accounting Systems." *Drexel Library Quarterly*. Summer, 1985, 21(3); pp. 61-74.

14. Brian Alley and Jennifer Cargill, *Keeping Track of What You Spend: The Librarian's Guide to Simple Bookkeeping*. Phoenix, AZ: Oryx Press, 1982.

15. G. Stevenson Smith, *Accounting for Librarians and Other Not for Profit Managers*,.Chicago, IL; American Library Association, 1983.

16. Jennifer S. Cargill and Brian Alley, *Practical Approval Plan Management*. Phoenix, AZ: Oryx Press, 1972. p. 75.

17. Alley and Cargill, pp. 21-25. (Source for procedures 1, 2, and 3.)

18. *Ibid*., pp. 25-26. (Source for procedures 3-7.)

19. Bookdealer-Library Relations Committee. Resources Section. Resources and Technical Services Division. American Library Association. *Guidelines for Handling Library Orders for In-Print Monographic Publications*. 2nd ed. Chicago, IL: American Library Association, 1984. pp. 10-11.

20. *Ibid*., pp. 9, 11, 12.

21. *Ibid*., pp. 6, 11.

22. Cargill and Alley, p. 73.

23. Ted Greider, *Acquisitions: Where, Who, and How*. Westport, CT: Greenwood, 1978. p. 18.

24. Charles A. Gardner, "Book Selection Policies in the College Library: A Reappraisal." *College and Research Library*. March, 1985, 46(2); pp. 143-144.

25. R.R. Hellenga, "Departmental Acquisitions Policies for Small College Libraries." *Library Acquisition: Practice and Theory*. 1979, 3(2); pp. 81-84.

26. Richard D. Johnson, "The College Library Collection." *Advances in Librarianship*. San Diego, CA: Academic Press, Vol. 14, p. 166.

27. Jasper G. Schad, "Fairness In Book Fund Allocation." *College and Research Libraries*. November, 1987, 48(6); p. 481.

28. Cargill and Alley, p. 75.

29. Cargill and Alley, p. 71.

30. Cargill and Alley, p. 76.

31. Dana L. Alessi, "Coping With Library Needs: The Approval Vendor's Response/Responsibility." *Issues In Acquisitions Programs and Evaluation*. Ann Arbor, MI: The Pieran Press, 1985. p. 103.

32. Cargill and Alley, p. 39.

33. Rebecca Lenzini and Judith G. Horn, "1975-86: Formulative Years for the Subscription Agency," *Serials Librarian*, in press.

34. Ronald Akie, "Periodical Prices 1986-1988 Update," *Serials Librarian*, 1988, 15(1/2); pp. 43-59. Other important sources of periodical pricing information include "Prices of U.S. and Foreign Published Materials" in the *Bowker Annual* and "Price Index for 1988: U.S. Periodicals" in the April issue of *Library Journal*.

35. Ibid., p. 13.

36. *Library Profiles* (Number 1), Faxon Collection Development Series, The Faxon Press, April, 1988; pp. 1-3.

37. Ibid., p. 12.

38. William Miller and Steven D. Rookwood, "Collection Development from the College Perspective," *College and Research Libraries*. July, 1979, 40(4); p. 321.

39. Bonk, p. 101.

How I Learned to Stop Worrying and Love the Budget

Judith F. Niles

SUMMARY. This article describes the realities of learning to manage a budget. Because there is little formal training in the graduate library school program, acquisitions librarians learn the necessary skills through observation, trial and error. Based on her own experience, the author provides a description and overview of the budget process and the various phases of it for which an acquisitions librarian may be responsible: budget development, committing the budget, and budget analyses and reports. She points out the typical difficulties which acquisitions librarians encounter in the budget management process, and suggests methods and strategies for coping with them. She concludes that it is a rewarding experience, despite the frustrations.

In fourteen years of experience in working with acquisitions in a variety of academic library environments I found that being a successful budget manager was the greatest challenge among many. It was also the task for which I had been the least prepared in my liberal arts and library science education. On entering the profession, I had no expectation that financial management was going to play a large part in my career as a librarian. I believe that the experience of the new acquisitions professional today is going to be a similar one. I hope that the following observations will be helpful to those new learners; that they will find in it new approaches to problems, or that it will give them a sense of perspective on their own situations. Other librarians who are "veterans" of the budget experience will also find it worthwhile to compare their own experiences

Judith F. Niles is Director, Division of Technical Services, University Libraries, University of Louisville, Louisville, KY 40292.

69

to mine, in the same way that I have found reassurance and encouragement in sharing experiences with my counterparts throughout my career.

TRAINING

It has always surprised me that I really enjoyed being involved with the "business end" of the library profession despite the inappropriateness of my training. My only related training prior to library school was a high school bookkeeping course, and that had not convinced me that I had a particular talent or inclination for a business or financial management career. Graduate library school provided me with a strong philosophical and conceptual understanding of the profession, and with a solid basic knowledge of information sources and systems. This is what it is designed to do. Unfortunately, it is less likely to provide significant training in the technical aspects of day-to-day library operations. Most librarians acquire that training "on-the-job."

Nonetheless, had I become a cataloger or a reference librarian, I would have started with basic training in the rules of cataloging and classification, or with a substantial knowledge of reference tools because there were courses designed to develop skills in those areas. I would not have found courses designed to train me to be an acquisitions librarian. It was my experience in library school that when the term "acquisitions" was used, it was defined as, or assumed to mean, selection of materials, or collection development, and did not deal with the realities of becoming a library purchasing agent and budget manager. Management courses sometimes touched upon the budget process, but avoided details relating to the materials budget and related activities. Recent library school graduates continue to confirm that my experience was not unique, and that curricula related to acquisitions have not changed in the intervening years. Unfortunately, library schools seem to be reducing, rather than expanding, training in all of the technical services, but that's another article.

So let us assume that the typical acquisitions librarian is a veritable novice when it comes to budgets. As in all jobs, it is useful to seek out a mentor who can explain, define and clarify all the mysteries. However, it is often hard to find a mentor. Ideally, it would be a supervisor who has a great deal of experience to draw upon. Very large libraries may have a hierarchy in the acquisitions department with entry level positions and supervisors to train them, but small and medium-sized libraries tend to have only one acquisitions managerial position. Coming up through the ranks in acquisitions usually means that one begins as a staff or paraprofessional employee, comes from a related department such as collection development or cataloging, or moves from smaller to larger library situations. In each of those situations, the individual usually learns about the budget by observing, asking questions, and having to solve problems.

BUDGET PROCESS – DEFINITION AND OVERVIEW

It seems appropriate next to look at the budget process as a whole and give it some definition. The *Random House Dictionary of the English Language* defines "budget" as follows:

As a noun:
- an estimate, often itemized, of expected income and expense, or operating results, for a given period in the future
- a plan of operations based on such an estimate
- an itemized allotment of funds for a given period
- the total sum of money set aside or needed for a specific purpose

As a verb:
- to plan allotment of funds
- to deal with specific funds in a budget

All of these definitions are appropriate but they only begin to describe the budget process. I think of budgeting as a process with a forward momentum, its pattern of movement spiral rather than linear in dimension. It is cyclical, but not a circle retraced upon itself over and over again. It progresses from one fiscal year to the next, in more or less the same pattern, building upon the information and processes already established. The budget is developed, approved, presented for use; it is then committed and expended; it is analyzed and reported on for management or collection development purposes. The spiral for each fiscal year overlaps the previous and forthcoming years, because development of the new budget must begin before the expending and analysis of the current year are completed, and because expenditure patterns will be used in budget projections for the future.

Size and Scope of the Budget

The budget process and the acquisitions librarian's role in it can also be affected by the size and scope of the budget, which can vary greatly from library to library. There are also many variations on how the materials budget is defined. In size, it can range from a few thousand dollars to several million. Typically, there are established budget lines for monographs, serials, binding, microforms, theses, and other formats or media. An acquisitions librarian may have responsibility for any one, for all, or for a combination of these budget lines, depending on the local organizational structure and the total amount of the budget. The monograph, serial and other budget lines may be fiscally separate, or they may simply be guidelines for expenditures, depending on institutional policies and regulations. Often the definitions of the categories will be very different in the accounting office than they are in the acquisitions department. The acquisitions librarian will find it necessary to understand, interpret and accommodate the differences in all payment and reporting functions.

The major portion of a materials budget, that which is supplied as part of the library's "general funds" or "base budget," is the share of total institutional operating funds which the parent institution has specifically designated for the purpose of purchasing library materials. It is sometimes referred to as "hard money" because there is some guarantee that it will be available every year. The amount is determined, ideally, from figures the library provides each year to demonstrate what funds are needed to continue to collect at established or increased levels. In reality, the amount is likely to reflect what the parent institution feels it can afford, and falls short of what is needed to achieve collecting goals.

The base budget provided by the parent institution is always very significant to the acquisitions librarian in this respect: it is only available for the current fiscal year. There are serious repercussions if it is not all committed within that time frame. If it is under-committed, the remainder of the money may revert to the parent institution, which may then infer that the library really does not require so much money in future years, and will accordingly reduce subsequent budgets. There are also repercussions if it is over-committed, primarily that the excess expenditures will have to be covered out of the subsequent budget, or from other funds. Ironically, the consequences are not quite as serious as with under-committing, since no money is actually lost. Nonetheless, the auditing body is likely to perceive over-commitment as fiscally irresponsible, and there may be serious sanctions against it in some institutions. Over-commitment is also going to complicate the bookkeeping for the acquisitions department and for that reason should be minimized even if there are no other consequences.

While speaking of committing the budget, it is important to point out that the definition of "commit" varies from institution to institution. In many libraries, it means only that there must be enough outstanding orders to encumber the remainder of the free balance of the budget at the end of the fiscal year. In others, it means that the entire budget must be expended (all monies paid out) at the close of the year. This distinction is crucial in planning the acquisitions process. Throughout this article, the term "commit" and its various forms is meant to imply whichever definition is appropriate to the local situation of the reader.

There are other types of funds which, though they are part of the total budget process, are not subject to the fiscal year requirements described above, but may have other restrictions. These may be known as "endowed," "gift," or "restricted" funds. Such funds are also often referred to as "soft money" because they are available on a one-time or short-term basis, rather than recurring annually as the base budget does. Typically, "soft money" funds come from outside donors, who have specified that they be used for certain types of purchases, or placed other restrictions on their use. Such funds are great boons to the library and allow collections to be enhanced, although their existence sometimes gives the parent institution an excuse to decrease general funding. The restrictions attached to them are often great headaches for the acquisitions manager, as we shall see further on.

Let us now take a more detailed look at the phases of the budget process and the accompanying role of the acquisitions librarian.

DEVELOPMENT OF THE BUDGET

The budget development process may be an integral part of the acquisitions librarian's responsibilities. It can start long before the fiscal year begins, with projections of needs for the next budget period, presentations to administrative officials at higher levels, and defense of the projected needs. It requires research into the anticipated average costs for materials in the coming years. It requires a knowledge of factors such as new collection development programs and goals. To be thorough the budget projection takes into account future trends in the national and international economies, currency fluctuations, and awareness of developments in the publishing industry. Once a final budget is approved, it is divided into subcategories, often called allocations. These subdivisions or allocations will be used to guide and/or track purchasing in support of subject disciplines, types of material, library location, etc. Often a combination of these are used, depending on the library's needs.

If the acquisitions manager is not the preparer of the budget proposal, s/he, more than likely, is still the provider of the bulk of the information for the person who does prepare it. Projecting the cost of library materials for a budget which will be in effect a year or more hence is only slightly more scientific than the use of a crystal ball. Most projections are based on historical patterns of publishing and cost increases. Until the 1980s this was a fairly reliable method which resulted in reasonably accurate predictions. In the current decade, however, international currency fluctuations, in particular, have made it extremely difficult to project costs precisely. In recent years historical patterns have been able to tell us only where we have been, and are not particularly helpful as a guide to the future. Currency fluctuations, serial price differentials, rapid changes in the publishing industry, the knowledge explosion and the development of new media and formats, have greatly complicated the projection process.

Average costs and projected inflation rates have traditionally been useful, but are becoming less so unless the context is very laboriously defined. What is average for the humanities? for the social sciences? for the sciences and technology? for trade publishers? for children's books? for university presses? for scientific and technical presses? for domestic materials? for foreign? In order to come up with a meaningful projection the acquisitions librarian has to combine separate cost figures for categories such as these and then factor in as well cost projections for a variety of formats or media types: monographs and serials, scores, audio and video recordings, microforms, realia, software packages, CD-ROM databases, and so on. The most significant projection in many libraries is for the cost of maintaining subscription and standing orders for periodicals, annuals and other continuing commitments.

To analyze expenditures locally in all these possible permutations is not an easy goal to accomplish. Vendors and professional organizations are providing more and more data broken down into these categories, but unless the acquisitions librarian can also categorize local expenditures in these same ways, vendor data are helpful only in a general sense. Automated systems are of some help in budget analysis and projection. Most frequently though, integrated or turn-key library systems provide us with "vanilla" and if we want a sundae, we must be prepared to make and provide our own toppings and additional flavors. If the librarian has a great deal of staff, time, and programming support, sophisticated projection packages can be designed and implemented. Rarely, however, are local resources adequate to allow this.

In the end, most budget projections are based to a greater extent on the acquisitions librarian's intuition from previous experience and current awareness of trends and patterns than on empirical evidence. In other words, it is an educated guess. Unfortunately, this is not always understood or appreciated by the fiscal authorities to whom the librarian reports.

COMMITTING THE BUDGET

Once the budget has been set up, the ordering and purchasing process begins. In this phase, the acquisitions librarian must ensure that there is an accounting system in place which interacts with the ordering system so that commitments and expenditures are accurately tracked. S/he must also provide ways to report data to offices of the parent institution to which the library must present its invoices for payment, and/or document commitments and expenditures. S/he must regularly monitor the status of the budget to assess whether it will be committed by the end of the fiscal year, taking steps to speed up or slow down the ordering process, as necessary. While there now exist many automated systems which facilitate this process, even the most sophisticated tend to be generic in their approach, so that they can be implemented in a variety of libraries. Frequently, even with an automated accounting system, a supplementary monitoring process may be required to coordinate staff activities of ordering and receiving to ensure that the budget balances. For instance, as the end of the fiscal year approaches it may be necessary to keep a manual log of orders placed and received throughout the department so that increases and reductions in commitments are known immediately.

One might assume that when the fiscal year commences, the acquisitions process can begin immediately, with a full twelve months to commit and expend those funds available for the year. In actuality, there are always delays of one sort or another that are beyond the control of the acquisitions librarian. The library administration may not know the budget figures at the beginning of the fiscal year. Even when the overall budget is known, the acquisitions librarian may need to wait for subdivisions or allocations to be set by the collection development department, or by the library administration. S/he may have the authority to set allocations, but have to submit them for approval to one of the aforementioned. The parent purchasing or accounting office may impose restrictions on the commencement of ordering and expending. Thus, typically, ordering may begin two or three months into the fiscal year. Similarly, at the end of the fiscal year the accounting office may impose early cut-off dates which further reduce the length of the commitment period.

Other events may also intervene. As we become more dependent on automated systems delays are often caused by software or hardware upgrades. If we have adequate control over the automation process, we can at least arrange to have the upgrade occur at the beginning of a fiscal year while we are waiting for the budget to be finalized. However, then we run the risk of problems in the implementation process which may delay the acquisitions process even longer into the fiscal year. In the worst case, the librarian may have no say in the timing of upgrades and may be given little or no warning that regular processes will be suspended at any time during the year.

BUDGET ANALYSIS AND REPORTS

Analysis of commitments and expenditures and the reports which result from it are major responsibilities for the acquisitions librarian. Budget analysis and reports are essentially inseparable from the first two parts of the process, budget development and commitment, because they provide the raw data from which projections can be drawn and the mechanisms by which the progress of commitment can be measured.

While acquisitions librarians will not usually have to develop a reporting structure from scratch, at some point it is likely that they will have to adjust established structures, or adapt them to automated systems. In my own experience, no established system that I inherited with my job seemed to answer all the questions that arose. I was continually tinkering with the system to obtain more data to help in managing the acquisitions department, to provide more management information for the library administration or collection development unit, or better reports for auditing bodies beyond the library.

If you are planning changes to an existing reporting structure, or implementing an automated system, you need to keep in mind that the reports will serve different purposes, and require different frequencies, for different audiences. The acquisitions librarian wants the most immediate access possible to ongoing changes in the status of each fund and allocation or subdivision (daily, if not minute-to-minute). The collection development units wants to know how much of each allocation is committed, and how much is left to spend (monthly, at least). The library administration is likely to be most interested in the bottom line: will it all be committed by the end of the fiscal year? The accounting office of the parent institution may not want to see the library's budget reports regularly. However, this data will be the library's primary documentation of commitments if there is any inquiry from the accounting office.

Annual reports will probably follow much the same structure as reports throughout the year, but it is useful to be able to extract some additional types of data, especially for projecting budget needs for future years. For instance, if the basic subdivisions of the budget are by subject, you may also need to be able to find out how much was spent by purchase type, format or media: serials and monographs, approvals and firm orders, microforms, AV materials, software, etc. If you have to keep track of the status of each gift fund separately from the base budget, you may still need to be able to determine how expenditures from that fund break down by subject. There are almost endless permutations on how reports can be structured, and you must find the best balance for your own situation.

Computers are providing many of us with the capability to extract different types of data. As mentioned earlier, an integrated system may provide an accounting package which automatically produces reports, once you have set up your basic fund structure. However, it is not likely to have enough flexibility to respond to all your needs. Additional manual research, or transfer of data to a microcomputer for analysis using other software, may be necessary. Either course can be complex and laborious. Neither may be feasible if the librarian has not anticipated local requirements enough to be sure that the various data elements are discretely identifiable or appropriately coded so that they can be extracted.

SURVIVAL TECHNIQUES

One of the best things an acquisitions librarian can do to cope with the responsibilities which have been discussed above is to be open to all sources of help and information. For general information there are the traditional means of continuing one's training: formal courses, professional publications in the field, and workshops, seminars and institutes. It is often harder to know where to find answers to specific local questions. Developing a network of reliable sources in other offices around the institution is the best solution. The beginning acquisitions librarian, or the more experienced professional seeking to become familiar with a new institution, will find that many institutional resources are available. The departments and offices with whom the librarian will work as a matter of course can provide much help in learning the ropes of budget management.

The library's accounting office can be a great source of information and assistance to the acquisitions librarian. S/he will often find that the library administrator in charge of the overall budget is willing and able to provide a great deal of information and background. That administrator may also be the library's primary liaison with the parent accounting office, and consequently can be a good source of information about institutional policies and procedures, which are often obscure and complex. Frequently that administrator also has more clout in resolving problems with the institutional accounting office than does the acquisitions librarian, and can therefore be a useful ally.

It is also very important to develop a good understanding of the operations of the parent institution's accounting office. A standard procedure which most acquisitions librarians must handle is the monthly and annual balancing of library expenditure and commitment records with those produced by the accounting office. In order to do so, it is necessary to learn the operating premises of the accounting system and to become educated, formally or informally, in basic accounting principles.

Unfortunately it is usually more difficult to develop a cooperative relationship with that accounting office than with the parallel office in the library. Procedures which this office insists upon, or regulations which it must enforce, can be a source of great frustration in expending the budget. Which is not to suggest that regulations should be ignored or sidestepped, but the staff of the accounting office may be totally unfamiliar with library purchasing and the ways in which regulations apply. In my own experience accounting offices have been known to question the expenditure of $5000.00 for a rare book because there is disbelief that a BOOK could cost that much. They have been known to insist that the purchase of a journal backfile be charged to the serial line in the budget, even though that line is set aside for the purchase of continuing subscriptions, because they did not understand the significance of that difference. Local regulations might require that every item be billed on a separate invoice, or, almost as bad, that all items for a given fund be invoiced separately from those for every other fund. The acquisitions librarian may spend many hours either negotiating local exceptions to those procedures, negotiating with a vendor to follow special invoicing requirements, or developing complex and time-consuming procedures in the acquisitions department.

The acquisitions librarian must be a diplomat in dealing with the various other departments and offices of the library and the parent institution, particularly for matters related to the budget. The librarian is likely to be held accountable for any and all aspects of the budget, whether s/he is endowed with real authority to control it or not. For that reason, the successful manager needs to establish and maintain good communication with other library departments which work with the budget. The collection development department, for instance, will have numerous questions relating to the budget. Monthly reports on the status of allocations will be questioned and have to be explained. In an academic library, the same questions may be asked by faculty from teaching departments who monitor allocations. The following are typical of questions that budget reports will provoke: why did the price increase so much? are all the orders turned in to Acquisitions reflected in the report? why can't I buy a periodical for just one year from the monographic budget? The acquisitions librarian may not know the answer or be unable to articulate it to the questioner's satisfaction. In these situations, it is tempting to build walls rather than open doors and thus isolate the acquisitions department from outside inquiry. While that strategy might seem to garner more time to get on with the work at hand without pesky interruptions, the long-term effect is to create dissatisfied patrons or colleagues, which eventually reflects badly on the library, or creates other problems for the acquisitions department. Through experience you do learn more satisfactory ways to explain unsatisfactory situations. The worst that can happen is that the same people will always ask the same questions and you will develop a thick skin about it. The best that can happen is that you may turn some interrogators into allies.

PUBLIC RELATIONS

If budgets were generous and grew from year to year to meet the needs of the collection, the acquisitions librarian might have little need to be concerned about public relations. Few other communications from the acquisitions department generate the emotional reactions that news about the budget does, especially when it is bad news (which it most often is!). The acquisitions librarian is often called to be accountable for a situation that is not of her or his making. S/he might be limited in what can be said publicly about the budget, making explanations almost impossible. Referring the irate patron or colleague to the director's office is only a temporary measure. Directors are usually more protected by their staff and the pressures of their schedules. The acquisitions librarian can almost always be found and the person who does not get satisfaction from the director is likely to vent his or her spleen on the librarian most directly associated with the problem. The inclination to build walls is particularly prevalent in this situation. But the answer once again is to develop a thick skin, and one's diplomatic skills.

In addition to the irate colleague or patron who may show up at one's door to complain about the budget situation, there are some less obvious problems that tight budgets cause. Budget problems are often reported to the local community, to encourage the citizenry to elect and support officials who will make library budgets a priority for public funds, or to stimulate financial support from other support groups such as alumni associations or "friends" organizations. Such publicity is often successful at achieving those goals. However, there is a side effect with negative impact as well. This is the dreaded flood of books and back issues of journals rained upon the library by donors responding to such publicity by clearing their attics, cellars and offices, as well as their consciences. And they want an appraisal and a tax deduction! Other articles have been and will be written about the difficulties of dealing with gifts and the ensuing paperwork.[1] Therefore, I will not dwell upon the topic except to say that these gifts rarely provide the books which the budget shortfall denies to us. Nonetheless, in dealing with these donors, the acquisitions librarian must be extremely careful that grievous insults are not inferred by the wealthy donor who really

MIGHT bequeath the library a large fortune. Since one often does not know in advance that the attic cleaner has a fortune, or the rejection of which item will be the unforgivable insult, the librarian must find a diplomatic way for donors to be handled by all acquisitions staff. Having an effective collection development or gift acceptance policy and a gracious manner are the best assets in this situation.

Donors of money are more rare and certainly more enthusiastically welcomed. Unfortunately, in most cases, it is not the acquisitions librarians who has the pleasure of being handed a check. Instead s/he is the one who finds that the check often comes with restrictions or obligations that make the money difficult to use or require elaborate procedures to fulfill. Restrictions might require that the money be used for subjects that are not appropriate to the collection, or that materials be selected only from certain lists, which may contain out-of-print or otherwise unavailable materials. Obligations could include elaborate title-by-title reporting of purchases, limited time in which to expend or commit the money, special book plates or acknowledgements, or even a separately managed room or shelving area. Again, strong collection development and gift policies supported by the director and the parent institution can be effective in avoiding such results. It is very important that the acquisitions librarian make efforts to communicate to the director, and to others who may accept donations, the difficulties of working under restrictions and the ensuing net decrease in productivity. However, there is no technique for saying "no, thank you" that does not risk causing a negative public relations result.

SATISFACTIONS OF WORKING WITH THE BUDGET

In looking back over my observations, even more frustrations come to mind than have already been discussed. They are not worth detailing, as they are variations on the same themes, but they do prompt me to ask the question: what made me like it enough to stick with it? I can't think of a long list of satisfactions, but I would sum it up for myself as follows:

Working with the budget is satisfying because it is like working with a puzzle. It is a real test of your ingenuity and tenacity, and provides powerful positive reinforcement when you succeed. Simultaneously, you have the thrill of being a risk-taker, of calling upon all your accumulated knowledge and experience and making your best estimate of what is going to happen in the ensuing years, then watching it unfold before your eyes. Even if all does not go as planned, if your skills are well developed, you have the satisfaction of coping with unforeseen events and still achieving your goals.

REFERENCE

1. For a recent good discussion of gifts, see "Buried Alive in Gifts," by Veneese C. Nelson, *Library Journal*, April 15, 1988, pp. 54-56.

Coping with a Decreasing Book Budget

Ian Edward

SUMMARY. This article discusses the nature of a library's declining book budget and the methods used to focus attention on a mechanism to alleviate the situation. The effect of budgetary decline on staffing requirements is examined along with an organizational structure suitable to fluctuating workflows.

Stagnant or retrograde funding will bring change to a library. Responses to change need not be detrimental to organizational routines or goals. Instead, changes can be seen as opportunities to become more efficient and to strengthen relationships within and around the library environment.

BACKGROUND

During the early 1970s, librarians and teaching faculty at Memphis State University were relatively content with the library material budget and with the level of collection development it maintained. Available funds could accommodate almost any request for a monograph, a new periodical title, continuation, or standing order.

The two major components of the material budget were designated for periodicals and for books. The periodicals budget (defined by the Libraries as titles published more than once a year) covered subscriptions for titles recommended by faculty over many years and was not allocated to specific academic units. The book budget covered mostly nonrecurring material such as monographs but also

---

Ian Edward is Head, Acquisitions Department, Memphis State University Libraries, Memphis, TN 38152.

85

included continuations and standing orders. These continuations made up a relatively small number of titles, but their costs grew quickly throughout the decade.

Also, the book budget supported several approval plans for Spanish, French, German, British and Latin American imprints, as well as a large domestic "selection plan." The selection plan differed from the approval plans in that monographs were ordered from bibliographic slips set out for faculty perusal rather than allowing an outside vendor to select material for the Libraries. Slips for the selection plan were screened by a librarian before the faculty's selection process began, making the material offered more appropriate to Memphis State Libraries' collections.

The remainder of the book budget was allocated to various academic units, including some of the Libraries' departments, for discretionary orders. For units external to the libraries, these allocations were derived from an adjustment of the previous fiscal year's dollar amount depending upon whether the book budget increased or decreased. For example, if a unit received 5% of $400,000.00 in a given fiscal year and allocatable funds the next fiscal year were $425,000.00 the unit would again receive 5% ($20,000.00 and $21,250.00 respectively).

Although the origin of this method of establishing percentages was unknown, there was a striking similarity between the old percentages derived from tradition and some new ones developed years later based on a formula using credit hour production, number of faculty, levels of programs taught, and relative costs of material to an academic unit. It seems likely that the traditional mechanism originated in some similar process.

The allocation process extant during the 1970s involved deducting amounts for approval plans, the selection plan, and continuations or standing orders from the total amount of book funds provided by the University administration. Then, the remaining sum was allocated to academic units after approval by a University Library Committee, the Vice-President for Academic Affairs, and the President. These approvals were more of a routing sequence than any forum for discussion and adjustment.

FUNDING TRENDS AND TACTICS

The shrinking book budget at Memphis State University Libraries came in the guise of a no-growth budget. The appointment of a new president in the mid-1970s was followed over the next two years by a substantially declining book budget which levelled off at two thirds its former size. Thereafter, funds budgeted for books and periodicals by the University's administration at the beginning of each fiscal year appeared static. These amounts were identical, to the dollar, from fiscal year to fiscal year, line item to line item. This appearance of a no-growth budget was deceptive because the phrase itself can be deceptive. The term implies changelessness: a static state. It begs an interpretation that, if a situation is not getting better neither is it getting worse. It tends to cloud the impact of annual inflation on day-to-day operations. The appearance of the same numbers on a budget document over subsequent fiscal years can help lull an administrator unfamiliar with unbridled periodical inflation into a sense of false security.

It would have been difficult for an interested party to determine the exact amount of newly appropriated funds that were available to be divided into book allocations in any specific fiscal year. Funds that had been obligated in a previous fiscal year and carried forward for subsequent deobligation were reported as part of the book budget total in some University reports. The inclusion of a "library books" item in the University's annual report gave the impression of a very healthy Memphis State University Libraries' book budget, unless one remembered that such an item included book funds for the organizationally separate Law School Library. It was important, therefore, to be specific when using the term "book budget" with faculty and other patrons.

The inclusion of so-called "year-end" funds was part of the book budget as reported in University reports for the Libraries. These funds ranged from a few thousand to tens of thousands of dollars and were added to the book budget during the last few months of the fiscal year. Usually, such funds arrived too late during the fiscal year to influence discretionary allocations. There was little or no opportunity for these funds to be used in the planned ordering of relatively inexpensive materials essential for collection develop-

ment. Often, "year-end funds" were used to cover existing or anticipated over-expenditures for approval or selection plans, for purchase of a few very costly retrospective sets, or to cover overages in periodical expenditures.

Despite apparent confusion caused by rapidly changing and shifting funds, an advantage did appear: clarification of expenditure priorities. The first priority was to pay for periodicals. To ensure there were sufficient funds for payment, periodical inflation was calculated at the beginning of the fiscal year. The inflation rate became the basis of a budgetary adjustment (budget revision) transferring funds from the book budget to the periodicals budget. The remainder of the book budget was then broken into its component parts.

The revised budget amounts became a foundation for a projection of the effects of periodical inflation on the book budget over the following four years. A table similar to the following accompanied allocation recommendations to the University Library Committee.

Year	Periodicals (Initial)	Periodicals (Revised)	Additional $ @ 15% from Books	Books (Initial)	Books (Revised)
Current	160,000	184,000	24,000	400,000	376,000
+1	160,000	211,600	51,600	400,000	348,400
+2	160,000	243,340	83,340	400,000	316,600
+3	160,000	279,841	119,841	400,000	280,159
+4	160,000	321,817	161,817	400,000	238,183

Since compounding inflation at fifteen percent over five years doubles a base, such projections served well to show the effects of inflation on the book budget whether or not it was first presented as static. Informing faculty of the effects of periodicals inflation and of the expanding continuations/standing orders base imbedded in the book budget and encroaching on discretionary allocations further intensified concerns. Additionally, the continuations/standing orders desk was transferred from the Periodicals Department to the Acquisitions Department on the assumption that the staff in a department with a reduced workload would have more time to handle and evaluate such material.

As an initial step toward addressing concerns over the budget, Libraries' administrators recommended a reevaluation and possible elimination of fixed areas in the book budget. During attempts to control spending, three unchanging collection development assumptions became more prominent.

The first assumption was that the individuals primarily responsible for collection development in most disciplines, the teaching faculty of the academic units, were better suited to evaluate the merits of a publication for inclusion in the collection than were purveyors of material such as approval plan vendors. Therefore, within the first two years of the "no-growth" situation, foreign approval plans were all but eliminated and funds for the domestic selection plan were drastically reduced. While faculty regretted the demise of the approval plans, none offered to forego their shrinking discretionary funds to sustain them.

The second assumption was that certain departments within the Libraries were responsible for selection of material so important to the Libraries and the University as a whole that their continued funding was essential. Thus funding for allocations of the Reference Department, Special Collections, Government Documents, and for replacement volumes continued to be allocated on an annual basis. While these allocations were cut along with those of academic departments, none were ever eliminated.

The third assumption treated periodical expenditures as fixed costs, much as rent or a utility bill to a small business: no matter if the organization's products were ten items or a thousand, these were costs that had to be sustained. Periodicals remained a relatively stable base in terms of numbers of subscriptions but were subject to extremely high inflation as were other commodities at the time. This assumption was proven true each time an attempt was made to curtail the number of subscription titles: the faculty wanted the "utility bill" paid in full.

Interestingly, however, the faculty did not object as strenuously to cutting continuations or standing orders. When a recurring publication was called a continuation rather than a periodical, the process of elimination did not seem nearly as painful to the faculty. On the assumption that monographs in series could be ordered from discretionary allocations and that funds would be saved because not every monograph in a series would be ordered, all such standing orders were dropped without many protests from faculty. Indeed, if the items in a series were of significant importance to faculty, they would be requested whether or not they were already on standing order. The cut in standing orders eliminated some wasted effort while avoiding the purchase of items unnecessary to the collection. Eventually all academic units were required to rank those standing orders and continuations attributed to them and most of the lower-ranked ones were dropped. Again, these adjustments were made with virtually no complaints. It seems likely that the nomenclature assigned to different types of publications has an impact on the emotional involvement of faculty with their material.

In addition to evaluating and eliminating approval plans and dropping continuations and standing orders another tactic that proved helpful in dealing with the shrinking budget was to inform the faculty that university administrators responded more to faculty comments about book budgets than they did to librarians' comments. Therefore, faculty members who voiced criticism of their new smaller allocations were invited to direct such comments toward the University's administration. It was suggested to faculty that such observations would be given more credibility coming from groups without the perceived vested interest that librarians had. University administrators received dozens of memos and letters from library consumers, rather than from librarians themselves, detailing how periodical inflation was eliminating the book budget. Also, if for no other reason than the strength of their ranks, there are more vociferous faculty members than there are librarians.

In keeping with the prevailing theme of tight money, faculty were informed about the Libraries' cost-cutting measures. Vendors were selected with greatest discount as the single most important criterion; speed of order fulfillment was no longer as great a concern. In some cases faculty were told cost cutting determined the format chosen to fill their orders. The acquisition of dissertations and periodical back runs in microformat was used to illustrate the conscientious manner in which librarians were helping to deal with the new poverty. Trade paper editions were preferred over hardbound because it was cheaper to bind after receipt and the cost was borne by a different line of the budget. Purchase of duplicate copies was curtailed as much as possible. A request for a branch library title found to be on order for the main facility would be returned so the requester might have the opportunity to spend those funds on another item. In a similar vein, a policy extant for years specifying requests for multiple copies be justified in writing began to be followed at a more intense level after several years of somewhat lax enforcement. The original purpose of this policy was to avoid purchase of books that were never circulated — the renewed policy was grounded in low funding. These cost-cutting activities became an effective method of keeping the budget problem before the faculty even though relatively few funds were saved.

Nitpicking one's way to faculty awareness of financial difficulties undoubtedly did not have the impact that publicizing realistic projections of the declining book budget had. However, the opportunity to communicate with faculty over minor budget matters occurred continuously throughout the year, thus maintaining faculty awareness at a higher level. This newfound knowledge was eagerly passed from the faculty to University administrators; by redirecting faculty complaints from the Libraries to the University administration, the librarians gained allies where they formerly had critics. Very likely there is no one individual today who could interpret whether or not this tactic had the desired result, but the current book budget at Memphis State has not come to be expressed in the negative numbers that loomed imminent in the latter part of the 1970s.

Budget documents contain messages vastly more important than mere numbers, especially as is the case with a publicly funded institution like Memphis State University where the funding of all operations' activities is a matter of public record and one can see the Libraries emphasis or de-emphasis in context with that of other activities on campus. In this case the message could have been interpreted as "we are decreasing your importance" but in context it was interpreted as an ignorance of the impact of periodical inflation. When this interpretation was communicated to the faculty, library funding became an agenda item for departmental, collegiate, and academic senate deliberations. While this increased dialogue was no simple cure to a complex problem, it certainly helped.

STAFFING

Prior to the period of no-growth budgets the Acquisitions Department had grown to eighteen members, including four professional librarians. Two of the librarians had the word "bibliographer" in their titles, but the duties assigned to them were connected more with the administration of approval plans, the selection plan, gift and exchange programs, and maintenance of out-of-print searching. There was little evaluation of the material received on the approval plans except screening for and return of duplicate material. There was a high level of contact between Acquisitions librarians and the individual faculty liaisons in various academic units. These associations proved to be valuable contacts for exchanging information between the Libraries and those academic units that gave voice to the Libraries' budgetary problems.

An impending long-term decline in the book budget caused speculation about the size of the Acquisitions Department staff needed for future conversion of dollars into books. The decrease in Acquisitions staff, however, was much more gradual than the decrease in funding. Over a five-year span, the professional staff dropped by 50 percent through transfer of positions, one of which was vacant because of retirement. The nonprofessional, or classified staff, dropped to eight from fourteen, a reduction of 43 percent due mostly to the transfer of positions as they became vacant.

The majority of the classified transfers were initiated from within the department with two goals in mind. First, if transfers of positions were initiated from within the department then control over such actions would most probably remain there, making transfers less subject to decisions of higher-level administrators and leaving staffing levels to be determined by those most closely involved with the work to be done. This posture served adequately for several years and was grounded in a more acute awareness of the seasonality of staffing needs in the Acquisitions Department. Simply, there was not much book ordering done over the summer months because most individuals responsible for book selection, the teaching faculty, were away then. Further, the approval of proposed allocations usually was not completed until early fall which helped render the summer months relatively inactive.

The second goal, grounded in the assumption that it is much more difficult to supervise workers with not enough to do, was the elimination of unnecessary staff. Conscientious employees constantly demand new tasks as they finish assignments while those less motivated spend their energies appearing busy or impeding the work of others. The cliche about work expanding to fill the time alloted works only up to a point. That point occurs when production drops or stops due to an overcrowding of workers around too few tasks. Therefore, positions were transferred to balance staffing with the uneven workflow.

Technological change made the decision to eliminate positions easier because some tasks were no longer essential nor even remotely necessary. For example, the advent of membership in the regional network affiliated with the OCLC system, SOLINET, and access to its database had the effect of releasing two full-time positions. One was a position for the operation of a camera used to enlarge National Union Catalog citations to catalog card size. The database made maintenance of the Library of Congress proofslip file, an Acquisitions Department responsibility, unnecessary, thus releasing hours equal to at least one full-time position. These positions, when vacant, were offered to library administrators for disposition elsewhere.

Technological change also created some new tasks that were much more interesting to Acquisitions staff than filing proofslips. The department's work with a retrospective catalog conversion project (RETROCON) provided a worthwhile use of Acquisitions' staff and occupied hours formerly devoted to other duties. Using the SOLINET database compelled anyone involved in bibliographic searching to learn keyboard skills and tasks. The RETROCON project helped maintain them.

Excess staff hours provided the impetus for undertaking some long-deferred projects, such as processing the stock of an antiquarian bookstore whose 20,000 volumes had been untouched for years. Appropriate staff, with more intensive training in bibliographic searching and verification techniques, began screening more than 15,000 items in the uncataloged backlog. Additionally, Acquisitions staff conducted a substantial use study on items received against a major foreign approval plan. The results of this study showed minimal use of material in most disciplines. This data made the decision to reduce coverage of material received on the plan an easier, and it was thought, better one. Such projects kept the department's staff engaged in useful, necessary work well into the period of drastic cuts in the book budget and during the summers.

Eventually, the Acquisitions Department could no longer afford to voluntarily surrender its vacant positions. In the absence of quantitative projections of future funding or levels of book ordering, further staff reductions could have caused an inability to cope with incoming orders were funding to increase. The level of departmental staffing allowed the processing of a high volume of orders in a relatively short time span. This was a satisfactory level of service provided to patrons. However, the demand for this level of service simply was not present toward the end of or at the beginning of any fiscal year. The demand for services provided by Acquisitions, with the exception of the receiving function, had stabilized at nine months of the fiscal year while staffing was fixed over a twelve-month span. The department, therefore, had a surplus of staff hours available for non-order oriented tasks from several staff members for about twenty-five percent of their time.

One approach employed toward solving this problem was to utilize a variant of the matrix organization. In a matrix organization, lines of authority for the accomplishment of a specific task cut across the existing traditional lines of authority in an established organization, drawing upon differing skills from various functional areas to accomplish that task. This concept has been common in management literature since the 1960s. Descriptions of matrix organizations often include cautionary comments that friction is associated with this arrangement as the participants are diverted from their normal work routines. The potential for conflict seems very likely for those at the level of supervisor or manager and remains a threat over the course of the *ad hoc* project's life.

It appeared that the Acquisitions Department had almost a reverse of the usual situation calling for a matrix organization: rather than a project without qualified staff there were qualified staff without a project. It was a safe assumption that bibliographic and other skills already developed could be put to good use elsewhere in the Libraries, and that the experience could stimulate good will and provide a measure of job enrichment to the participants. Such job enrichment could accrue to those on the receiving end of those efforts, as well as to those whose time was loaned to other units.

Since the basis for and direction of such activity would be focused toward other units as opposed to drawing upon their resources, it was anticipated that the potential conflicts mentioned as a drawback of matrix organizations would be avoided. There was, in fact, almost no friction among participants.

To avoid false expectations by any Acquisitions' staff and by staff in Libraries' units receiving assistance, a brief series of interviews with the various prospective participants was conducted. Eventually, some units within the Libraries were identified with requirements seemingly well-suited to the activity at hand: short-term projects that required skills to be found among Acquisitions staff that could not carry a "busy work" appellation. Acquisitions staff were assured that this activity was not an effort to ease them out of their jobs nor that they were being shunted aside, but instead that they were being temporarily placed where skills were most needed. Those who were lacking confidence were offered the simplistic but effective argument that smaller staffs in smaller libraries had to possess a wider range of skills to be effective.

By the end of the second summer after these temporary reassignments had been in effect, the process had become routine and familiar. Indications were that the process was considered a worthwhile endeavor by its participants. Over 2,500 Acquisitions staff hours were reassigned to seven other library units and more than 2,200 of these hours were allocated among three units. While the result of this action had a net effect of reassigning one full-time staff member to duties outside the department for over a year, the actual reassignment involved four to five individuals performing other duties outside the department for two to three months. The goal of finding meaningful work for a large number of Acquisitions staff over the slack summer months had been accomplished.

The three units in the Libraries that received most of Acquisitions' staff hours were a branch library, the centralized bookkeeping facility, and the Special Collections Department. The bookkeeping facility shared a workflow that crossed many organizational lines from several Libraries' operations. Much of the work originated in Acquisitions as books received turned into accounts payable. The seasonality of book ordering at Memphis State became evident as increased activity in book ordering was followed by activity in receiving and then in bill payment. A knowledge of business language and of specific university financial procedures proved helpful for efficient processing in this unit.

A sudden need for additional hours arose in a branch library with the departure of the public service staff member assigned there. An existing hiring freeze undoubtedly increased the attractiveness of the surplus hours offered by Acquisitions. Two staff members with prior experience in the supervision of student employees covered operating hours for the branch library throughout the summer. The experience was positive for all concerned since one of the participating staff members applied for and attained the branch position after the hiring freeze was lifted. While this was not the goal of the reallocation of surplus hours within Acquisitions, it suggests the concept was both successful and beneficial to the Libraries.

The largest portion of reallocated hours were used by the Libraries' special collection, the Mississippi Valley Collection. The staff there were faced with a large quantity of unprocessed collections of family and business manuscripts or records. One Acquisitions staff member quickly developed a talent for weeding, organizing, and creating guides to such collections under the guidance of the Curator of Special Collections.

A series of informal progress reports on the reallocated hours was maintained. The most enthusiastic reaction came from Special Collections, where one individual remained assigned even after her services were needed in Acquisitions at the end of the summer. Since it should be acknowledged at the onset of any such project that a matrix organization brings with it some degree of inconvenience to the lending agency, the reassignment in this case was maintained to complete the work in Special Collections and to leave a favorable impression. Goodwill gained from the extension of the assignment outweighed any adverse impact on Acquisitions.

The need for reallocating surplus hours from Acquisitions Department staff was eliminated after three full-time staff were transferred to other duties elsewhere within the Libraries. This permanent solution to an intermittent short-term problem changed staffing in Acquisitions to a level that no longer generated such a prominent number of surplus hours. While the time necessary to process a routine book order from receipt of the request to the point of ordering increased, Acquisitions staff nevertheless managed to process all orders that funding permitted.

Initiating a series of deadlines wherein academic departments had to meet percents of their allocations during the fiscal year was instrumental in spreading incoming requests over a greater portion of the fiscal year. For example, an academic department with a $10,000.00 allocation would have to submit requests totaling $4,500.00 by the middle of the fifth month of the fiscal year, an additional $4,500.00 by the end of the seventh month, and the remaining $1,000.00 at the beginning of the tenth month. This procedure was adopted shortly after the last Acquisitions staff cut left the department with only three Bibliographic Searchers. Acquisitions statistics illustrated the very real possibility that the department might be unable to process enough requests to obligate the book funds unless requests were forthcoming over a greater portion of the fiscal year. In fact, more uniform monthly inflows have allowed fewer staff to process orders. Surprisingly, there was very little faculty resistance to meeting three deadlines when they formerly had but one.

But even with the improvement in the inflow of requests, the matrix organizational concept still has had a place in Acquisitions' operations. Additional staff were sent to Acquisitions when a larger-than-normal book budget greatly increased the number of requests to be processed one fiscal year. The communication of realistic expectations to the extra staff and their supervisors was the key to a successful effort. The urgent need to obligate funds that would otherwise be lost after the end of the fiscal year was a compelling, and heeded, reason to implement a matrix organization. Participants from three other departments were quickly trained in pre-order searching procedures and, with the help of an additional typist, all funds were obligated and orders were placed.

The experience with the matrix concept in the Acquisitions Department has been a positive one. Although large university library staffs tend toward a high level of specialization, virtually anyone can learn enough allied skills or build on those they already possess to make an effective difference over the life of a short-term project. Although some of these short-term projects covered two to three months, one week seemed ample time for participants to become useful in their new assignments. Intangible and unquantifiable by-products such as job enrichment and appreciation of others' jobs were beneficial and grew directly from these activities.

There are many good reasons for selecting permanent or long-term reassignments over temporary ones, such as, continuity of supervision, better accountability of personnel, and better-realized learning curves. However, a matrix organization or a permutation of one can be a useful method of using staff until long-term reassignments become a necessity.

CONCLUSION

Coping with a declining book budget can be a demoralizing endeavor; many factors come into play, some beyond the influence of the acquisitions staff. Trying to bring about any funding change requires considerable outside assistance. At Memphis State University the most influential segment of the patron base, the teaching faculty, served to focus needed administrative attention on the issue. In using the faculty to best advantage, it is important they be kept well informed, both about local financial procedures and about economic forces influencing the book trade.

Coping with staffing in a time of a diminishing book budget was an easier process since it was relatively self-contained. No matter how successful other tactics are in slowing the book budget decrease, the staffing area needs attention. In the case of Memphis State University Libraries, improving staff skills in acquisitions and enhancing staffing levels in other departments through the matrix concept was of significant benefit.

Stretching and Restretching the Materials Budget: Trying to Do More with Less

Noreen S. Alldredge

SUMMARY. The director's perspective of the problems and dilemmas which libraries have confronted in trying to provide a continuing base of information resources is addressed. Factors contributing to the reduction in purchasing power are reviewed and campus/library relationships are discussed. The author calls for routine planning for and review of library services and collections, as well as an examination of the issues related to on-site ownership versus access to information.

BACKGROUND

The greatest challenge for most library directors has been the management of human resources and the introduction of appropriate technologies. However, the most perplexing problem since 1985, especially at institutions where the sciences play a major role, has been providing for and controlling the materials budget. Acquisitions have bounced to the forefront of challenges for several reasons:

1. the continuing escalation of the amount of information being published and the inherent proliferation of journal titles;
2. fluctuation in international currency rates;
3. the increased presence of commercial publishers in the print-

Noreen S. Alldredge is Dean of Libraries, Roland R. Renne Library, Montana State University, Bozeman, MT 59717.

ing and distribution of the publications of scientific and scholarly organizations;
4. exploitive and differential pricing practices.

While these factors are beyond the control of libraries, they have had a profound effect on the scope of collections in academic libraries.

Initially, before the full impact of these factors was felt, much less understood, libraries strove to stretch their existing acquisitions dollars. Some of the more common techniques for making fiscal resources go farther included:

1. prepaying monographic and serial vendors in return for a discount on purchase price;
2. cancellation of duplicate subscriptions;
3. cancellation of serial titles which were most expensive and least used;
4. reduction or full suspension of retrospective purchasing;
5. temporary freezes on new serial subscriptions;
6. trimming of monographic acquisitions to ensure adequate funds for renewal of existing serial subscriptions;
7. reallocation of personnel or operations to the materials budget;
8. petitioning the parent institution for "bail-out" funds.

While prepaying of vendors is an excellent continuing strategy, the other techniques are usually only effective the first time they are employed—thus they are only an immediate triage. A freeze on new purchases ensures a cap on the number of titles but does nothing to generate the funds necessary to cover the seemingly steady increases of costs for the "core" serials. Cuts in monographic acquisitions have an immediate negative effect on those academic programs which are largely dependant on monographic sources of information. A more significant long term impact is a gradual increase in the number of requests for some of the missing materials via interlibrary loan. In addition, another subsequent negative effect is the fact that nearly all of the materials budget becomes dedicated to serials. Reallocation of personnel and operations funds frequently endangers the base budget, effects the level and quality of services, and lowers staff morale. Bail-out funds can usually only be tapped one time and use of the practice contributes to the future credibility of the library's requests since the "bottomless pit" concept is raised by institutional administrators or governing boards.

RELATIONSHIP WITH PARENT INSTITUTION

Libraries are sometimes very isolated from the campus community. They are seen as storehouses, not as an integral part of the system of the scholarly communication process. Sometimes they appear to exist, in part, because of tradition and because national and professional accrediting groups call for them. In 1984 Patricia Battin, then at Columbia University, wrote that

> the most striking feature of traditional academic organizations, and one that I believe is most misunderstood and ignored by our academic colleagues, is the virtual isolation of the library in the organization. Despite rhetoric about it being "the heart of the university," the library and librarians have been for years isolated from the policy councils of most institutions.[1]

Thus, with not much participation in the policy and no immediate constituency (like a department or college would have), the library is dependent upon the sole advocacy of its administrator or the occasional specialized interest group that springs up when a single service is threatened (e.g., reduction of hours).

A recent report from the U.S. Department of Education on higher education administrative costs is revealing. It indicates that the percent of funding for libraries at institutions of higher education has been declining for ten years. "In contrast, there has been an increase in administrative costs among all types of institutions."[2] The decline in library funding may be a reflection of the perceived place (importance) of the library, or may be due to a lack of advocacy. Whatever the reason(s) the tremendous change in fiscal need has been slow to be acknowledged by administrators.

A further dilemma faces the academic community because the faculty are creators of information and libraries are frequently automatic purchasers of that same information. The publish or perish syndrome in institutions of higher education becomes the ultimate

"Catch-22" for the library. Serials have always been the "sacred cows" — with a myth that they must be protected at the expense of other information sources. Also, some faculty maintain loyalty to specific journals, even when those same journals have changed focus or price, or even ceased to exist!

DILEMMA OF THE LIBRARY ADMINISTRATOR

No one should be surprised that there are other budgetary needs today besides serial subscriptions. Major efforts must be made in areas of preservation and technology. Existing services need to be reviewed and redefined and expanded. Decreases in collection resources usually creates additional work for library personnel, and thus staffing levels must be maintained or even increased. A reduction of on-site materials will mean that access to bibliographic utilities and reference sources will become even more important. Consequently operations resources must also be protected or garnered.

All information sources must be viewed as competing for a portion of the materials budget — e.g., video, micro, CD-ROM, monographs — yet many librarians and faculty adhere to the principle that a serial, once started, must be continued, and any gaps must be filled in, no matter what the cost or probable usefulness to the collection. Thus, screening committees who were charged with balancing collections are now, and will continue to be, important internal action groups.

The mission of the institution has, or should have, a direct effect on a library's collections. However, in many institutions new programs or centers are initiated without consideration of the library's ability to provide resources for the students, faculty and services of the program. Perhaps because libraries have, in the past, managed to limp along without calling much attention to their inability to meet the needs of clients, they have been expected to continue to do more with less. In addition to the problems noted above, the increasing interdisciplinary work under way at many universities makes it exceedingly difficult to identify unique titles which can be cancelled without jeopardizing the instruction and/or research of some campus unit.

The effect of the demands on the materials budgets since 1985 has been a subtle reduction of collections and some services—but not enough for most of the scholarly community to realize the full import of the problem. Research and instructional efforts in the coming years will most likely be hampered by the lack of on-site or even regional resources.

ACTION PLAN FOR THE LIBRARY ADMINISTRATOR

If a comprehensive serial review project has not been undertaken, it should be. If we are to have the confidence of faculty and institutional administrators in the future, we must demonstrate an ability to provide them with the detail which they, and we, need to effectively manage our resources (fiscal and physical). When conducting serial review, it is particularly useful to include the following information to faculty:

1. old and new subscription rates;
2. regional holdings, if any;
3. use (in and out of library) if available;
4. old and new size and/or number of issues for each subscription;
5. titles of other holdings which may adequately cover the subject area.

While serial reviews and cancellation projects are never easy to conduct, the cause and process will be more easily understood and accepted if information is provided as to why such a review is underway and how the faculty can assist in the process.

Planning for the future of the library requires an examination of the mission of the institution since this will have a direct effect on a library's collections and services. Once the mission has been defined the administrator can consider:

1. redeploying existing resources by utilizing a zero-based approach to every unit and service. For example, a lesser grade of binding might be sufficient, or acquisitions funds might be transferred to access funds, so that interlibrary loans and data base searches can be supported.
2. cooperation with sister institutions. Regional holdings of even

moderately used titles may be adequate if document delivery can be upgraded. Reciprocal access and circulation policies should be pursued.

3. planning the future. Access to campus program reviews, college level prioritization of departments, etc. may allow for changes in collections and services.
4. educating funding authorities and faculty regarding the role of the library in the scholarly communication process.

FUTURE ACTION

Electronic publication will provide for distribution of some research and also may become a substitute for some reference services. The amount and quality of scholarly publication should be monitored and discussed with faculty so that better appraisals can be made of information sources.

Funding sufficient for the existing "core collections" (serial and monographic) must be found. Additional fiscal resources for new titles (serial, micro, CD, etc.) is equally essential.

Reviews of serials and standing orders can be a healthy process. All too often libraries don't assess the usefulness of their collections until economic conditions mandate hasty examinations.

A closer look at the advantages and disadvantages of on-site ownership versus access is needed for each individual library. As we identify and address immediate and long term campus needs we must also strive to participate in the provision of information resources necessary for the region.

REFERENCES

1. Patricia Battin, "The Library: Center of the Restructured University," *C & RL* (May 1984): 172.
2. Thomas P. Snyder, *Higher Education Administrative Costs: Continuing the Study*. (Washington, U.S. Department of Education, 1988) p.5.

The Implications for Acquisitions of Stagnant Budgets

Murray S. Martin

SUMMARY. Libraries have not been able to keep up with inflationary and other price increases for library materials. As a result their purchasing power has declined. Because the rates of price increase vary by subject and type of publication, acquisitions budgets are being distorted. Strategies for containing the worst of these side-effects are discussed. The most important of these is the establishment of a meaningful dialogue with administrators and faculty to determine priorities and directions to go. Cancellations of serials are not the only answer, though a necessary first step is the re-evaluation of all subscriptions. The longer-term implications of new technologies are examined and a new approach to budgeting is recommended.

Recent substantial price increases for serial subscriptions have sent shock-waves across the academic community.[1] Budget increases over the years have generally been able to keep pace with inflation and the sudden inability to match increases of 15% or more came as an unwelcome touch of reality.[2] The reasons for this change are complex and out of scope for this article. The fact, however, is real. As a result librarians have had to adopt emergency measures while assessing the longer-term implications. Behind this unfortunate situation lie many issues that have yet to be usefully discussed. Debate so far has tended to look for scapegoats, whether price-gouging by publishers, bad management by librarians, or even tenure-driven pressure to publish. More disturbing to librarians is the questioning of library priorities, particularly the retention of infre-

---

Murray S. Martin is University Librarian, Tufts University, Medford, MA 02155.

105

quently-used periodicals. The question strikes at the heart of existing collection management strategies, and raises issues that involve
freedom of access, copyright, royalty fees, and alternative sources.
The resolution of such issues will take time. In the meantime the
realities of financing higher education, whether public or private,
ensures that libraries are unlikely to return to the days of rising
budgets. Regardless of individual actions and decisions the patterns
of collection management will change over the next decade.

Although we are concerned primarily with the effects of budgets
that cannot match expectations, there are important differences between budget strategies. Most budgets allow for some increase,
whether in the form of mandated salary increases, economic adjustments (a euphemism for inflation), or selective program increases.
There may also be matching decreases or mandated savings for return to a central account. All such budget styles leave purchasing
power relatively intact, that is, they cover cost increases. This represents the "steady-state" approach. By stages, usually by under-
stating inflation, but also by selective program cuts, a budget may
be reduced to a "no growth" level. At this level there is no increase
in the dollars available, which means that some other way has to be
found to handle inflation. The means employed by the librarian in
either case will depend on the degree of flexibility that can be exercised, the size of the existing budget, and its distribution among
categories. If the librarian is allowed to shift money between lines,
the situation is easier to handle. Where this is not allowed, there are
likely to be severe dislocations, with some parts of the budget un-
derspent and others overspent, or a lot of unpaid bills. This is less
the result of bad managerial planning than because library transactions tend to spread over rather more than a year and any drastic
change of course needs two or more years to implement successfully.

There are many variations within steady state and no growth budgets, but what they have in common is that they do not contemplate
program expansion. Without overtly intending to do so, they pro-
mote program contraction. Unless this is understood, their effect on
libraries will not be understood either.

THE EFFECTS OF INFLATION ON VARIOUS BUDGETARY STYLES

Most institutions use some formula to calculate inflation. The information used to develop this formula is often incomplete. For example, most book price indexes cover all subjects and levels of publishing, regardless of their relevance to a particular institution. There are several excellent articles by Frederick Lynden and others on the use of price indexes.[3] One of the messages they convey is the importance of developing one's own index based on the library's own buying history. If possible, budget planners should then be persuaded to use this index. While that may ensure more realistic projections, it cannot take into account sudden perturbations such as those of the last three years in serial prices. As a result the various strategies recommended under no growth budgets must still be used.

Inflation, of course, is never evenly spread across the whole range of library materials. Study of the various price indexes indicates an irregular but continuing higher rate of increase for scientific and technical materials. Periodicals have also tended, as a group, to rise in price faster than books and other materials. Finally, over the last few years, the weakness of the dollar and other international economic trends have increased the differences between rates of price increase in the U.S. and abroad. If no action were taken to counteract these trends, over a short period of time scientific and technical books and periodicals would come to dominate the budget. While that might be appropriate for a highly specialized institution it would be entirely inappropriate for a general college or university. Tables 1, 2, and 3 represent various such scenarios.

No institution is likely to follow consistently one or other of these scenarios. The most likely pattern is a succession of different approaches, reflecting the institution's budgetary situation each year. Changes of this sort from year to year are even more disruptive of library programs.

The figures in these tables are, of course, greatly simplified. In reality there are many more categories of expenditure, and whole areas such as binding have been left out of consideration. They

Table 1

Budget Distribution under a No Growth budget
No Serial Cancellations
Stable Distribution by Area

Category	$ First Year	%	Rate of Inflation	$ Third Year	%
Engineering					
Books	50,000	5	10	15,000	1.5
Periodicals	150,000	15	11	185,000	18.5
Subtotals	200,000	20		200,000	20.0
Humanities					
Books	130,000	13	8	117,000	11.7
Periodicals	70,000	7	9	83,000	8.3
Subtotals	200,000	20		200,000	20.0
Reference/General					
Books	40,000	4	8	27,000	2.7
Periodicals	60,000	6	10	73,000	7.3
Subtotals	100,000	10		100,000	10.0
Science					
Books	50,000	5	10	–	0.0
Periodicals	250,000	25	12	313,000	31.3
Subtotals	300,000	30		313,000	31.3
Social Sciences					
Books	120,000	12	8	103,000	10.3
Periodicals	80,000	8	10	97,000	9.7
Subtotals	200,000	20		200,000	20.0
TOTALS	1,000,000	100		1,013,000	101.3

Notes: Despite the attempt to hold distribution
constant without cancelling serials, the result is a
deficit of $13,000.   Since a no growth budget is one
of the givens, the only possibilities open are to re-
distribute within the budget to pay for the Science
serials, or to cancel some subscriptions, not
necessarily in Science.   Either of these solutions
violates one or another of the principles set out as
governing the allocation of funds.

What is even more striking is the shift of
expenditures between books and periodicals.   Including
the overbudget of $13,000, the cost of serials has
risen from $610,000 to $761,000.   In percentage terms,
the increase has been from 61% to 76.1%.   Within each
area the ratio has also changed.

Table 2

Budget Distribution with a Modest Funding Increase
No Serial Cancellations
Stable Distribution by Area

Category	$ First Year	% First Year	Rate of Inflation	$ Third Year	% Third Year
Engineering					
Books	50,000	5	8	37,000	3.2
Periodicals	150,000	15	10	185,000	16.8
Subtotals	200,000	20		220,000	20.0
Humanities					
Books	130,000	13	8	137,000	12.5
Periodicals	70,000	7	9	83,000	7.5
Subtotals	200,000	20		220,000	20.0
Reference/General					
Books	40,000	4	8	37,000	3.4
Periodicals	60,000	6	10	73,000	6.6
Subtotals	100,000	10		110,000	10.0
Science					
Books	50,000	5	10	17,000	1.5
Periodicals	250,000	25	12	313,000	28.5
Subtotal	300,000	30		330,000	30.0
Social Science					
Books	120,000	12	8	123,000	11.2
Periodicals	80,000	8	10	97,000	8.8
Subtotals	200,000	20		220,000	20.0
TOTALS	1,000,000	100	5	1,100,000	100.0

Notes: While the severe distortions evident in the no
growth budget table are less noticeable, they are still
present and can be expected to become more evident each
year.   Serial subscriptions have risen from 61% to 68%
of the budget.

The amounts allocated for books in each area
reflect money not committed to serials.   In no case do
they match inflation, so the purchasing power of the
library has been diminished. particularly in the case
of Science.

Table 3

Budgetary Distribution under a Steady State Budget
No Serial Cancellations
Stable Acquisition Rate by Area

Category	$ First Year	%	Rate of Inflation	$ Third Year	%
Engineering					
Books	50,000	5	10	61,000	5.0
Periodicals	150,000	15	11	185,000	15.3
Subtotals	200,000	20		246,000	20.3
Humanities					
Books	130,000	13	8	152,000	12.5
Periodicals	70,000	7	9	83,000	6.8
Subtotals	200,000	20		246,000	19.8
Reference/General					
Books	40,000	4	8	47,000	3.9
Periodicals	60,000	6	10	73,000	6.0
Subtotals	100,000	10		120,000	9.8
Science					
Books	50,000	5	10	61,000	5.0
Periodicals	250,000	25	12	313,000	25.8
Subtotals	300,000	30		374,000	30.8
Social Science					
Books	120,000	12	8	140,000	11.6
Periodicals	80,000	8	10	97,000	8.0
Subtotals	200,000	20		237,000	19.6
TOTALS	1,000,000	100	10.4	1,212,000	100.0

Notes: Although the distributional changes are small,
over time they will increase, particularly if there are
any sudden price increases in a single sector.   Even
the marginal expansion of periodical expenditures from
61% to 62%, represents the transfer from books to
periodicals of more than $12,000 in two years, thus
changing the budgetary base.   Note that the average
rate of budget increase is tilted towards the highest
level because of the proportion of the whole budget
affected by such expenditures.

nevertheless illustrate the kinds of changes that result from different budgetary strategies. Above all they show the effect of having chosen to protect one field, periodical subscriptions. As can be seen, inaction, the decision to do nothing, results in widespread changes, whether in distribution by category or by subject. As I pointed out in 1977[4] it is possible, over a short period of time, to shift the entire budget to the support of subscriptions. Of course, such a dramatic change is unlikely, because some actions will be taken to counter the trend.

Where the money available is insufficient to meet all desires a program of serial containment is essential. Just what level should be thought satisfactory is a matter for each institution to determine. Every effort should be made to keep annual commitments such as serial subscriptions within limits that the budget can sustain.

PRIMARY EFFECTS OF NO GROWTH BUDGETS

A no growth budget in dollars, because there will nevertheless be price increases, means a decline in library purchasing power. The rate of the decline will depend on the rate of inflation and the degree of flexibility permitted to the library.

The effects of no growth budgets are relatively easy to understand. If the acquisitions budget stays the same for two or more years, the library will lose purchasing power equivalent to the rate of inflation over that period. Presuming a 5% rate of inflation what costs $100 today will cost $110.25 in two years' time. If, however, you still have only $100 to spend you will be able to buy the equivalent what today would cost you $90.70, which represents a loss of 9.3% in purchasing power. Since inflation rates have been as high as 20-25% for significant parts of their acquisitions, the actual change will be even greater.

BUDGETARY RESPONSES

Several corrective measures are available. First, the library administration should review the entire budget looking for funds which can be transferred to library materials. In most library budgets the amount of money likely to be so available is small, but the action is, as it were, an earnest of good faith, a necessary preparation for approaching the institution for added funds. The most common way is to assign salary savings to acquisitions. At best, however, any such strategy is available only once. It simply establishes a new base.

Second, the institution and the library administration should conduct a rigorous review of library/academic program match. Since this involves the examination of academic priorities and library priorities, it is likely to take some time. It is also highly political and seldom achieves the needed degree of specificity. Nevertheless it can provide some guidance as to broad priorities and future directions.

Third, the existing expenditure distribution should be examined in great detail. Despite the many statistics kept, libraries often do not know how much is being paid for what on a subject basis. One of the commonest failures is to regard periodical subscriptions and standing orders as sacred territory. Their cost is simply scooped off the top and the rest of the budget allocated according to some formula. Also, general funds and approval plans interfere with the subject analysis of the acquisition program. They are useful tools for acquiring materials, but should be subject to the same scrutiny as any other allocation. Difficult as it is, however, the effort to break down the total budget into its component parts is essential if any rational plan is to be followed.

Fourth, having completed the previous analyses, the librarian, in consultation with the appropriate faculty committees and representatives, should work to correct the most obvious imbalances. This requires the re-examination of subscriptions and the book-periodical balance in the various subjects. Most faculty can identify periodicals which are no longer relevant, because of program or content changes. Such titles can seldom achieve the savings likely to be needed, so there remains the harder task of identifying important journals that can be discontinued. In some cases interlibrary loan (within copyright limits) or database access can be substituted, and such possibilities should be explored. More will be said about the broader implications of such decisions. Not all faculty are aware of the implications of such assertions as: "We depend on periodicals for our information." Faculty and librarians do not always share the same definitions. For example, some faculty do not think of proceedings or conference papers as "books" and consequently do not realize that such purchases are charged against book funds. The need is to re-explore the current needs of the departments, to see whether there have been program shifts, making investment in new areas essential, or discontinuation of older investments possible.

Long and difficult as such a process may be it is needed to set up policy guidelines for the future. The process of consultation has brought others into the game, and to the extent that they have been consulted they tend to assume some responsibility for the future. The final decisions have to be made within the library on the basis of information received.

Finally, new consideration has to be given to the role of consortia and cooperative groups.[5] The long and somewhat unsuccessful history of cooperative acquisition in this country has been caused for the most part by the desire to be too specific. All libraries must serve their own constituency first and anything which interferes with that priority is going to come off second best. Vague as they may seem, agreements providing for mutual access and use, or information about specializations can be very helpful in determining the levels to which the library should collect in many academic areas. Such cooperation must work both ways to be effective.

STEADY-STATE BUDGETS

A steady-state budget implies providing enough money to cover price increases. If, however, the institution allows too low a rate of increase, the library may well find that its purchasing power is reduced. Second, because the rates of inflation are differential by subject or type of material, there will be shifts in spending patterns and, depending on the individual situation, there may have to be trade-offs resulting in maintaining purchasing power in some areas while losing it in others.

Steady-state budgets would not seem to present the same problems as no growth budgets. While it is true that they attempt to maintain current purchasing power, they do not provide for new programs and areas of study, nor can they always take into account the effects of differential inflation. If periodical prices increase more rapidly than book prices, a generalized inflation allowance will tilt the budget towards periodicals, in the same way as a no growth budget, though less rapidly. (See Tables 2 and 3.)

The actions taken will depend on the situation of the individual library. Most have taken the decision to exercise restraint on serial subscriptions, seeking to limit such expenditure to a given percentage of the total budget. There are no totally reliable guides as to what this percentage should be, but in general as serial expenditure exceeds 55-60%, all other parts of the budget will start to erode. Within disciplines the proportion spent on serials will vary, ranging from 10% to 90%. These facts must be kept in mind when allocating funds. Unfortunately they frequently mean that, in order to maintain an equitable distribution by discipline, some will have to sacrifice book money to maintain serials.

Explanations of budget changes are more difficult to make and to defend when there is clearly more money than when the budget remains static. The facts given above are the beginning of such explanations, but many of the reasons for a particular distribution lie deep in institutional history.

STANDARDS AND FORMULAE FOR COLLECTIONS

One other factor should be taken into account, particularly in larger research libraries, namely the figures derived from standards and formulae.

Most of the formulae for collection size and collection growth were developed in response to the perceived needs of the post-Sputnik era, particularly for state systems where there was a need to develop new and bigger institutions to provide for a rapidly growing student body. These conditions are unlikely to repeat themselves, but the formulae remain. The largest libraries have long since passed even the most ambitious interpretations of the Clapp-Jordan formula and the old rule of 5% annual growth would result in unattainable annual acquisition figures. A library with 10,000,000 volumes would, by that rule, have to add 500,000 volumes a year, a totally unrealistic expectation. Conversely, adherence to the 5% figure might understate the real needs of a smaller library, which is struggling to meet even minimal program needs. Because of the changes which have overtaken library materials prices in the last few years, older views of allocation and other management policies are no longer relevant. These statements do not imply gross error on the part of those who set our great libraries on the road to that greatness. All they mean is that all received wisdom must eventually be re-examined. Standards or formulae can no longer be the sole guides for collection development. Each institution must work out its own library destiny. Reference can be made to expectations, as embodied in earlier statements, but the present reality is that there is not enough money to maintain most libraries even where they are.

COLLECTION MANAGEMENT
IN THE LARGER CONTEXT

So far acquisitions has been discussed in somewhat of a vacuum. Whether in a steady-state or a no growth setting, acquisitions must compete with other library and nonlibrary programs for scarce dollars. By focusing narrowly on buying materials, we may be doing libraries and their parent institutions a disservice.

Many administrators have responded to the current serial crisis by providing one-time money for books or a special supplement to pay for the serials overage. This is a variation on the lump-sum budget treatment, and means "I am not taking responsibility for the problem, here's some money, go away and don't bother me." Instead of looking at the underlying problems of program imbalance, unrealistic expectations and the need to re-examine the institution's information needs, the short-term solution was preferred. Being short-term it has merely delayed the day of reckoning.

There are wider considerations. At the International Conference on Contemporary Issues in Academic and Research Libraries (Boulder, March 1984) several speakers stressed the need to review budget concepts. My own paper[6] suggested that a total revamping of the budget might be necessary to cope with the changes taking place in the information industry. If we think of information *access* as the touchstone rather than *purchase*, collection management must then include database use, interlibrary loan, cooperative purchases, processing costs, equipment, maintenance and a large part of the costs of automation. To a limited extent the Association of Research Libraries has recognized this fact by including data access costs under the rubric of library materials. Further change was examined in *The Changing State of Scholarly Communication*.[7] Most library budget making has still not reached this point. What it implies is that librarians must think more clearly about the part each format must play in the provision of information.

In response to a questionnaire prepared by Faxon[8] many librarians expressed anxiety about the effects of new technologies on budgets. The expectation of many was that automation, document delivery, databases and the like, though essential parts of the library program and ways in which the materials budget problem could be addressed, might have long-term effects on the ability of the library to sustain that budget.[9]

Whatever the specific outcomes, these new technologies are here to stay. It has been difficult enough for librarians to see the connection between increased database searching and increased interlibrary loan. The need now is to make even more connections in ways that run across budget lines. CD-Rom products (some with accompanying microfiche collections), purchase-on-demand services, consortium memberships or library cards, all present legitimate alternatives to purchasing for retention. Each must be fitted into its niche among library services and such a process takes time. If, however, the process is not begun, library budgets will become more and more fragile.

CONCLUSION

The task of collection management has grown more complex. Some cherished beliefs, such as the inviolability of serial subscriptions, can no longer be sustained in the face of declining purchasing power. New alternatives to acquisition, some of them available to the casual user, have matured and must be taken seriously. Goal-setting for the future must be more detailed and must involve many more people than in the past, both inside and outside the institution. In the short-term there are few alternatives to reducing serials expenditures, but the longer-term objective should be to establish a new balance between formats, including those which the library will not own but must lease or pay for on a use basis.

REFERENCES

1. Rebecca T. Lenzini, "Periodical Prices 1985-87 Update," *Serials Librarian* 13(1): 49-57, 1987. Also "Paying the Piper: ARL Libraries Respond to Skyrocketing Journal Subscription Prices," *J of Academic Librarianship* 14(1): 4-9, 1988.

2. Douglas M. Knight and E. Shepley Nourse. *Libraries at Large: Tradition, Innovation, and the National Interest.* New York: Bowker, 1969. Especially Part 2, Chapter 5, "The Costs of Library and Informational Services," (pp. 168-227) is a particularly good overview, which has not been dated by the passage of time. A later study by William J. Baumol and Matityahu Marcus, *Economics of Academic Libraries* (Washington D.C.: American Council on Education, 1973) contains more recent analyses of library costs.

3. William H. Axford, "The Validity of Book Price Indexes for Budgetary Predictions," *Library Resources and Technical Services* 19:5-12, Winter 1975. Frederick C. Lynden, "Library Materials Cost Studies," *LRTS* 27:156-162, April 1983, and "Prices of Foreign Library Materials: A Report," *College and Research Libraries*, 49: 217-231, May 1988. *Pricing and Costs of Monographs and Serials: National and International Issues* ed. by Sul H. Lee. New York, The Haworth Press, Inc., 1987. D. Smith, "Forecasting Price Increase Needs for Library Materials: the University of California Experience," *LRTS* 28:136-148 April 1984.

4. Murray S. Martin, "Budgetary Strategies: Coping with a Changing Fiscal Environment," *J of Academic Librarianship* 2(6): 297-302, 1977.

5. An interesting development is represented by the report, "Serials Cancellation Clearinghouse Set Up by UT-Austin," *Library Hotline* 17 no 30, p.1, July 31, 1988. More such can be expected, but they still depend upon individual library actions within legal, programmatic, and financial restrictions.

6. Murray S. Martin, "Financial Planning—New Needs, New Sources, New Styles," in *Financing Information Services . . .* ed. Peter Spyers-Duran and Thomas W. Mann. Westport, Conn.: Greenwood Press, 1985, pp.91-108.

7. *The Changing State of Scholarly Communication.* Washington, D.C.: Assn. of Research Libraries, 1986.

8. *Library Profiles: Number 1.* (Faxon Collection Development Series) [Boston], The Faxon Press, 1988. Publishers (*Publisher Profiles for 1989.* Faxon, 1988) on the other hand "feel that many librarians misjudge them," but they share similar feelings over future trends. They are concerned about the effects of consortia and resource sharing on publishing. Oddly, they are much less committed to new technologies, and do not expect a rapid move away from print. While librarians remain committed to high-use periodicals, publishers are only slowly realizing that something has to give, and it will first be low-use periodicals.

9. Richard M. Dougherty, "Electronic Journals Won't Bring Relief," *American Libraries* 18(7): 21-22, 1987.

A Maintenance Budget:
Living Within Your Means

Twyla Mueller Racz
Walter Hogan
Mary Meernik

SUMMARY. In the 1980s libraries have been affected by reduced library budgets and have shifted funds from monographs to serials to pay the escalating serial costs. This article examines the positive approaches taken in one library by the Collection Development and Technical Services units, working cooperatively, to gain control over a maintenance/austere budget, and mitigate its effects. It discusses the crucial need for internal controls and the economical operations that can be performed by Acquisitions. Also presented is the creation of in-house management databases that can produce the information essential for careful planning of selection and deselection which is necessary in order to stay within the strict budgetary limits. In addition, there is the recognition that without an inflation factor calculated into the library's budget regression will inevitably follow.

Joseph Nitecki has written that "our attitude toward austerity ought to be positive . . . it is very important to replace a passive and custodial approach to resource scarcity with an active and creative approach focused on containment."[1] The latter is the approach which the staff at Eastern Michigan University Library wish to pursue, but it is a difficult, time consuming and laborious process to reach this goal. Perhaps relating our experiences in handling our problems will be beneficial to other librarians facing similar problems.

Twyla Mueller Racz is Coordinator, Collection Development, Walter Hogan is Coordinator, Technical Services, and Mary Meernik is Acquisitions Librarian, Eastern Michigan University Library, Ypsilanti, MI 48197.

BACKGROUND

Eastern Michigan University evolved from a teacher's college into a university which now serves approximately 22,000 students of whom 5,500 are graduate students. There are no PhD programs. Unfortunately the library's acquisitions budget has never been more than just adequate even in its "good" years when funds were more plentiful than they presently are. Emphasis has always been on meeting the instructional needs of the faculty and students and there has been no endeavor or funds to support faculty research needs. This inadequacy is somewhat alleviated by the proximity of the University of Michigan Libraries which extend borrowing privileges to EMU faculty and pressure to accommodate faculty research requests is probably lessened because of these privileges.

Although during earlier times no formal collection development structure or systematic periodical review procedure existed, there was an attempt to keep a budgetary balance between serials and monographs. Whenever serials consumed too large a portion of the monograph funds cancellation projects would be initiated. In effect, we carried out Cameron and Roberts' "cancellation exercises" which were then "dissipated by the gradual creep of new subscriptions" ordered during "periods of financial respite."[2]

Several years ago, however, the library administration established a collection development unit and reorganized technical services. It was obvious to both units that a serials deselection program would have to be undertaken, but before plans could be completely formulated disaster struck. At the beginning of the 1986/87 fiscal year the library was informed that it was overexpended. The reasons for the overexpenditure are as follows: First, all university departments with overencumbrances suddenly had had the total amount subtracted from their current budget allocations. There was no rule stating that encumbrances would be carried forward without penalty and the possibility of this action had always existed, but in reality it had never occurred. Second, the overencumbrances were partly due to the new university accounting procedures which did not mesh completely with those of the library's, and confusing, inaccurate reports had been generated for library use. Third, dependence upon an archaic order system had allowed a large payment to go unrecorded by Acquisitions. Fourth, the major serial vendors had been paid, thus limiting timely serial cancellations. The result of these converging factors left the library overspent at the beginning of a fiscal year and totally without funds to buy monographs.

Under these crisis conditions options were limited. The days of shifting monograph funds to cover serial costs had ended. The library had to execute emergency procedures: primarily the cancellation of "big ticket" items and specialized cooperative projects (e.g., Michigan Newspapers on Microfilm) that could be eliminated without damaging the collection. A few recommended cuts were so politically sensitive and unpopular that action by the library administration was required.

SERIALS ASSESSMENT

While the subject selectors were agonizing over their deselection decisions, Technical Services and Collection Development were designing systematic methods of gathering information for analyzing the collection, especially serials, and correlating the analyses to program needs.

Because standing order and periodical expenditures had never been differentiated by subject, we knew little about this aspect of our continuing orders beyond an unscientific impression that the science and technology areas accounted for the lion's share. The expansion of these program areas within the university necessitated the purchase of very expensive monographs and serials and consequently reduced the total number of items that could be acquired. In order to gain control over our commitments it would first be necessary to have a subject breakdown of all continuations and their respective prices.

A rough subject breakdown by departmental funds was available for unitary book purchases, but nothing comparable existed for our continuations. The effort to establish subject control proceeded in several stages. First, we consolidated most of our journal subscriptions with vendors who could provide sophisticated management reports from their computers. We were then able to obtain reports that sorted our titles in rough LC classification order. Next we undertook a project to assign our own subject codes to the journals.

After we communicated our code assignments to the vendors for inclusion in customer-defined fields of their respective databases, we were able to order management reports sorted on our own subject identifiers.

CREATION OF DATABASES

The next stage was the creation of in-house databases on microcomputer to report on those continuing orders that had not been consolidated with major service vendors. Two databases were built: one for journals, and a second for standing orders. These were carefully constructed for maximum compatibility with one another and with our vendor-supplied reports. We designed spreadsheets that total all of our standing order and periodicals expenditures by subject. Graphic displays such as pie and bar charts have been derived from the spreadsheets.

Once the alignment of serials to subjects was completed, an allocation formula could be applied to discern if a subject was receiving a disproportionate share of funds in relation to its program needs. An in-house allocation formula for monographs had been adopted several years ago, but Collection Development recommended abandoning it in favor of the fund distribution formula used at Western Illinois University[3] which included serials. The formula is applied separately to monographs and to serials for each subject area, which then receives the total allotment. The allocation can be manipulated between monographs and serials as long as the total is not exceeded.

Therefore, the formula was utilized this year on a trial basis for both serials and monographs; the results, including the serial subject alignment prepared by Technical Services, were distributed to the library subject specialists for their review. As might have been foretold, the serial subject allocation has not met with unanimous support from those whose serial expenditures are greater than their allocations. Efforts continue to find additional strategies, e.g., citation indexes, use studies to either incorporate into the serial formula or to replace it, etc. Nonetheless, reality clearly indicates that whatever methods are selected, serial costs must be contained, and serial titles must be correlated to program requirements.

The library's inability to purchase monographs and the resulting recommendation that the library revert to allocating a fixed percentage of the materials fund to monographs intensifies the pressure to reduce the serials budget. To accomplish this goal, deselection will have to continue until the serial budget is in line. All new serial requests are under a moratorium until the refinements are concluded. In addition, any periodical that changes from free to priced is to be treated as a new subscription. All serials with price increases above the inflation rate are to be reevaluated. Also under investigation is the possibility of expanding database searches in exchange for dropping expensive indices. Subject selectors are encouraged to complete their collection assessments which should give them better insight into collection discrepancies.

With the accelerating speed of change in a technologically volatile era, the library must respond positively or face a deterioration of service. But it does add another element to the budget puzzle. EMU Library has been a test site for a CD-ROM service which has been heavily used by the business students and faculty. Based on need and demand the decision to purchase has been made, but the method of incorporation into the budget plan as either a separate line item or as a continuation remains unresolved at present.

STRUGGLING AGAINST THE TIDE

The vocal dissatisfaction expressed by the teaching and library faculty over the lack of any money for monographs, the fact that the library had had no additional acquisitions funds in four years, plus a bit of White's risk management[4] on the part of the library dean resulted in an increment to the materials budget base for 1987/88. As a one-time addition it was a substantial (in EMU terms) increase, but a five percent inflation component each of the four years would have raised the base even higher. Regrettably the increase created the false expectation that this sum solved all of our problems: monographs could be purchased, new subscriptions could be placed, and deselection was no longer required.

Without an inflation factor the library can only slide backward; each year will bring higher costs and reduced purchasing power. The library administration must and will continue to fight to have an inflation adjustment calculated into the budget, and Collection Development and Technical Services must provide the necessary data. Meanwhile, the library is obliged to make the best use of its funds and to show that they are used appropriately. The search for accountability in the management of library resources must continue. "Libraries must respond positively to the financial crisis as well as to technological innovations."[5]

TECHNICAL SERVICES ROLE

While the subject specialists continue to grapple with the painful problem of maintaining a static serials budget in the face of 10-15% annual price increases,[6] Technical Services has pursued a variety of strategies to keep acquisitions costs down, and to provide Collection Development with timely and accurate management information.

INTERNAL CONTROLS CRUCIAL

Our library must reconcile its records with those of the University's Accounting Office, which controls the payment system. Unfortunately, we do not have online access to Accounting, and our only glimpse of its records arrives in the form of monthly printouts. For a number of reasons, the printouts are of minimal help in monitoring our budget:

1. These monthly reports are a frozen snapshot of the budget at a point in time. They are out of date even before they arrive at the library in the campus mail.
2. The reports are based upon Accounting's internal payments schedule, which varies dramatically in response to staff attendance, seasonal workload, computer downtime, and other factors. As a result, the timing of the entry of encumbrances, payments, and adjustments is unpredictable. Payments are sometimes not recorded until long after the library has authorized payment. Interrelated data entry operations may be out of the proper time sequence: for example encumbrances often are not deleted until long after the associated payment has been

made, with the result that twice as much of the library's money appears to be tied up than is actually the case.

3. Our existing batch acquisitions system is based on ancient software and punchcard technology. Errors sometimes occur when it fails to dump our data properly into University Accounting's sophisticated new Financial Records System. (Of course, there is no guarantee that our upcoming online integrated system will interface any better with FRS.)

4. The reports are inflexible. The library staff cannot sort or reformat them in different ways.

Aside from these particular problems we face at EMU, it is simply bad business practice for any acquisitions operation to rely entirely upon a separately administered office to monitor its budget. Even if our University's Accounting Department were up-to-date in all of its postings, and never made errors, Acquisitions should still have some means of tracking its expenditures internally, if for no other reason than to maintain knowledge and control of its own activities.

To this end, an acquisitions database was developed on the same software that had been used for the journals and standing orders databases previously mentioned.

AUTOMATING WITH MICROS

At this point, perhaps a brief mention of our library's microcomputer environment might be of some interest. As with many libraries, our earliest exposure to PCs came about through the use of OCLC M300 terminals. Later, our Administration installed IBM-compatible PCs in staff offices throughout the library, and provided training in the use of Enable, an integrated software package that includes word processing, database management, spreadsheet, and graphics components, all using similar command language. (This article is being composed in collaboration by the three of us, each using Enable word processing at our respective terminals. The databases, spreadsheets, and graphs referred to in this article are also in Enable, although we also sometimes use a MacIntosh for graphics.)

The acquisitions database, like those we designed for our continuation orders, provides useful management information such as a breakdown of our encumbrances and expenditures by department fund. However, it is more than a supplementary file used to generate reports. The acquisitions database is a live, constantly updated file that contains a record for every purchase order we issue. It has replaced files of $3 \times 5''$ slips and various paper ledgers to become our basic source of financial information. The database and its records are of a manageable size because no bibliographic elements are included among its ten fields:

PURCHASE ORDER NUMBER
ACCOUNT NUMBER
VENDOR CODE
DEPT. FUND CODE
NUMBER OF COPIES ORDERED
NUMBER OF COPIES RECEIVED
AMOUNT ENCUMBERED
AMOUNT SPENT
DATE RECORD CREATED (System-supplied)
DATE OF LAST EDIT (System-supplied)

We can now immediately obtain information about total funds encumbered and spent as well as expense breakdowns by subject areas for books and by type of material—monographs, standing orders, periodicals, etc. This breakdown by material type has proved invaluable because the reports from Accounting are arranged in this manner (i.e., separate funds for binding, monographs, periodicals, and microforms). On a monthly basis, these accounting figures are compared with our own internal reports to verify that items have been paid for and charged to the correct fund. If fund totals between the two reports differ, we can generate more specific reports that can be qualified by the fields listed above. It is obviously more helpful with tracking problems if data can be manipulated in this manner rather than having to deal with the inflexibility of paper records.

If orders cannot be filled, we want to be able to clear encumbered amounts and use the money to buy other items as soon as possible. Accounting must be provided with a list of cancellations on a regular basis so that those commitments can be liquidated. Instead of requiring staff to keep written records, we indicate cancellations in the database and can obtain a listing, with whatever qualifications we may choose, in a matter of minutes.

In order to estimate costs for the year, libraries must also be aware of price changes in materials. Besides checking published price indexes, we now use the database to generate specific cost data that reflect our own buying patterns. By knowing the average price of the titles we are ordering, we can more accurately estimate the number of book orders that must be placed to keep pace with available money. This data can also be refined to show average cost by subject—a crucial consideration when formulating fund allocations.

In addition to streamlining Acquisitions' own operations, the department's databases are also proving a great asset to the Collection Development Coordinator in evaluating the current distribution of funds and in formulating subject allocations. Previously the Coordinator had to rely on printouts from the University's Computer Center, our partner in the batch acquisitions system. These reports were arranged by subject fund for books but grouped standing orders and periodicals together into single funds. Not only did we lack subject breakdown for these materials, which represent the majority of our expenditures, but also the reports were prone to the same type of errors as the Accounting reports. The acquisitions database provided us with a reliable basis for evaluating expense breakdowns by subjects for our monographs, and we wanted to obtain similar data about our continuations. In order to make the standing order database compatible with the acquisitions database, the same subject classification was applied. Using the standing order database, we can immediately supply the Collection Development Coordinator with a wide variety of information about our continuations—data that would formerly have taken hours to pull together from card files. These database reports can be general or extremely specific in scope, ranging from a simple tally of items with total costs to complete documentation for each title, including main entry, publisher, vendor, cost, division, subject, bibliographic type, call number, etc. When the Coordinator requests subject breakdowns of standing orders, we can construct reports to provide such listings, complete with cost data.

We have found that, in addition to the anticipated benefits of the micro databases—getting control of our budget and developing management information about our collections—these new resources have provided some valuable fringe benefits. First, the existence of computerized files has proved helpful in recruiting and developing new Acquisitions librarians. The PC database represents a simple and inexpensive tool for organizing information into a rational system that is presentable to outsiders and to newcomers. If, as in our case, a decision is made not to develop full-fledged acquisitions ordering or check-in systems as an intermediate step before the installation of an integrated mainframe system, the creation of acquisitions databases on a standard commercial software package is an excellent investment.

The databases are extremely useful as bridges to our eventual integrated online environment. To begin with, management information is essential in pre-implementation planning. The possession of basic statistical facts about our operation allows the Acquisitions Department to quickly provide administration, vendors, and consultants with accurate information that assists in determining the scope of the library's implementation project. In addition, we have found that the creation of PC databases gives the library a head start in organizing its files into machine-readable formats. These databases provide good practice for mainframe automation, and it weans the staff from dependency upon the idiosyncracies of the old manual system. Staff members begin to see logical connections between files that may look very different in the manual environment, and to realize that the familiar, old card files do not represent the only way of organizing the library's records. The establishment of PC databases to supplement, rather than replace, existing files has allowed a gentle, gradual introduction to the brave new world of automation. Especially for veteran staff, this approach has made the prospect of change much less abrupt and threatening than it might otherwise have seemed to them.

ECONOMICAL OPERATIONS

Although we have been very pleased with the enhancements made possible by microcomputer technology, we have not lost sight of our fundamental obligation to apply sound, traditional management principles to the business of purchasing library materials. Any Acquisitions Department concerned with economical operations requires vendors who can supply books efficiently, accurately, and inexpensively. In a situation where the materials budget is a scarcer resource than staff time, there might be some logic in placing a higher value upon discounts than upon service. Fortunately, we have been able to find both booksellers and subscription agents who provide good service at the most competitive prices, and so we have not experienced any deterioration of service as a result of our need to obtain the most favorable book discounts and lowest subscription charges available.

It is the library's policy to purchase paperback editions of titles when available. Since many paperbacks are priced at less than half the cost of hardcovers, this practice represents a substantial savings. We have an agreement with our vendor to supply paperback versions, and that company has been very cooperative in fulfilling that request even when it has not been possible for us to absolutely verify that a paperback edition exists (i.e., discrepancy between OCLC records and other bibliographic data). We have also stipulated that if the price of any title is more than $15.00 higher than the estimated price on the purchase order, we are to be notified before the book is shipped. This notification permits us to reevaluate ordering items that are priced significantly higher than expected and also prevents us from underencumbering funds.

A static budget also necessitates careful monitoring of standing order expenditures. In addition to accommodating inflationary increases, we must judiciously use what monies may be available for adding new continuations. When we are notified about a new series, annual, etc., we frequently hold off on placing a standing order, and purchase instead the first volume or two on an individual basis. This practice allows us to evaluate the usefulness of the title before committing to the purchase of additional volumes. We also have the practice of skipping some volumes of annual publications in cases where a continuous run is not necessary in our library.

We are now in the process of transferring the majority of our standing orders over to our book vendor. Of our approximately 1100 titles, over 750 have been ordered directly from publishers in the past. With this changeover not only will there be more uniformity when processing the paperwork, but the flat discount we have negotiated with our jobber will also apply to these items. Since we have been receiving little or no discount on the majority of these titles and frequently must pay shipping and handling charges, we hope to realize a substantial savings with this change. Our standing order database proved invaluable in the transferral process. We wanted to provide the vendor with a list of our standing order publishers in advance to determine whether their titles could be supplied. Instead of going through our records manually, we were able to generate a report in minutes that provided us with a list of publishers and their respective titles.

Although many libraries question the cost effectiveness of their gift programs, we rely upon donations, especially when faced with lean budgets, to supplement our book and periodical collections. We encourage all gifts provided they have no restrictions attached and we will add those that fit our collection development policies. Faculty and staff have proved excellent sources for copies of recent titles that would otherwise have had to be purchased. (We take pains to process recently-published gifts immediately, in order to avoid duplication while the gift is in process.)

No-growth budgets can result in down-time for acquisitions staff, especially at the beginning (before funds are released) and at the end (when all monies are spent) of the fiscal year. An economical operation necessitates that all resources, including staff, be well utilized. We therefore have a variety of on-going projects in which all employees participate as time permits. These include book mending and relabeling, processing of gift books and database creation and maintenance.

CONCLUSION

There are a number of factors that can adversely affect an acquisitions budget, but we were not alert to all of them until a number of them happened to coincide during a single year, in our library, effectively bringing our discretionary ordering to a complete halt. Inflation is one of these factors. And, although we are all almost daily apprised of the inflation rate in our country, at times the rate of increase for published materials, and particularly for foreign publications, can be considerably greater than the general U.S. inflation rate. This problem worsened recently due to differential pricing as well as to the falling dollar. Awareness of these factors, however, does not guarantee accurate prediction of the cost increases that will impact on any particular library's unique mix of orders and subscriptions during a particular year.

Price increases for journals are especially problematic for several reasons. First, a subscription to a serial publication is generally expected to be a long-term commitment, and the cancellation of a journal run for reasons of financial exigency is disturbing to both users and staff of any library. Furthermore, the typical payment schedule for subscriptions is not conducive to financial flexibility. A library usually pays for the next year's subscriptions several months in advance. This payment immediately commits a huge percentage of the budgets of most libraries. Worse still, debit memos for additional subscription costs will trickle in unpredictably throughout the year.

As we discovered when the magnitude of our budget crisis became apparent, it is impractical to cancel subscriptions once payment has been made. In effect, there is a built-in delay of as much as a full year from the time that a library decides upon a cancellation, until the library can actually achieve a reduction in its committed funds. If the library is not in a position to make cancellation decisions speedily, the lead time needed to effect such reductions can easily extend beyond a single fiscal year.

Although there is no way to remove the pain from the imposition of austerity measures, we have found that the process can be greatly aided when accurate, thorough, and objective information concerning the library's purchases is made available to subject specialists. The collection data we have gathered from vendors and from our new in-house databases has not only given our bibliographers the essential information they require in order to make informed decisions, but it has also reduced arguments over the division of our scarce resources, because the information has been presented in an open, objective manner.

Along with these collection development efforts, Acquisitions has made major efforts in two areas to maximize collection growth despite budgetary constraints. First, we have developed a highly responsive in-house bookkeeping operation, which allows ready analysis of our purchasing activities, and enables us to quickly identify and request correction of inaccuracies in the University's official Accounting records. In addition, we have sought to apply traditional principles of sound management to every aspect of the acquisitions operation, to ensure that we are obtaining library materials in the most cost-effective manner possible. Unfortunately, there are real limits to the savings that can be achieved even under the most efficient management. The bottom line is that a no-growth budget will purchase fewer materials each year during an era of inflation. If most of the library's funds are committed to serials, cancellation of subscriptions ultimately represents the only means of protecting some funds for discretionary monographic purchases.

We have learned a great deal from our budget crash, and certainly the experience has motivated us to improve some of our procedures. However, now that the lessons have been learned, we cannot help but ponder how nice it would be if we could count on some small but predictable annual increase as a hedge against inflation — the one factor over which we have no control.

NOTES

1. Nitecki, Joseph Z. "Creative Management in Austerity." In *Austerity Management in Academic Libraries*, edited by John F. Harvey and Peter Spyers-Duran, 43-61. Metuchen, NJ: The Scarecrow Press, 1984.

2. Cameron, Kenneth J. and Michael Roberts. "Amputation: By Consent?" *Library Review* 35 (Summer 1986): 91-103.

3. Goehner, Donna M. "Allocating by Formula: The Rationale from an Institutional Perspective." *Collection Management* 5 (Fall/Winter 1983): 161-173.

4. White, Herbert S. "Library Materials Prices and Academic Library Practices: Between Scylla and Charybdis." *Journal of Academic Librarianship* 5 (March 1979): 20-23.

5. Cameron, "Amputation," 91-103.

6. Various sources have reported recent annual increases of 10% and over for domestic journals, and at least 20% for foreign journals. Our own increases have been closer to the 10% mark, presumably because we are not a research library, and maintain a fairly basic collection.

Establishing, Monitoring, and Spending the College and University Acquisitions Budget

Mildred McGinnis
Mary Faust

SUMMARY. This paper covers the topic of establishing, monitoring and spending the college and university acquisitions budget in addition to briefly examining the working relationships of those personnel charged with these budgetary tasks. Following a brief history of recent economic considerations, the paper deals with allocating and monitoring the budget, using manual and automated systems. Two goals for expending the budget are: (1) spending the budget effectively; and (2) spending the money in a timely fashion. Both collection development and acquisitions personnel are responsible for helping to meet these goals. Establishing, monitoring, and spending the acquisitions budget efficiently and effectively is a joint effort by all personnel concerned.

INTRODUCTION

Most library schools devote certain courses to some discussion of collection development activities; however, little time is normally spent covering day-to-day acquisitions processes. This paper emphasizes one of the important, yet often neglected aspects: establishing, monitoring, and spending the acquisitions budget. In addition to addressing the issue of establishing the budget and spending

Mildred McGinnis is Acquisitions Search and Order Librarian, and Mary Faust is Acquisitions Fiscal Control Librarian, Ball State University Library, Muncie, IN 47306.

it effectively, some attention is given to the working relationships among personnel charged with budgetary tasks. Comprehensive coverage of all matters related to budget processes cannot be covered in such a short paper; rather, its purpose is to stimulate thinking regarding the importance of closely scrutinizing budgetary goals and seeking methods for reaching these goals.

RECENT HISTORY OF LIBRARY
ACQUISITIONS BUDGETS

During the sixties and seventies, price increases of library materials were at a double digit level. Materials costs remained high in the early eighties; then, for a short time the dollar strengthened and there was actually a decline in the price of foreign materials. In the mid-eighties, when the exchange rate for the dollar fell, the cost of foreign materials rose to new heights. This was especially true for periodicals. A study reported in *Library Journal* for the period, 1967-79, showed that the overall price increase of journals for this period was 250.7%. During a previous period, 1957-69, prices increased only 89.7%[1].

According to an Indiana University National Science Foundation survey, materials budgets were increased by an average of 9.4% for major academic libraries during the period 1973-76. The same study showed that library administrators responded to shortages in the library materials budget by canceling duplicates and shifting funds from monographic to serials accounts. Another common tactic was to halt new subscriptions for periodicals in order to renew old ones. In 1969, two dollars were spent on serials for every dollar spent on monographs; by 1976 a steady decrease in the purchase of serials had reduced the spending ratio to $1.23 for serials compared to one dollar spent on monographs[2].

With 1977 as a base year, the 1987 *Bowker Annual* indicates that U.S. periodical prices increased 104.3% by 1983 and 164.3% by 1986. This compares with book price increases of 62.3% by 1983 and 62.4% by 1986.[3] (See Chart 1.) Thus the price of periodicals has continued to climb at a rapid pace even in the most recent years. With this increase in the price of periodicals during the mid-eighties, acquisitions librarians have had to continue to deal with consid-

CHART 1. Periodical and Book Price Increases, 1977-1986

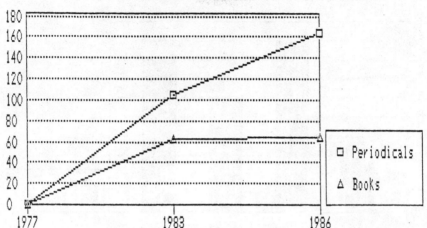

erably larger cost increases for serials than for monographs. In 1975, the median figure for serials expenditures for ARL member libraries was about 48% of the total library materials expenditures. By 1981 that figure had grown to 58%. The rate then dropped steadily until 1986, when 52% of materials budgets was spent on serials. Then in just one year — 1987 — serials expenditures rose to 56% of the budget, nearly returning to their highest point. (See Chart 2.) Should serials continue to demand ever greater proportions of the library budget, there will be a significant impact on academic libraries and the resources they are able to provide for scholars in the future[4].

ALLOCATING THE ACQUISITIONS BUDGET

In allocating the library budget, two important factors should be kept in mind: inflationary costs of books and periodicals, and the percentage of monies to be allocated for serials versus monographs. Rapid serial increases have forced libraries to decide whether to cut back in serial purchases or to spend ever larger percentages of materials money on them. An additional consideration is that library materials have had greater percentage increases in certain disci-

CHART 2. Percent of Total Budget Spent for Periodicals, 1975-1987

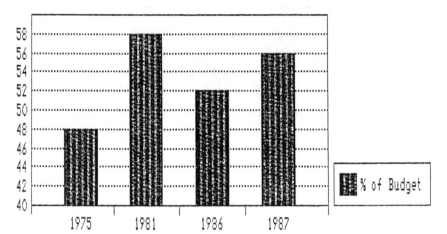

plines than in others. From 1979-80 to 1985-86, periodicals in chemistry increased 64.4%; fine and applied arts, 48.2%; and industrial arts, 11.5%[5]. A yearly analysis of the balance between serials and monographs should be a routine part of the budget projection.

Formula Budgets

Another important consideration in allocating library budgets is the type of budget system to use. It is common for academic libraries to divide their materials budget among the academic departments. There are different ways to establish this division. Often the budget is based on formulas, some of which are rather complicated. These formulas may include: size of the collection for a discipline based on a periodic shelf list count; number of students in a departmental major; number of faculty in a department; number and type of graduate degrees offered (as well as the number of courses offered by the department); circulation statistics; and other considerations peculiar to the individual institution. Some of the above factors may also be weighted. Once a formula is applied and the budget established by the library, it is wise to monitor this budget periodically.

Incremental Budgets

Usually the budget allocation for the new fiscal year is based to some extent on the previous year's expenditures by department/college and library area. The person charged with allocating funds for the new year examines each college/department's expenditures from the previous year, considers the overall budget, evaluates collection needs for the college/department, and then makes a determination of the allocation for that particular unit. Those departments/colleges which did not spend all of their allocated money the previous year may not receive increases; in fact, these units may have their allocations cut.

Preliminary Allocations

Often an appropriate library administrator or college dean may consider what percentage of the total departmental materials budget will be spent for monographs and what percentage for serials. This percentage may vary from department to department. Science departments may desire to allocate more for serials and less for monographs since scientists rely more on the latest research findings than is true for the humanities. Conversely, departments in the humanities may wish to spend more on monographs and not as large a percentage on serials because information is not as rapidly outdated in these fields.

After preliminary allocations have been assigned by the library, input from the deans of the colleges may be sought to determine how the college budget will be distributed to individual departments. It is important that the deans have knowledge based on an appropriate formula, or other significant information if no formula is applied, to determine which departments need more money and which need less.

Other Considerations in Budget Allocations

Important to consider when allocating funds are the library's use of approval plans and recent price trends. Approval plans allow the library to efficiently obtain current books in specific disciplines and on specific levels based on a profile established with an approval vendor. Disciplines for which an abundance of books are received on an approval plan may not need so large a departmental allocation as disciplines that rely on material outside the scope of approval plans.

If possible, a percentage of increase should be incorporated into the entire budget, but for monographs and serials, based on projected inflation factors for each type of material. Book and periodical prices have historically increased at a greater rate than library salaries or supplies. Sources of information, such as *Bowker Annual* or *Publishers Weekly* may help establish such projections. Programs that need to be enhanced are another factor to be taken into consideration. Increases in the purchase of costly materials (e.g., audio-visuals), will also need to be considered when formulating the total budget.

Sources such as suppliers, jobbers and subscription agencies can be contacted for their estimates to determine how inflation will impact on the budget. These firms may have reliable estimates in advance of the operational year. Information in the *Bowker Annual*, and articles covering U.S. periodical and serial price indexes appearing in *Library Journal*, are excellent sources of information on historical price-increase trends. This information will allow justification for larger-than-inflation increases in the acquisitions budget. These sources offer more reliable data for cost projections of library materials than does the standard rate of inflation.

METHODS FOR BUDGET MONITORING

Manual Budget Control

It is very difficult to accurately monitor the budget in an entirely manual mode. When purchase orders are typed, at least one of the multi-part forms is designated as the fund slip. Those slips may be filed first by fund and then by title in an "on order" file until the material is received and the invoice is ready to be paid. At that point the slip is pulled from the "on order" file and the invoice is processed in a manual mode. The fund slips are totaled by fund for a total of weekly expenditures, and these weekly fund expenditures are later compiled into a monthly report. Fund slips may also be sorted to total expenditures by vendor. The fund slip is then refiled into a "received" file. Thus, it is possible to know how much is outstanding for each fund and how much has been spent for each vendor. This practice, however, is time consuming and would probably have to be performed on a weekly basis. Cumulated reports can be typed and distributed on perhaps a monthly or quarterly basis.

Monitoring the budget in a manual mode is inconvenient because reports are only current on the date they are typed and it is difficult to get interim information between reports. Serials and other irregular publications on standing order may not be monitored at all in a manual mode because it is cumbersome to produce and manipulate slips for materials of this kind. Since these types of materials may not be monitored, it is difficult to determine how much of the acquisitions budget must be retained to spend on these materials and how much can be encumbered for additional monographs or large sets.

Semi-Automatic Budget Control

The budget may also be monitored semi-automatically. With this method, the actual ordering and receiving is still manual, but the fund accounting is automated to some degree. The acquisitions department continues to handle all of the manual slips; however, the fund accounting can be set up on a personal computer, logically on a spreadsheet program. Using a spreadsheet, the bookkeeper can post the invoices when they arrive in the department. After posting, the invoices can be returned to the receiving unit to be used when checking in the material. When invoices are ready for payment, the bookkeeper will post the invoice against the proper vendor on the spreadsheet which will then show the invoice as paid. The amounts from the invoices also need to be recorded by fund on another spreadsheet program. As with the completely manual mode, reports can be generated on a regular basis, only this time they can be printed from the PC spreadsheet program.

It may be advisable to print the fund report weekly, as each weekly posting of invoices is entered into the computer. Fund slips are then filed the same way as in the completely manual method, i.e., by fund and then by title in the "on order" file, until the invoice is ready to be paid. At that time, the individual slips will be pulled, used in the payment process, and then refiled into the "paid" file.

Outstanding encumbrances can be totaled at the beginning of the new fiscal year from the outstanding "on order" fund slips and entered on the new spreadsheet for that year. Problems with monitoring this type of budget are similar to those of the manual system, i.e., serials and irregular standing order funds are difficult to control, and therefore may not be monitored at all, or only estimated at best. The librarian monitoring the budget must constantly keep in mind the amount that remains to be spent for such categories. Failure to do so may result in having to expend large amounts of remaining funds with less discrimination.

Automated Budget Control

A good automated system can make a tremendous difference in monitoring an acquisitions budget. To accommodate management information needs, funds may be allocated and formatted on the system (i.e., subdivisions by college/department/format, etc.) and the system is then ready to manipulate this information. As orders are placed, the proper amount is automatically encumbered against the correct fund. When material is received, the invoice can be entered on the system to disencumber the proper amount from the correct fund and post the payment against this fund. The system provides up-to-the-minute information about allocations, expenditures, encumbrances, free balances, and cash balances.

With an automated system, reports can be printed on a regular basis or on a demand basis. It is also possible to set up departmental funds for approval plan(s) and even for each segment of the approval plan (i.e., notification slips, claim on approvals), if that is desired.

It is also possible to monitor serials and periodicals for each department by encumbering an amount at the beginning of the fiscal year to cover all ongoing standing orders. Funds for new standing orders could be set up in several ways. For example, for the first year, new standing order titles could come out of a library's general fund; in succeeding years, the title would be paid out of a departmental budget. Another method for funding new serial or periodical orders might be to establish a "new standing order" fund for each department from which orders would be paid the first year. As above, in the succeeding years, the title would be paid out of the departmental fund.

One type of material that is still difficult to monitor, even with an automated system, is the monographic series/sets category. Because these titles are so irregular, it is impossible to accurately allocate an amount for ongoing standing orders with any certainty that this designated amount will be spent during that fiscal year. The publisher may initially issue two books in a given year. If the library encumbers for two books the following year, the publisher may actually publish five books in the set or series, or no books at all. In fact, the next book may not be available for several years. Thus expenditures can be tracked but exact allocations are hard to establish.

SPENDING THE ACQUISITIONS BUDGET

In a very small library, one person would probably handle all aspects of collection development and library acquisitions duties as described in the foregoing pages. At the other extreme, in a very large library, several professionals would deal with both collections development and acquisitions processes.

Although specific job responsibilities for collection development and acquisitions personnel are outside the scope of this paper, it is important to note that all professionals should have a clear understanding of their job responsibilities. It is also advantageous for each librarian to have an understanding of tasks to be performed in both the acquisitions and collection development units. By having some conception of the whole process, each person can make better professional decisions.

Goals for Spending the Budget

The collections development and acquisitions units should each have their unique goals. In addition, there are some joint goals equally important to both departments. Two of these are: (1) spending the budget effectively; and (2) spending the budget in a timely fashion. To reach these goals, it is important that the steps taken in each unit be coordinated. Perhaps the "how to" in the steps of coordination is not so important as the recognition that coordination is a very important and necessary function. The acquisition of materials is sometimes thought of in pure business terms with ordering, receiving, and paying as primarily clerical procedures. To oversee these procedures in such a way that the goals of acquisitions and collection development are met, however, the acquisitions librarian needs to view the job from a wider perspective. Among other duties, the acquisitions librarian should be familiar with the trade literature, be actively involved in consulting with book vendors, and should take an active part in book selection.

General Considerations for Spending the Budget

Some considerations for spending the budget are: how much of the budget should be devoted to standing orders and what percentage should be spent on nonprint materials, e.g., CD-ROM, audiovisual material, and the associated equipment? Answers to these questions will vary from library to library, but a conscious decision should be made regarding the amounts to be set aside for these purchases.

Vendor discounts are another area of concern for the acquisitions librarian. With an automated acquisitions system, vendor performance can often be monitored on a regular basis and purchasing decisions made accordingly. To be fair to vendors, however, one needs to be very careful in comparing them unless the mix of materials ordered is as nearly identical as possible. To ideally compare, one would send each vendor the same requests, but this is unrealistic unless more than one copy of a number of books are ordered at the same time.

Discounts are only one area of consideration in measuring vendor performance; of equal importance is the quality of service rendered. Some aspects of service to be considered are: average delivery time; rate of delivery (how many filled orders in a given time frame); clarity of reports; invoicing procedures; and availability of vendor personnel to resolve problems. Only with very careful monitoring of all these factors can one make the best vendor selection.

There are also some mechanical aspects to consider in spending the library budget. When the parent institution is on a cash accounting system, the library's encumbrances must be cleared before the end of the budget year, i.e., ordered items must be received and paid for before the end of the budget year. Items encumbered but not received must be canceled, rather than carried over into the next year. However, when an accrual accounting system is in effect, encumbrances may be carried over to the next fiscal year. In this case, items still "on order" need not be cancelled, but left "on order" to be received and paid during the new fiscal year.

Monitoring Free Balances and Cash Balances

Free balances should be monitored during most of the fiscal year to assure full expenditure of all allocations. Moreover, cash balances need to be monitored closely *throughout the fiscal year*, but especially toward the end of the year since it is difficult to know which encumbered materials will be received. These decisions should be made early enough for ordered materials to have a likely chance of being received before the end of the fiscal year. Over-encumbering to the extent that a large portion of a department's funds are committed for the next fiscal year should be avoided. Likewise, it is useful to check departmental budgets on a weekly basis to prevent encumbrances from going over a prearranged specific amount. Even with careful monitoring, it can be difficult to plan the workflow in such a way that over-encumbrances do not occur.

Other Monitoring Factors

In addition to the day-to-day monitoring of the library budget, best managed with an automated system, there is a "judgmental" type of monitoring which is far more inexact and difficult to achieve. Some of the factors affecting this type of monitoring are: receiving requests which may exceed the allocation of one department, or receiving too few requests from another to spend that department's budget; making decisions on how to use a given department's unspent funds; underestimating the costs of current periodical subscriptions and thus having to "rob" other budgets to obtain the necessary monies; and, avoiding the preparation of orders which cannot be placed due to overspent accounts. There are many variables controlling the foregoing factors. In a small library, where one person has control over several functions, coordinating the goals of spending the money effectively and in a timely fashion may be more easily facilitated than in a larger library. In the latter, it is crucial for those involved in making acquisitions decisions to work as a team, so that each person clearly understands the operation as a whole.

CONCLUSION

To establish, monitor, and spend the acquisitions budget in the best possible manner, a joint effort is needed by all personnel in the acquisitions and collection development units of the library. Selecting and purchasing books/periodicals/media is an inexact science at best. At worst, acquisitions processes can be well-intentioned but needlessly inefficient. Acquisitions and collection development librarians need to combine their professional efforts to ensure the desirable goals of spending the budget effectively and efficiently.

REFERENCES

1. Michael R. Kronenfeld and James Thompson, "The Impact of Inflation on Journal Costs," *Library Journal* 106:7 (April 1, 1981) 714-717.

2. Herbert S. White, "Library Materials Prices and Academic Library Practices: Between Scylla and Charybdes," *Journal of Academic Librarianship* 5:1 (March, 1979) 20-23.

3. *Bowker Annual of Library and Book Trade Information*. New York, R. R. Bowker Co., 1987, 434-5.

4. "ARL Statistics Confirm Trend of Rising Serial Prices," Association of Research Libraries, May 20, 1988, 1.

5. *Bowker Annual*, 1987, 438-9.

Administering the Allocated Acquisitions Budget: Achieving a Balanced Matrix

David C. Genaway

SUMMARY. This article will outline the problems of administering a systematically allocated library acquisitions budget in an academic environment in the context of multiple formats and fund accounts. It is roughly divided into two parts. The first section deals with the variable components in allocation or options for allocating the library materials acquisitions budget. The second section is concerned with issues and problems involved in administering an allocated budget based on these variables. Some brief guidelines for dealing with these issues are provided in the conclusion.

When funding becomes sparse and library acquisitions budgets approach a steady state, allocation of resources becomes even more important than in affluent times. While allocation of the library acquisitions budget is a logical way of dealing with limited resources, it is not without problems in its administration. Since all budgets are, at one time or another, allocated, this article will help identify the problems and issues common to all academic libraries.

TO ALLOCATE OR NOT TO ALLOCATE IS NOT THE QUESTION

Library materials budget allocations are in too many cases determined by what the accountant terms FIFO (first in, first out) or by historical precedent rather than a rational systematic procedure.

David C. Genaway is University Librarian, William F. Maag Library, Youngstown State University, Youngstown, OH 4555-0001.

Whether the budget is spent by collection development librarians, faculty or a combination of faculty and collection development librarians, there is no such thing as an *un*allocated materials budget. Every library acquisitions budget is allocated. If it is not allocated prior to expenditure, it becomes a post-expenditure allocation, in which data used in self-study and accreditation reports must be laboriously compiled after the fact. So the real question becomes a question of timing, i.e., "When to allocate?"

Allocation is a means of systematic collection development, since allocating a budget is in essence determining the thrust of collection development. In the most rudimentary sense, the basic premise of a pre-expenditure allocation is that there is some conceptual, theoretical, idealistic basis for a "balanced collection" and that allocation will help to achieve it. It presumes that there is an ideal ratio of library acquisitions to needs of an academic department. It assumes that "library intensiveness" can be defined and measured by the variables described below either independently or collectively.

Whether such an ideal balanced plan for collection development really exists is subject to considerable debate and is an even heavier topic than the definition of a serial publication. It is not the purpose of this article to discuss whether a philosophical ideal exists. Rather, this article will examine several practical components commonly used in allocation, prescribe a method for combining them to minimize their individual flaws, and outline the issues involved in administering an allocated acquisitions budget. Further, it is not the purpose of this article to discuss the advantages and disadvantages of allocation or indeed a comprehensive collection of formulas or procedures. These are covered in-depth in the author's previous works and other articles listed in the References section. This article assumes the pre-disposition of the reader toward the application of some method of allocation.

If the acquisitions budget is allocated in a systematic manner before expenditures, then one must deal with some basic administrative decisions regarding enforcement of the allocation. The budget must be expended by the end of the fiscal year, regardless of the degree of activity of departments. This fact alone may still ensure that those who spend more will get more. If the entire allocation is not spent, be assured that you will get less next year because of the perceived lack of need. Yet, the librarian is legally constrained from spending more than the budget.

The first part of this article will deal with some of the various components available for allocating the budget, the flaws of each and some procedural options. A method of overcoming the individual flaws through a comprehensive but flexible formula combining all these components will be suggested. The second part will concentrate on the issues and problems associated with the administration of an allocated budget.

ALLOCATION OPTIONS AND VARIABLES

Who should decide the how the library budget is allocated: The president? The library dean or director? Faculty only? Faculty and librarians? Faculty, librarians, and students? Librarians tend to seek balance, strive for evenness and have a broader view. Faculty generally will seek greater involvement, but have a more myopic view and vested interests.[1] How much of the budget is to be allocated and what areas are to be included in the allocation? Should the entire acquisitions budget be allocated or only 50% to 80%? It is assumed that a portion of the budget will be held for "contingencies," such as new programs, excessive inflation or foreign exchange rates, etc. How much should be kept in a contingency fund? How much should be allocated to general works and/or reference? It is not our purpose to debate definitions here. Suffice it to say that these are general interest works or reference tools too expensive and/or general to be assigned to a given allocation unit. Once these basic questions have been dealt with some of the components or variables commonly used in allocation should be examined.

Several studies are currently under way regarding the allocation of library resources, including those by Kay Adams at Southeastern Louisiana University and Thomas Loven at the University of Scranton.[2]

Once the amount of the budget to be allocated is determined, the procedure or method for allocating the budget should be determined: historical precedent, a single variable, multiple variables by formula, according to FIFO, etc.

FORMULAS AND PROCEDURES

The methods for allocation can be divided into two groups: procedures and formulas. A procedure is where different factors are combined with mathematical applications to arrive at a quantitative figure, be it a percent or a dollar amount for each allocation. The application of the FTE (full time equivalent) or any of the library standards[3] used to determine the number of volumes that should be in a collection according to field or level could be considered a procedure. (Full time equivalent is derived by dividing the total number of credit hours offered by the university by the number of credit hours considered to be a full load.) The use of the same percent that each department gets from the administration to determine the same ratio for library allocations is another example of a procedure.[4] The use of *Choice* as a basis for determining distribution of funds is another example of a procedure, although the latter is closer to a formula.[5]

A formula assumes an equation, i.e., that the sum of the parts will equal the whole. The application of a formula to determine percentages or ratios will always equal 100% of the total amount allocated when the percent allocated to each academic unit is added together.

COMPONENT VARIABLES

Virtually every variable used in any formula has its drawbacks. Some of the most commonly used variables and their weaknesses are outlined below.

Circulation which is frequently touted as the chief barometer for measuring library intensiveness totally ignores those items that are most heavily used but do not circulate: reference books, periodicals, and microformat items, for example. Periodical intensive disciplines, such as Chemistry and Physics, might show far less library use than traditional library users, such as History or English, by applying this variable alone. Also, circulation statistics by department may be difficult to obtain unless circulation is automated. There is also a significant difference in the procedure used to obtain use statistics. If the home, school, college or department that the student indicates on his borrowing card is used as a basis for determining circulation, then any book on any subject is credited to his/her department even if it is only recreational reading. If the count is measured by analyzing circulation of specific classification numbers, then it may be difficult to assign class numbers to departments for purposes of allocation.

Faculty: Full time or Actual. The use of the number of full-time equivalent faculty (total course load in university/normal course load for faculty) or the headcount of faculty in each department as a variable is complicated by some part-time faculty, who may use the library more extensively than some full-time faculty. Full-time faculty do not reflect class size. A freshman English class taught by a part-time faculty member would indicate less intensive because he/she is only .5 FTE. Yet his/her class would require more library resources than one FTE faculty teaching flute, algebra, typing, etc. If this statistic is intended to reflect faculty research, bear in mind that faculty research interests may or may not reflect teaching interests.

Students as a variable falls into two types: raw headcount or FTE (full-time equivalent). The FTE is the most commonly used figure since it represents a standard statistic, but one might also argue that headcount is a more valid figure. FTE may or may not indicate a direct correlation between actual students. In most universities actual headcount is greater than the number of FTEs because of a significant number of part-time students taking less than a full load. In some cases, however, such as Miami University in Ohio, the opposite is true because many students take an overload, yielding a higher FTE than enrollment. In any case, if the amount per FTE is divided first and then weighted by level, the result will not be a balanced equation, and the total amount will not equal the amount to be allocated. (See Figures 1 and 2.) FTEs must be weighted throughout the application prior to determining the unit amount per FTE much like GPA. As an algorithm, the total funds to be allocated is divided by the weighted FTE to determine the dollar value of each FTE or weighted FTE.

When FTEs are used to determine allocation, the allocation process is said to be enrollment-driven. It is assumed that the more students there are taking a course, the greater the need for library

Figure 1

Allocation by Unadjusted FTE Full Time Equivalent Student

Youngstown State University

FTE Fall 1987

Level	CAST	A & S	School/College S.B.A.	EDUC.	ENGIN.	F.& P.A.	TOTAL
TECHNICAL	942.3	0.0	0.0	0.0	0.0	0.0	942.3
GENERAL	1.5	3977.7	0.0	73.6	0.0	190.7	4243.5
BACCALAUREATE	368.5	2666.1	1053.2	344.8	361.4	563.3	5357.3
MASTER	6.9	99.3	64.4	165.6	24.5	14.0	374.7
TOTALS (RAW FTE)	1319.2	6743.1	1117.6	584.0	385.9	768.0	10917.8

Amount of library budget to be allocated $665,000.00

F.T.E.   10,917.8

Dollar amount per F.T.E. (Amount/FTE) $ 60.91

Weighted F.T.E. dollar value

TECHNICAL	0.5	$ 30.45
GENERAL	1.0	$ 60.91
BACCALAUREATE	1.0	$ 60.91
MASTER	2.0	$ 121.82

1988-89 ALLOCATION (WEIGHTED F.T.E. DOLLAR VALUE * F.T.E.)

	CAST	A & S	S.B.A.	EDUC.	ENGIN.	F & P.A.	TOTAL
TECH	28,697.61	0.00	0.00	0.00	0.00	0.00	28,697.61
GEN	91.36	242,280.54	0.00	4,482.95	0.00	11,615.48	258,470.34
BAC	22,445.23	162,391.37	64,150.10	21,001.67	22,012.77	34,310.44	326,311.57
MASTER	840.55	12,096.67	7,845.17	20,173.29	2,984.58	1,705.47	45,645.73
TOTAL $	52,074.75	416,768.58	71,995.27	45,657.92	24,997.34	47,631.39	659,125.26

* Note difference in total allocation and total amount to be allocated. This is due to unequal
distribution of weighted F.T.E.s

Figure 2

Allocation by Adjusted Full Time Equivalent Student

Youngstown State University

FTE Fall 1987

School/College

Level	Weight	CAST	A & S	S.B.A.	EDUC.	ENGIN.	F.& P.A.	TOTAL
TECH	.5	471	0	0	0	0	0	471
GENERAL	1	2	3978	0	74	0	191	4245
BACCAL.	1	369	2666	1053	345	361	563	5357
MASTER	2	14	198	128	332	50	28	750
TOTAL		856	6842	1181	751	411	782	10823
TECH		28939.76	0.00	0.00	0.00	0.00	0.00	28939.76
GENERAL		122.69	244421.14	0.00	4546.80	0.00	11735.66	260826.48
BACCAL.		22672.55	163807.63	64699.71	21197.91	22181.00	34592.53	329151.34
MASTER		860.21	12165.76	7864.73	20599.15	3072.16	1720.41	46082.42
TOTAL $		52595.40	420394.53	72564.45	46143.86	25253.16	48048.60	665000.00

WEIGHTED FTE AMOUNT = $ 61.44

Note: Enrollment figures were multiplied by weight, totaled and then divided into the total amount available. The result is that the sum of all allocations equals the total amount allocated.

materials. One flaw is that some classes require vast library resources while others are taught solely from textbooks. There may be an inverse relationship between the size of classes and the need for library resources, although this is an untested hypothesis. Programs that are highly selective by screening out weaker students suffer because reduced FTE leads to reduced funding, while programs with more open enrollments may fare better in library allocation. This is why raw headcount is sometimes considered a more accurate reflection of the library needs of a department, because each student will presumably have the same assignment.

Student credit hours (SCH) produce the same allocations as FTE students.

Courses. The number of courses offered by level has been suggested as a factor in allocations. Quite obviously the departments with the greatest number of courses will receive the largest allocation. The Music department with a separate course for each instrument and each year of instruction could receive 50% or more of the allocation on that basis.

Figure 3 is an example of the application of the number of courses to the allocation of the budget in a typical mid-size university. Note the amount allocated to Fine & Performing Arts using courses by level—approximately one-third of the total budget.

Inter-Library loans have sometimes been viewed as an indicator of deficits in the collection. These statistics have been used to increase allocations to departments with the highest number of interlibrary loan requests, since these requests show the need for materials not in the library. These statistics can be greatly skewed by surges of research activity based on short term needs and could misrepresent longstanding needs.

Historical precedent is probably the most common way of allocating the acquisitions budget. Whatever departments spent last year they will get this next year, perhaps increased by 5% or 10% across the board. The problem is that this procedure perpetuates the past needs in a college or university where there may be changing curricula and programs. However, this could be used in conjunction with other variables' weights to reduce the effect of dramatic shifts when a single variable is used.

Formula. If one chooses a formula to allocate the budget, then

Figure 3

Allocation by Courses Weighted by Level

WEIGHT	CAST	A & S	SBA	ED	ENG	F & PA	TOTAL
500	650	1065	10	30	30	1175	2960
600	1308	1212	420	12	216	1848	5016
700	714	3241	336	126	504	2625	7546
800	832	2768	400	1544	1112	2688	9334
900	270	2250	675	927	927	1908	6957
1000	0	270	0	540	0	0	810
	3774	10806	1841	3179	2789	10244	32633
	$ 76907.12	220206.23	37516.16	64782.12	56834.65	208753.72	665000

UNIT WEIGHTED COURSE ALLOCATION = $ 20.38

Allocation = Total number of courses x weighted course allocation the question of what to include as variables emerges. Virtually any statistical element of the university could theoretically be used as a variable and probably has. It is possible, however, to combine as few variables or as many as desired into a single formula that will provide a ratio or percent based on the combination of all of them. Weights can be assigned to each to indicate the degree of importance placed on each variable at a given institution.

Although each of these variables used independently has advantages and disadvantages, they might be used collectively to determine allocations. Collective use of all or most of them would help distribute the shortcomings of each. They might be combined into a single formula based on proportions in each department versus proportions for the college or university, such as the Q formula shown in Figure 4 below.[6] Also, the greater number of variables used to determine an allocation the greater acceptability and leveling effect of each.

Figure 5 shows the effect of changing weights on the percent allocations. The same data are used in each case.

As one can see by the above illustrations, a formula such as the Q formula can be quite flexible, can amortize the disadvantages of several component variables, and can win wider approval by including all the most commonly accepted variables. By assigning weights, if desired, one can place greater emphasis on any given variable.

There are at least three schools known to be using the same variation of the procedures found in the Q formula: Ohio University, Northeastern Illinois University, and Youngstown State University.

PRODUCTIVITY AND PRICE: A ZERO-BASED APPROACH TO ALLOCATION

Through the application of productivity and price statistics it might be possible to determine an allocation in a kind of zero-based budget approach. This concept might be extended to develop a zero-based budget, but that is another topic. This section is an expansion and continuation of a concept suggested in an earlier article.[7]

How many new titles are published annually? In all disciplines?

Figure 4

Q Formula

$$Q = a(CD/CT) + b(FD/FT) + c(SD/ST) + d(ID/IT) + e(ND/NT)$$

a,b,c,d,e = Weights

CD = Total number of departmental courses
CT = Total number of university courses
FD = Total number of FTE departmental faculty
FT = Total number of FTE university faculty
SD = Total number of FTE students enrolled in a department
ST = Total number FTE students enrolled in the university
ID = Total circulation checkouts in a department
IT = Total circulation checkoust for the university
     Circulation includes graduate students. Figure represents the
     number of items checked out by a student from the school in which
     he/she is enrolled. Does not include faculty circulation.
ID = Total inter-libraryloans for a department
IT = Total number of university inter-library loans
HD = Average departmental allocation for past three years
HU = Average university library allocation for past three years

Sample weights:

```
COURSES   A =             .01
FACULTY   B =             .01
STUDENTS  C =             .95
CIRCULATION  D =          .01
INTER-LIBRARY LOAN  E =   .01
HISTORICAL AVERAGE  F =   .01

                         1.00
```

Allocation based on sample weights.

SCHOOL	PERCENT	ALLOCATION
CAST	12	$ 79,800.00
ARTS & SCI.	61	$ 405,650.00
S.B.A.	10	$ 66,500.00
EDUC.	5	$ 33,250.00
ENGIN.	5	$ 33,250.00
F & PA	7	$ 46,550.00
TOTAL	100 %	$ 665,000.00

Figure 5

Q Formula

Percent Allocation With Reassigned Weights for Each Variable
Using the Same Data

SCHOOL/ COLLEGE	Unweighted	Courses	Faculty	Students	Circulation	Inter-library Loan	Historical Average
		.95	.95	.95	.95	.95	.95
	✗	✗	✗	✗	✗	✗	✗
CAST	13	14	15	12	20	7	9
A & S	55	50	50	61	35	67	62
SBA	10	7	9	10	14	6	10
EDUC.	7	8	8	5	11	10	5
ENGIN.	6	5	6	4	11	3	8
F & PA	9	16	12	8	9	7	6
TOTALS	100	100	100	100	100	100	100

157

In each discipline? What would it cost to buy the entire output of all academic books produced in the U.S.? In Europe? The rest of the world? What would it cost to buy all biology books produced in the U.S.? Assuming that the answers to these questions could be found, this data could be used in allocating the materials budget. In other words, the total production and price for a given discipline would be compared with the sum of the total production and price for all disciplines. Once this was determined for monographs the same procedure could be applied to periodicals. Total productivity and price could even be tied to previous and present inflation rates to determine a projected budget for next year. The ratio of the costs of all books published in biology to the cost of the total value of all books published could be used to determine the percent of the local budget to be allocated to biology. Periodical price data could be combined with monographs in the same manner or treated independently. As the reader can see, it is just a short step from this procedure to developing a zero-based budget. Yet, another approach might be to take the average price of all monographic and periodical titles and use a factor that incorporates the deviation (positive or negative) from the average cost of books or periodicals in a discipline.

The problem with attempting to develop an allocation based on this approach has to do with obtaining data for all disciplines. Historical data for one's own institution might be used, if available. The advantages of such data are that they reflect local needs and disciplines and are likely to be relatively complete. *The Bowker Annual* might also be used, but difficulties will be encountered in matching defined subject categories in the annual with specific disciplines at the local university.[8] Also, there may be gaps for which there are no matching data. In this case, one could use an average for all disciplines or the next broader subject area under which a specific discipline falls. Several vendors also provide price data via their statistical analysis or management packages. The wide variation in the cost of out-of-print material is another factor difficult to anticipate.

Most of these problems are not insurmountable and the effort might be worth it. A particular statistic such as academic books might be applied or the eclectic approach of combining several categories, such as textbooks, college books and mass market books might be used.

Northeastern Illinois University[9] and Ohio University[10] have attempted to include average book price and title production in their formula but stop short of using it as a basis for a zero-based budget.

The Consumer Price Index, the *Higher Education Price Index*,[11] and library materials index are also useful statistics that could be applied in attempting to develop a budget.

ADMINISTRATION OF THE ALLOCATED BUDGET: ISSUES AND PROBLEMS

How the budget is allocated and the flexibility or rigidity of adherence to allocations by discipline and by format will greatly effect the number of problems associated with its administration. If there has never been an allocation, the introduction of such could cause reactions from those who were accustomed to unlimited spending in a given discipline and who are suddenly curtailed to achieve a more balanced budget. Also, how the budget is allocated will have a great deal of impact on the significance of the response to an allocation. If faculty from the various schools or colleges are involved in the allocation process, there may be aggressive interest in the amounts each department receives. This also could have an interesting side benefit of greatly increasing support for additional library acquisitions budget by a broader base of faculty than if allocations were made by the director or dean alone.

Some of the issues involved in administration of the allocated budget are outlined below.

Level of Specificity

How finely do you allocate the budget? Should allocations be made at the macro level by school or college or at the micro level to each department within a school or college? What about interdisciplinary programs, institutes, etc.? Do you allocate to school and/or college and let the dean or a committee within the school or college subdivide the allocation to departments? Is there a floor for some disciplines, a minimum allocation a school, college or discipline must have regardless of the number of students it has?

Maintaining the balance between competing departments and competing formats (books, periodicals, etc.) could become quite tricky. If the budget is allocated at the school or college level and the library has responsibility for balancing the budget only at that level, then it is quite possible that individual departments, if they have an internal allocation, may not be able to spend their full allocation because the total college or school expenditures have been spent. It then becomes very difficult to tell the Mathematics Department, who can add and subtract in binary, decimal, and hexadecimal, that it cannot spend a positive balance of $5,000 because the total for its parent, the College of Arts and Sciences, is overspent due to other departments overspending. This produces a case where the sum of the parts becomes greater than the whole, even though some of parts are underspent.

Degree of Flexibility

How tightly do you control the allocations and make departments adhere to them? This will, of course, be governed to some extent by the amount of the library-wide budget allocated. If the entire acquisitions budget is allocated, then there will have to be a more rigid enforcement than if departments over budget can be bailed out with a contingency fund. Bear in mind that overspending by any department can seriously countermand the whole intent of an allocated budget, i.e., to balance the collection.

Category of Format

Once the level of specificity has been decided, how much of the budget should be allocated by format: audiovisual, microforms, books, periodicals? Are each of these separate line items when allocated to the library? If so, should the same ratios be applied to each departmental allocation? First, how rigidly should you adhere to the various formats? If no more than the classic 60% should be spent for periodicals, should this be interpreted to mean across the total library budget? Or should each department be held accountable for maintaining that ratio? English or History might be hard pressed to spend 60% of its allocation for periodicals while Chemistry and Physics would be equally hard pressed to limit periodical subscriptions to 60%. Would it be fair to require Chemistry or Physics to adhere to the 60:40 rule? Yet, an accreditation team may be concerned if ten years from now it discovers that the entire Chemistry budget has gone for periodicals and there are few new books on the shelves in this field. If departments are not forced to reduce periodical subscriptions when 90% of their allocation is spent for periodicals and the inflation or exchange rate exceeds 10%, then next year 100% will be spent for periodicals.

Again the rigidity with which the allocation is adhered to by format could cause considerable difficulty. Chemistry, along with other sciences, relies most heavily on the most recent information, which is found only in periodicals. Should a given department that has spent only 20% of its budget for periodicals and has a large reserve unspent not be allowed to enter a new subscription because the university-wide allocation or ratio for periodicals has been expended?

Serials prices and percentages of increase by disciplines will be found in the "Annual Survey of Periodicals Prices" published in *Library Journal* in mid-April.[12]

Should there be a cutoff date beyond which all departmental allocations become college-wide allocations, i.e., as long as there are funds in the college any department may still purchase library materials? Should there be yet another cutoff date, beyond which all unencumbered funds at the college or school level can be spent library-wide? Whether specified or not, this becomes the case, if the practical realities of June 30 cutoff date must be adhered to rigidly.

The 624 Cell Spreadsheet Matrix

Visualize a gigantic spreadsheet with one row for each department, college and/or school and one column for each format, plus a column for the status of expenditures in each format. As with any spreadsheet the intersection of each row and column is a cell. Expenditures for microformat items in the Biology department would constitute one cell. If each allocation is subdivided by format and expenditure status, then the spreadsheet has a 600 plus cell matrix. For example, if there are six schools or colleges, and a total of 33 departments, allotting one cell for each school or college and each department's total budget, in a typical medium-size university there would be 39 cells for budget allocation alone (6 schools or colleges plus 33 departments). Setting up a spreadsheet by allocating a column for budget, payments, budget less payments, and encumbered for each of the 39 lines or rows makes 156 cells for all rows and columns (4 columns × 39 rows). Further allocation and fund accounting by four formats (books, periodicals, etc.) yields four more columns or 4 × 156 or 624 cells in the spreadsheet matrix.

Although it is impossible to show such a spreadsheet on this page a partial example is given in Figure 6. Note that there would be another separate sheet depicting the same information for books, periodical, and microforms independently.

These detailed records come in very handy when the accreditation teams arrive and ask for such data. It is all pre-compiled and does not have to be derived retrospectively with inexact data. It also makes accounting of finely divided allocations very precise.

Other Considerations

Scheduling Expenditures

In automobiles and library allocations, timing is important to smooth operation. How does one maintain an even flow of orders and expenditures throughout the academic year? Obviously, various cutoff dates to ensure that orders are processed and paid before June 30. But the publishing industry is not necessarily geared to the academic calendar nor indeed is the dissemination of information about available titles.

It is quite possible that freezing and releasing funds before and after a certain date can create a feast or famine situation in which the big spender still takes all and the underspender loses due to timing? Supposing special funds become available either through grants or internal windfalls, should these also be allocated or used for special needs? Another question is who's responsible for maintaining the balance, the departments or the library? Bailing out an

Figure 6

The 620 Cell Matrix (Partial display)

William F. Maag Library Acquisitions Report
July 1, 1987 through August 31, 1987

BOOKS, PERIODICALS, MICROFORMS

School/College Departments		TOTAL BUDGET ALLOCATION	PAYMENTS TO DATE	BUDGET LESS PAYMENTS	ENCUMBERED TO DATE
CAST	Allied Health	$10,222.00	$5,866.64	$4,355.36	$4,021.11
	Bus. Ed. Tech.	$8,608.00	$1,437.14	$7,170.86	$2,696.30
	Crim. Justice	$9,146.00	$3,734.79	$5,411.21	$7,119.86
	Engr. Tech.	$8,608.00	$4,922.73	$3,635.27	$2,099.04
	Home Economics	$8,608.00	$4,200.55	$4,407.45	$2,916.56
	Nursing	$8,608.00	$1,775.65	$6,832.35	$7,017.41
	Sub total	$55,800.00	$21,937.50	$31,862.50	$25,870.28
Arts & Sci.	Biol. Sci.	$48,620.00	$34,892.14	$13,727.86	$14,046.30
	Black Studies	$2,690.00	$659.73	$2,030.27	$675.49
	Chemistry	$64,940.00	$57,505.53	$7,636.67	$10,703.92
	Economics	$13,780.00	$5,722.31	$10,057.69	$10,276.53
	English	$44,570.00	$17,695.71	$26,974.29	$12,725.67
	For. Language	$14,375.00	$6,031.63	$8,343.37	$9,359.66
	Geography	$10,170.00	$6,605.64	$3,564.36	$3,628.87
	Geology	$7,800.00	$4,802.24	$2,997.76	$2,641.33
	Health & PE	$3,079.00	$699.29	$2,379.71	$1,671.14
	History	$44,370.00	$18,666.71	$25,703.23	$14,950.39
	Math./Comp.	$28,755.00	$14,649.06	$14,105.94	$5,371.58
	Philos.& Relig.	$13,390.00	$3,787.54	$9,602.66	$5,873.29
	Physics & Astr.	$20,860.00	$23,096.60	$-2,536.60	$330.45
	Pol. Sci.	$23,620.00	$11,041.63	$12,578.57	$14,396.38
	Psychol.	$16,430.00	$4,390.65	$12,039.35	$6,745.53
	Soc. Antro.	$13,110,00	$6,308.33	$6,801.67	$7,914.09
	Sub total	$370,559.00	$214,352.34	$156,206.66	$121,370.68
S. Bus. Ad.	Sub total	$61,054.00	$32,335.46	$28,718.54	$27,563.87
Education	CRC/Dean	$4,625.00	$1,335.39	$3,289.61	$186.99
	Elementary	$5,549.00	$1,432.08	$4,116.92	$2,132.63
	Foundations	$8,324.00	$5,352.31	$4,371.63	$4,459.55
	Guidance	$3,391.00	$640.77	$2,750.23	$1,899.66
	Sec. Admin.	$2,158.00	$889.67	$1,268.33	$1,522.74
	Spec. Ed.	$6,783.00	$2,784.34	$3,998.66	$4,818.45
	Sub total	$30,830.00	$11,034.56	$13,795.44	$15,010.02
Engineer.	Sub total	$45,942.00	$31,762.42	$14,179.58	$16,439.09
Fine & P.A.	Art	$10,156.00	$904.32	$9,251.68	$4,885.09
	Music	$22,003.00	$15,093.51	$6,909.49	$9,635.78
	Speech, Comm.	$10,156.00	$6,061.25	$4,094.75	$3,091.86
	Subtotal	$42,315.00	$22,059.08	$20,255.92	$17,612.73
Gen. Wks./Ref.		$85,000.00	$53,679.65	$31.320.37	$23,308.02
Refer. Devl.		$20,000.00	$17,029.62	$2,970.38	$2,994.50
Replacements		$10,500,00	$2,576.97	$7,923.03	$6,195.81
Total	Grand total	$720,000.00	$406,767.58	$313,252.41	$256,365.00

overspent department can cause comments of favoritism or upset the intent of the allocation process.

THE BALANCED ALLOCATION: THE ELUSIVE SEARCH

This article does not provide any definitive method of achieving the balanced allocation, simply because there does not appear to be a universal definition of the term. Once defined, it is doubtful as to whether such a goal could be uniformly and consistently achieved. By dealing with the problems in striving to achieve such an ideal, it is the author's intent to suggest several methods of attempting to achieve it. It is like happiness or heaven, there is probably no universal agreement as to what constitutes either, but this does not prevent a significant portion of the population from trying to achieve them.

Is the effort to obtain a systematic allocated library materials budget worth the trouble? It is better to have tried and fallen short, than never to have tried at all. The question ultimately reduces to that of expenditures determining the allocation or letting allocation determine the spending pattern and consequently collection development.

CONCLUSIONS

It will be helpful to summarize some of the issues involved in administering the allocated acquisitions budget.

Autonomy versus autocracy: In a setting where faculty are active in helping to allocate or spend the acquisitions budget, departmental autonomy, as far as the budget is concerned, could become a significant issue. How much control over allocation and, hence, collection development should the librarians have versus the faculty? Can library collection development by professionals be compatible with faculty autonomy? Obviously, a separate amount allocated to each group or a close library-college approach using the expertise of both librarians and faculty would be one solution.

Flexibility or rigidity: Once a budget is allocated the degree of rigidity or flexibility in its enforcement can have a profound effect on its success. The tensility of the administration regarding an allocation is related to the seriousness of belief that a theoretical, ideal, balanced collection can be achieved. The stronger the belief in the hypothesis that the formula or procedure accepted will achieve this, the more rigid will be adherence to the allocations. Conversely, skepticism of this concept will be reflected in one's commitment to enforcement. All of which has to be weighed against the realities of end-of-year closures.

The problem of containing periodical costs in an era of rising inflation and foreign exchange rates will be partially resolved when the determination of the proper ratio between monographs and periodicals is determined and enforced.

Productivity and price: One would expect an inverse relationship between productivity and price. That is, the disciplines wherein the greatest number of titles were produced would have the lowest cost, and the most costly disciplines would be those with limited production. This would be true if the economist's elasticity of demand were functioning in a pure vacuum. This would make it easier to determine allocations because fixed amounts could be spent for each discipline. While there is some degree of truth in this axiom, it does not uniformly hold true. Yes, Chemistry titles are generally more expensive than History titles, both monographs and periodicals, but the budget required to purchase the total output of each is not equal. Nevertheless, this ratio should not be totally ignored when considering allocations.

Guidelines

An allocated budget that allows for some degree of autonomy and flexibility while attempting to balance the collection is more likely to be successful. Contingencies are key factors and can be used for special needs such as new programs, research, etc. Someone has said that administration is the ability to function in the midst of ambiguity, the ability to make valid decisions before all the facts are in. In the search for the perfect method of allocating and administering the allocated budget all the facts may not be in, but this is no reason not to strive for an allocated budget. It is certainly better than the alternative of unbridled, post-expenditure allocation.

Allocations procedures should be dynamic rather than static, have stability while accommodating change, should be broadly based to incorporate several variables rather than based on a single element, and data should be readily available.

Administration of the budget should be flexible, consider the university wide periodical to monograph ratio, should allow for some autonomy in expending the budget, and ideally should consider price and productivity. In all cases, involvement of and communication with the library staff and faculty will help facilitate the administration of the allocated budget.

Although post-expenditure allocation is all too often the case, and the perfect allocation method may be an elusive theoretical ideal, the benefits of attempting to allocate the acquisitions budget based on some rationale in order to balance the collection is worth the effort, despite the unanswered philosophical questions: What is a balanced collection? What are the criteria that determine such a collection? These could be debated *ad infinitum*. It is the writer's belief that any attempt to achieve some kind of balance in the collection, however flawed, is better than leaving collection development totally to the most enthusiastic faculty member, who resigns after his/her area of special interest is developed, or the most aggressive collection development librarian.

REFERENCES

1. Oslobe, S. A. The Faculty Versus Librarians in the Acquisitions Process: A Comparative Analysis. *Library Acquisitions: Practice and Theory*, 5 (1981): 9-13.

2. Kay Adams, Assistant Director, Technical Services, Southeastern Louisiana University and John Bud, Assistant Professor, University of Arizona. "Allocation of Library Resources: A Questionnaire." This survey seeks to determine dollar amounts expended by category. "Library Acquisition Survey" issued by the Center for Book Research, University of Scranton, Scranton, PA 18510 for the Professional and Scholarly Publishing Division of the Association of American Publishers. Conducted by Thomas J. Loven, Assistant Director. An in-depth study to determine who actually allocates the budget, the most important factors in selecting titles, percentages of alternative formats, etc.

3. Downs, Robert B. and Heussman, John W. "Standards for University Libraries," *College & Research Libraries* 31 (January 1970): 28-35. See also "Standards for College Libraries," *College & Research Libraries: News* 36 (Oc-

tober 1975): 277-301; "Standards for University Libraries," *College & Research Libraries: News* 39 (April 1979): 101-110; "Standards for College Libraries, 1986," *College & Research Libraries: News* 47 (March 1986): 189-200.

4. Genaway, David C. "P.B.A.: Percentage Based Allocation for Acquisitions: A Simplified Method for the Allocation of the Library Materials Budget," *Library Acquisitions: Practice and Theory*, vol. 10, no. 4. (1986): 287-292.

5. Scudder, Mary C. "Using Choice in an Allocation Formula in a Small Academic Library," *Choice* 24 (June 1987): 1506-1512.

6. Genaway, David C. "The Q Formula: The Flexible Formula for Library Acquisitions Allocations," *Library Acquisitions: Practice and Theory*, vol. 10, no. 4. (1986): 293-309.

7. Genaway, David C. Op. cit. p. 305.

8. "Book Trade and Research Statistics," *The Bowker Annual of Library & Book Trade Information*. 32nd ed. 1987. Compiled and edited by Filomena Simora (New York: R.R. Bowker Co., 1987), p. 411-452.

9. Memos from Joseph Gregg, Northeastern Illinois University. "Library Book Budget Subject Allocation Formula" (December 10, 1986) and "Book Budget Formula Data, FY87 and FY 88." (August 13, 1987).

10. Mulliner, Kent. "The Acquisitions Allocation Formula at Ohio University," *Library Acquisitions: Practice & Theory*, Vol. 10 (1986): 315-327.

11. *Higher Education Prices and Price Indexes: 1987 Update*. Research Associates of Washington, 2605 Kingle Road, N.W. Washington, DC 20008.

12. Knapp, Leslie C. and Rebecca T. Lenzini. "Price Index for 1987: U.S. Periodicals." The 27th Annual Survey of U.S. Periodical Prices. *Library Journal* (April 15, 1987): 39-44. For monograph prices see: Grannis, Chandler B. "Title Output and Prices: 1987: The Year in Review," *Publishers Weekly* (March 11, 1988): 30-33.

The Research Library
Materials Budget:
Management of a Shrinking Resource

Stella Bentley

SUMMARY. Materials budgets in research libraries are a shrinking resource as a result of increased costs and demands for nontraditional materials. It is vital that librarians manage effectively the allocation of the materials budget and the development of the collections as the purchasing power of the materials budget declines.

The decline of the purchasing power of research library materials budgets has been well documented. The combination of the increasing publishing output and the increasing prices for all types of materials has meant that most research libraries have been able to acquire fewer materials with their materials budget each year. Price data reported in the *Bowker Annual*[1] shows the price increases for both U.S. hardcover books and U.S. periodicals purchased by college and university libraries over the ten year period from fiscal 1975 to fiscal 1985 (see Table 1). Prices of foreign periodicals have increased at an even greater rate, as we all know. The average prices for 1986 and 1988 for the science and technology journals subscribed to by Case Western Reserve University were recently supplied by our principal vendor. The average prices and the increase over two years for some countries are listed in Table 2.

Statistics gathered from ARL libraries[2] show the impact of these price increases on the purchasing power of the libraries' materials

---

Stella Bentley is Assistant University Librarian, Collection Development, University Library, University of California, Santa Barbara, CA 93106.

TABLE 1

Fiscal	U.S. hardcover Ave Price	U.S. Periodicals Ave Price
1975	$14.09	$34.55
1976	16.19	38.94
1977	17.20	41.85
1978	18.03	45.14
1979	20.10	50.11
1980	22.80	57.23
1981	23.57	67.81
1982	26.88	73.89
1983	30.34	78.04
1984	29.00	82.47
1985	29.96	87.93
Pct. Increase	112.6%	154.5%

TABLE 2

	N	1986	1988	% Inc
Australia	9	70.97	90.85	28.0
Canada	31	48.88	67.94	39.0
Denmark	7	180.29	285.49	58.4
France	34	170.70	244.32	43.1
German Dem Rep	12	208.49	272.12	30.5
Fed Rep of Germany	68	331.27	499.94	50.9
Japan	26	140.43	245.51	74.8
Netherlands	115	418.99	659.52	57.4
Sweden	7	118.28	203.00	71.6
Switzerland	29	524.24	855.65	63.2
United Kingdom	283	262.83	325.18	23.7
United States	871	183.32	226.96	23.8

budgets (see Table 3). While the funds expended for materials have increased 142% in this time period, the number of total bound volumes added increased by only 4%.

It is also useful to note the shifts taking place within the materials expenditures over the same 1975/76-1985/86 time period. The impact of rising serials prices, which have outstripped the increases in the materials budget, is clearly evident (see Table 4).

The shifts of funds from monographs and binding to help cover the increasing costs of subscriptions are also clearly evident from the ARL data (see Table 5).

Additional strain is placed on the materials budget by the demands of new technologies. As research libraries have begun to emphasize the provision of access to information as well as the acquisition of resources, the materials budget is seen as the funding source for optical disk technologies, online database searching, and even bibliographic utilities. An excellent summary of the argument to expand the use of the materials budget is presented by Beltran:

TABLE 3

	Total Materials Expenditures	Total Gross Volumes Added
1975/76	$136,374,468	8,237,834
1985/86	$330,545,622	8,593,571

TABLE 4

Total ARL Materials Expenditures

	1975/76	1985/86	change
Serials	$50,884,028	$165,322,209	+224.9%
Monographs	75,065,242	133,270,989	+77.5%
Binding	11,325,198	19,095,453	+68.7%
Total	$137,224,468	$317,688,651	+131.4%

TABLE 5

ARL Libraries Materials Expenditures

	1975/76	1981/82	1985/86
Serials	37.1%	49.0%	52.0%
Monographs	54.6%	44.8%	42.0%
Binding	8.3%	6.2%	6.0%

The academic library is funded to support the teaching and research missions of the university, to provide access to the intellectual record, to organize that access, and to preserve that record. In support of this effort, we have devised budgeting mechanisms which set aside a part of our funding for something we once most commonly called "books" and currently most commonly call "materials." That shift came about to accommodate areas about which we felt quite uncertain: microforms, audio and video media. It is clearly time for another shift for which it would be nice to find a satisfactory and elegant name. An inelegant but useful compromise adopted by some libraries is the label materials/access budget.[3]

The extent to which libraries fund information access from the materials budget is reflected in recent changes in the materials expenditures categories for the ARL statistics. After a trial to determine if such information could be separated from traditional materials expenditures, ARL added two categories for the 1985/86 statistical report which are defined in the following ways:

— other materials — audiovisual microforms, serials backfiles, maps and charts, electronic media
— miscellaneous materials — nonmaterials expenditures from the materials budget such as bibliographic utilities, literature searching, and memberships.

The ARL libraries that could separate these two categories from other materials expenditures in 1985/86 reported spending over

$22,000,000 for them. The result of these additional demands on the budget is that research libraries have a shrinking resource available for traditional materials.

THE COLLECTION MANAGEMENT PROBLEM

The challenge for those responsible for the collections is to manage that shrinking resource, the materials budget. The challenge is not a new one. There have been periods in the past when budgets have not kept up with rising prices and increasing publications and formats. Look in any research library's files, and one will find documents produced during the '70s that discussed the pressures on the materials budgets — the information explosion, inflation (especially in the publishing industry), the decline of the dollar — which were eroding its purchasing power, and the challenge for the libraries to maintain their status as outstanding research collections. I recently came across a document prepared in 1978, which concludes:

> all these factors have combined to place the library in the difficult position of balancing increasing needs against limited resources and rising costs. The University Library has already strained selectivity to the limit in its effort to restore its losses, meet current scholarly requirements, and maintain its high standards. A comprehensive and suitably funded collection is essential to the tradition of excellence in teaching and research long established at the University.[4]

As conditions changed, however, and funding became more plentiful for higher education, many research libraries had good periods even quite recently when the number of current subscriptions and volumes added increased. Shaugnessy has suggested, however, that the present financial crisis is different from earlier crises for several reasons:

— many publishers are now part of large conglomerates interested in the profit level
— the decline in value of the dollar against foreign currencies
— big science is spawning more and more journals
— the impact of the current financial crisis is not appreciated or

understood by university administrators or by the research libraries' users.

He believes that libraries have reached the point where no manipulation of the budget will allow the library to do any more than retard the destruction of the collections.[5]

Others feel that librarians must convince the university community that the impact of escalating prices on collections is their problem and not just the library's. Proponents of this position argue that since U.S. researchers and scholars are the source of the majority of scholarly manuscripts, and since the process of scholarly publishing is so vital to their work, they should take an active role in helping to solve the problem.[6] Dougherty has advocated steps to change the scholarly communication process to sidestep commercial publishers and their inflated subscription prices.[7]

Regardless of how one views the dilemma, however, and what solutions one tries, we must approach it as a collection management problem. We should take the necessary steps to control costs, to manage the materials budget, and to manage the development of the collections. An important first step in such a process for academic librarians is to understand the changing role of the research library.

ROLE OF THE RESEARCH LIBRARY

The role and mission of the research library is changing as the university changes. Talbot has pointed out that the percent of the operating budget of research universities devoted to their libraries has been a fairly constant figure over time.[8] There is little reason to expect this amount to increase, especially with computing facilities and resources becoming increasingly important, and also often perceived as another "bottomless pit" requiring extensive funding increases each year. Research libraries generally have two parts to their mission statements — to provide information and to provide access to information to meet the research and instruction needs of their faculty and students. As the resources available for collections shrink in their purchasing power, collection managers must make decisions between the need to provide the sources and the need to provide access to the sources. There are real trade-offs in making such decisions, and it will be impossible to make everyone happy no matter what choice is made. For example, is it better to purchase an expensive cumulation of an important index, or provide searches of the online index at no cost to the users (using the funds that were saved by not purchasing the index)? Should materials funds be spent on equipment (e.g., workstations for CD ROM indexes or other technologies) to improve access to information rather than on serial journal subscriptions, 1000 monographs, or other traditional materials that provide the information? What is the core collection necessary to support instructional needs? Research needs? To what extent can we set up consortia, networks, etc. to insure rapid access to the basic source materials that we have determined we do not need as part of the core collections? We talk about resource sharing and we have set up various mechanisms for coordinated collection development and resource sharing. Certainly the efforts of the Research Libraries Group (RLG) with the development of the conspectus to inventory research collections and the establishment of the North American Collection Inventory Project (NCIP) by the Association of Research Libraries (ARL) to involve the entire research library community are extremely positive steps. The assumption of primary collecting responsibilities (pcr's), rapid delivery of materials, and equitable compensation (incentives) for the library which assumes primary collecting responsibilities must follow quickly.

ALLOCATING THE MATERIALS BUDGET

Positive, fundamental initiatives are necessary in allocating the materials budget, especially in times of retrenchment. Not only are funds being allocated, they should be reallocated to maintain important collections, provide access to new information sources and technologies, and to support developing research and instructional programs. The process and procedures should include the following elements:

— both objective data and professional judgment are part of the decision making process.

— the process is open to participation and review by interested parties.
— the reallocation of resources to maintain priority collections and to support developing programs.[9]

The crucial point is that across the board increases must never be made. Because the materials budget is a shrinking resource and budget increases are inadequate to maintain the current collection levels, choices must be made about individual subject collections. Nor should monographs be seen to be suffering so journals can be maintained, or broad subject categories (e.g., humanities) be seen to suffer for others (e.g., sciences with high journal inflation rates). Hard decisions must be made about specific areas to support and those to cut back. Our process encourages each collection manager to identify and analyze the problems facing his/her particular subject collection and to develop long range plans for the collection. This procedure entails gathering data on the developments in the programs supported by the collection and the concomitant collection needs. Each collection manager gathers the following information about the collection and the university's programs:

— recently developed/discontinued programs and courses
— recently recruited/reported faculty or new directions in faculty research
— increasing, decreasing, or shifting enrollments
— other programmatic factors
— development of cooperative arrangements, including cooperative collection development and interlibrary lending
— increasing/decreasing average cost and inflation rates
— increasing/decreasing publishing output
— foreign versus domestic purchasing
— serials versus monograph balance
— media and other nonbook formats (including microforms, audio and video programs, online services)
— any other factors not covered above which have an impact on the collections.

The information is reviewed by a peer group of collection managers representing the humanities, social sciences, and sciences.

They are asked to assess the needs of each subject collection relative to the needs of the other subjects, based on the resources available. Recommendations are then made for the level of increase — high, medium, low, or no increase. These recommendations are reviewed by the library administration and the faculty library committee, and allocations made from the increases received for the budget. The process has enabled the collection managers to establish collection priorities, to be responsive to the changing environment in the University and in the information world, and to supply their professional judgment to the development and management of the collections.

MANAGING THE COLLECTIONS

The key concern is to manage the development of the collections — to know and understand what we are doing and why, to have a rational basis for the methods chosen and for the impact of all collection management decisions on the collections and on the provision of access to information.

Schad has offered guidance as to what to consider in managing the collections:

— what are the information needs of the institution?
— what is the condition of the collections at this time?
— what material is available?[10]

In order to determine the information needs of the institution, the collection manager must understand thoroughly the instruction and research goals and programs of the institution. The current condition of the collection requires an inventory and assessment that provides information about the strengths and weaknesses of the collections, and how these compare with the institution's instruction and research goals. Finally, to know what material is available requires that the collection manager understands the methods and trends in research in a field, the information seeking behavior of researchers in the field, and how to best provide access to the information needed by the discipline's students and faculty.

There are a number of steps that collection managers can take to control costs. Each of these steps is well known to collection managers:

- cancelling serials
- cancelling approval plans
- reducing monographic purchases
- seeking larger discounts from vendors
- cutting back on binding
- seeking other funding internally and externally.

None of these steps will solve the financial crisis, but they enable a collection manager to manage the process and manage the development of the collections even in the face of the crisis.

The collection manager should seek expertise and information from technical services units and from vendors to assist in the process of managing the materials budget.

The technical services units of the library should play a major role in assisting with the management and development of the collections in a period of declining resources. The personnel in these units can provide some of the research and analysis that is needed for decision-making, particularly if the information is not available from the vendors used by the library. Of vital importance to the collection managers is information about what is happening to each subscription and standing order, including cost increases, time period covered by invoices, added charges as a result of devaluation of the dollar, and other pertinent information that often comes only to the technical services departments and then needs to be compiled and distributed to collection managers for their use.

As purchasing power declines and the library needs to make hard decisions about serials, subscriptions, the appropriate level of monographic purchases, and juggle the other demands on the materials budget, the library should take advantage of the services offered by the vendors. Many of the vendors offer a large range of services and are oriented toward the needs of the libraries. With the advanced technology that some of the vendors are using, they can provide a great deal of information to a library about that library's monographic acquisitions, standing orders, and subscriptions.

The collection manager is crucial to the process of managing the materials budget at any time, but especially when it is a declining resource. Farrell has stated that "collection managers who reshape their roles in accordance with the realities of fiscal retrenchment and the true needs of their clientele will create a new, more professional, more authoritative presence in the university."[11] The subject expertise, professional judgment, and departmental contacts that the collection managers have should be critical elements brought to decision-making. They should be intimately involved in deciding what specific steps should be taken for their own subject — cancellations of subscriptions, reduced monographic purchases, developing cooperative agreements with other libraries for shared resources, etc. Those who work most closely with the libraries' users must know and understand the problem, be able to explain it to the users, and be able to respond to the situation in ways that keep the users' needs foremost.

REFERENCES

1. "Average Prices and Indexes for College and University Library Acquisitions, FYs 1975-1985," *Bowker Annual of Library and Book Trade Information*. New York: Bowker, 1986.

2. Association of Research Libraries. *ARL Statistics*. Washington, DC: ARL, 1975-1985.

3. Ann Bristow Beltran. "Funding Computer-Assisted Reference in Academic Research Libraries," *Journal of Academic Librarianship* 13:4-7 (March 1987).

4. Unknown.

5. Thomas Shaugnessy. "Management Strategies for Financial Crises," Conference presentation, Oklahoma City (February 1988).

6. Robert L. Houbeck, Jr. "If Present Trends Continue: Responding to Journal Price Increases," *Journal of Academic Librarianship* 13:214-220 (September 1987).

7. Richard M. Dougherty. "Scholarly Publishers Who Charge Outrageous Prices for Journals May Get Some Unexpected Competition," *Chronicle of Higher Education* 33:40-41 (June 3, 1987).

8. Richard J. Talbot. "College and University Libraries," *Bowker Annual of Library and Book Trade Information*. New York: Bowker, 1984.

9. Stella Bentley and David Farrell. "Beyond Retrenchment: The Reallocation of a Library Materials Budget," *Journal of Academic Librarianship* 10:321-325 (January 1985).

10. Jasper G. Schad. "Allocating Materials Budgets in Institutions of Higher Education," *Journal of Academic Librarianship* 3:328-332 (January 1978).

11. David Farrell. "Why There is a Crisis in Collection Management," *Options for the Eighties*. Greenwich, CN: JAI Press, 1982.

Money, Manure, Squeaky Wheels, A Paucity of Grease and Possibly Grit!

Henry M. Yaple

SUMMARY. The acquisitions process in academic libraries functions optimally when adequate funds support library needs, local political realities and faculty needs and demands. It often requires careful diplomacy by acquisitions librarians to balance sharp faculty interests, but their needs and demands can and should be used to develop and enrich library collections. This process is traditional in academic libraries, and it should not be regarded as unusual. Rapidly escalating costs for serial subscriptions over the past five years have consumed larger and larger portions of most academic libraries acquisitions budgets. As a consequence, librarians have less funds available to balance collections. Can the library profession utilize modern technology to reduce, if not eliminate, the problem of high costs for serials? A partial solution to the serials problem is suggested.

For nine years, 1978-1987, I was Acquisitions Librarian at the University of Wyoming Libraries. A happy task that went with that position was to help the Wyoming State Library appraise collections in various parts of the state. As a result, I sometimes found myself with the sort of individuals one does not find inhabiting academic libraries. For some reason, these individuals have a gift for arresting turns of phrase. Some expressions I heard include, "It's a damn poor outfit that can't afford a boss!," or "Don't kick a rattlesnake!," "He's gunny sack crazy, or she's a terror to snakes." I treasure one phrase especially. "Money and manure can only do

---

Henry M. Yaple is Director, Penrose Memorial Library, Whitman College, Walla Walla, WA.

good when they are spread around.'' I enjoy this last phrase because it seems a somewhat crude, but not entirely inaccurate, paradigm of acquisitions activity in academic libraries.

Funds are allocated, usually in a large pile, for each fiscal year. The spreading begins. Every library does it according to their own customs and by their own set of traditions, but the spreading process allocates funds to internal library accounts, serials, reference, general books, etc., and then to external accounts for the various academic departments, English, History, Chemistry, etc. Next Acquisitions generates orders for the multitudinous items libraries purchase: periodicals, scholarly journals, serials, annuals, monographs, pamphlets, government documents, videotapes, electronic data bases, CD-ROM discs, etc., etc. Ultimately, the money or manure is spread on the vendors. The economy grows and prospers.

SQUEAKY WHEELS

Squeaky wheels are not uncommon in academe. They may be presidents, provosts, vice presidents, department chairs. These individuals have clout. They lobby for their constituents and/or for their favored subject areas. As a result more money (or manure) is allocated into their favored subject areas. Over time, some strangely lopsided bulges develop in acquisition budgets. Librarians may deny this fact, and proclaim loudly and proudly at professional meetings that "their" budgets are balanced and controlled by the librarians. Don't believe it, not even for a minute! Humans are political animals. Squeaky wheels do get the grease, or the money or the manure. Some continue to be squeaky even when well greased.

My own favorite form of the squeaky wheel are the professors who haunts the acquisitions department almost daily. They are extremely conscious of any new publications in their subject area. They read out-of-print antiquarian catalogs assiduously. They are often well acquainted with book dealers. They become good friends or valued enemies of the paraprofessional staff in Acquisitions. In brief, they care about the library or more accurately that portion of the collection devoted to their own disciplines.

Some of the squeaky wheels I have been fortunate to work with include Russel Nye and Arthur Sherbo at Michigan State University, Larry Cardoso, Bill Gienapp, Eric Nye, and John Grunefelder at the University of Wyoming. To be candid, these individuals educated me so that I knew enough to acquire some notable materials for their respective libraries. Russel Nye tutored me in the fine points of popular culture, and that led to some exciting discoveries at the annual East Lansing AAUW Book Sale. Arthur Sherbo's fascination with the 18th century editors of Shakespeare enabled me to nab an especially fine copy of Isaac Reed and George Stevens' 1793 edition of Shakespeare's works from an antiquarian catalog. Larry Cardoso's patience and willingness to compromise enabled us to outwait the British Museum in the acquisition of the *Archivo de Porfirio Diaz* from several dealers. Bill Gienapp inspired us to collect the microformed papers of Civil War statesmen, and the newspapers which support and inform these papers. Association with Professor Gienapp, by the way, forced me into some amazing, and too often futile correspondence and telephone calls with the Photoduplication Service of the Library of Congress. Eric Nye, by persistence and diligence, led us to the acquisition of some first rate manuscripts of Samuel Taylor Coleridge and Thomas DeQuincey. Unfortunately, we missed a large collection of materials John Grunefelder knew about from a British bookseller. These books would have greatly enriched Wyoming's source material for the study of 17th and 18th century British history and political theory. However, Professor Grunefelder has patiently assembled a remarkably complete collection in microformat of early 17th century British state papers.

I characterize these academics as "squeaky wheels," but it is not meant in a pejorative sense. They were "squeaky" only because they frequented the Acquisitions Department and were vitally interested in the acquisitions process. It may be significant that they were either from the disciplines of English and American Literature or History. However, the library is the primary resource, read laboratory, for individuals working in these subject areas so that may be only normal. Certainly, it may be necessary to "balance" the efforts and zeal of these "squeaky wheels" but their interest and knowledge are invaluable. For that reason, they should be cultivated, even assiduously.

There are, of course, as many ways to grease squeaky wheels as there are methods to skin proverbial cats. One method that has helped to tame the zealous academic is the letter of introduction. When I have known that members of the faculty were going to travel to foreign countries or even to large cities with concentrations of bookstores, I arm them with letters of introduction to booksellers. Normally, this letter goes over the library director's signature. It authorizes the bearer to select from the book dealer's stock for the library. Most important, the book dealer is carefully instructed to *quote*, NOT SHIP, those titles selected to the Acquisitions Department of the library by title and author. Title, we have found, is more accurate. The quotation letter with prices permits the Acquisitions Department to check the public catalog accurately, eliminate duplicates, and purchase only those titles actually desired. It is my impression that faculty agreeing to this task enjoy it immensely. They like to look over books, new or old, and it makes them a very real part of developing the collection. Indeed, in two cases, I allocated more than $1,000 to cover their purchases. However, these were for extended trips. One was Professor Grunefelder's sabbatical in Britain, and the other was for an Eric Nye commando assault on the book dealers of Northern Britain and Scotland. Finally, Acquisitions staff seem to enjoy the project as well. As the letters arrive from the booksellers quoting titles, it is possible to track the geographic progress of the squeaky wheel.

THE PAUCITY OF GREASE AND MAYBE GRIT!

The methods of acquisition and collection development outlined above are most likely idiosyncratic and probably outmoded. They were fun. And, they taught me a good deal on many subjects. The high-powered types engaged in cooperative collection development with other research libraries would probably deplore them. Better that they rely upon their computers and battalions of use statistics. But it doesn't really matter. Whatever method acquisitions and collection development librarians have used in the past five to eight years, everyone must know that the inflating costs for scholarly serials and journals, especially journals published abroad, have reduced sharply our grease, money, manure, and fun. Whether we acquire monographs from antiquarian catalogs, faculty requests, approval plans with vendors, selection from reviewing journals, or by letters of introduction, one of our most important professional responsibilities, book selection, has been hindered badly by the insatiable appetite of the scholarly journal publishers for more money each year.[1]

What are we going to do about it? It is heartening to see that some individuals in the library profession are aware and are working to reduce the high cost of serials. Charles Hamaker of LSU, Phyllis Brown, Idaho State University, Jim Thompson of UC Riverside, Richard Dougherty of University of Michigan are some names which come to mind. Their actions are important. They have aroused our profession and hopefully they will motivate it to substantive action. Does the library profession have the grit to conceive and execute some actions to resolve the problem of high serial costs?

Yet, I am impelled to ask, does this profession have the grit or pluck to resolve the serious problem of costly serial subscriptions which continue to increase each year? Given that librarianship has many clever minds, and an absolute plethora of high technology equipment, we ought to be able to reduce our dependence upon these serial publishers and their high priced subscriptions. If I may be so bold, I would suggest an experimental method of serial publishing.

The Council on Library Resources (CLR) exists to benefit libraries in this country. They provide excellent management training programs. They offer collection analysis projects. They fund a management intern trainee program that has produced an interesting cadre of professional library managers. CLR ought to regard the high cost of serials as a serious challenge. Could they not lend their resources? their management interns? their clout? to help resolve the problem?

Would it be possible for CLR to publish, or perhaps make available would be a more precise term, a Fax on demand serial? The purpose of the project would be to determine if this kind of serial publishing is feasible and what it would cost. Perhaps five years might be a good period of time for experimental purposes. The good people at CLR would create a staff for a publication. Could they use a new crop of management interns for this purpose? The publication—let's call it *Aspects of SnoEngineering*—would have an editorial staff but it would not have a cadre of referees. According to a survey published in the August 6, 86 issue of *The Chronicle of Higher Education*, "There are far too many journals published and most of what they publish is 'ignorant drivel.'" Why bother to referee? Every article submitted would be prepared for publication. Most important, each article submitted must have a tautly edited abstract. If it did not, it would be edited mercilessly or one could be crafted carefully from the article.

Next, the editors at CLR would create a Table of Abstracts from the article submitted. The Table of Abstracts would be published serially—monthly, bimonthly, quarterly, whatever schedule seemed optimal. The Table of Abstracts would be circulated to a subscription list as current serial publications are now. Certainly, it would take time to develop a subscription base, but if the libraries of this country understood that this was an experimental effort designed to reduce serial costs, there ought to be at least 200-300 serious subscribers to *Aspects of SnoEngineering*. What should a subscription to *Aspects of SnoEngineering: Table of Abstracts* cost? Perhaps $50 to $200 per year would be possible. If that doesn't seem substantive enough to the research libraries of this country, the price could be raised easily enough.

When the readers of *Aspects of SnoEngineering: Table of Abstracts* discovered an abstract that piqued their interest, they would go to the library and request that a complete copy of the article be telefacsimiled to them. *Aspects of SnoEngineering*, Issue I, article 6, pages 50-72. Fax it to me! The advantage of this method of serial availability should be apparent. Patrons would know what was available and when they wanted an article they would get exactly what they wanted. They would pay a nominal fee for the copy and the telecommunications charges. Royalties could be built in if necessary. If the costs were not too clear, libraries might pay costs for obtaining the article. However, the serial costs libraries must bear now for editorial fees, referee fees, printing, paper, mailing, binding, and/or microfilm and space to house multiple volumes of serial backfiles could be sharply reduced. Most important, those individuals who must publish so they will not perish from this earth would know they were legitimately "available." Their resumes could list their citations to the pertinent Table of Abstracts. Tenure committees or hiring committees could secure complete copies of relevant articles. Conceivably, they could also know how many times an author had been Faxed, if that information seemed important.

It is, of course, possible for a Table of Abstracts availability program to be established as part of an electronic or computer network. Such a program may be only a brief time in the future. Some directors of large libraries also now control their campus computer facilities. What does that bode for the rest of us without these facilities under our control? The key is to wean ourselves from the tenaciously held concept that libraries must have "in hand" on the premises actual copies of the entire serial publication. Modern technology has eliminated the need for paper or microformat copies. The highly profitable serial industry as perpetuated upon us by Pergamon, Elsevier, Springer Verlag, Taylor Francis et al. is a monster. Let's show some grit and stop taking the manure some of these publishers have spread so freely.

REFERENCE

1. "Paying the Piper, ARL Libraries Respond to Skyrocketing Journal Subscription Prices," *Journal of Academic Librarianship*, Vol. 14, no. 1, pp. 4-9.

Bread Not Butter:
Funding Online Searching
in Hard Times

Gloriana St. Clair
Jay Martin Poole

SUMMARY. While it is the best of times in the variety of appropriate items available for purchase from a materials budget, it is the worst of times in the adequacy of those budgets. Many external factors impinging on library budgets have eroded buying power until both steady-state and moderately increasing budgets have become de facto retrenchment budgets. In such a situation, the budget manager must choose between cutting some programs and reducing all programs, possibly to a level of mediocrity. One new program, frequently targeted for cutting, is funding of online searching from the materials budget. Philosophically, the online search serves legitimate educational and research needs and should be funded from the print materials budget. Practically, online searches allow resource-poor institutions to fulfill user demands more completely. The example of one research library reacting to a budget reduction is provided. Relationships between freedom of information and the continuance of democracy are noted.

BACKGROUND

"It was the best of times, it was the worst of times" says Charles Dickens in his touching, if somewhat melodramatic, classic *A Tale*

Gloriana St. Clair is Assistant Director for Technical, Automation, and Administrative Services, William Jasper Kerr Library, Oregon State University, Corvallis, OR 97330. Jay Martin Poole is Assistant University Library for Public Services, Library, University of California, Irvine, Irvine, CA 92713.

The authors wish to thank Mary Steckel for creating the graphs and editing and re-editing the paper and the Faculty Women's Writing Group for their critiques.

of Two Cities.[1] This widely-quoted beginning of a story about personal courage and sacrifice in a time of bloody revolution serves as a metaphor for the dilemma of the library budget officer in the 1980s and 1990s.

The variety of materials suitable and desirable for both academic and public libraries has expanded collecting limits in the last few decades. Collection of mainly print materials has given way to a broad and rich melange of formats selected to meet the information needs of an increasingly sophisticated public. The university library's stock-in-trade — academic journals, academic books, and a few long-playing records to support the music appreciation class — is ceding to diverse collections of mixed microforms, laser disks, videocassettes, CD-ROM databases, online searching, and software programs. Similarly, in public libraries, core collections built solidly on books from standard lists with multiple copies of current bestsellers and on magazines indexed in the *Reader's Guide* are relinquishing suzerainty over materials budgets. Less closely programmed mixtures of records, tapes, compact disks, videocassettes, films, filmstrips, software packages, games, toys, puzzles, pets, fotonovella, realia, and trade paperbacks are now common. Clearly, entry into the information age has created the best of times for appropriate expenditures of materials budget monies.

Concurrent with this explosion in the availability of suitable materials for libraries has been an implosion in the buying power of the always scarce library dollar. In *Library Issues,* Ronald G. Leach demonstrates that prices for serials have risen 164.3% on the consumer price index from 1977 to 1986.[2] Serials doubled the average of all other goods and services.

Category	Percentage
Books	68.7%
Food	65.8%
Clothing	34.7%
Transportation	73.8%
Housing	93.1%
Medical	114.1%
All Items	80.9%

The average price of a periodical has gone from $24.59 in 1977 to $65.00 in 1986. The years 1987 and 1988 saw even higher increases especially in foreign periodicals; many libraries have been forced into serials cancellation projects. Both domestic and foreign periodicals are expected to undergo a 10-15% increase in 1989.[3] Book prices have also been fairly high in the categories of inflation.

Factors contributing to this divergence in the rate of inflation include:

- Increases in costs of paper, printing, and related production costs for monographs.
- Increase in numbers of monograph titles available.
- Desire of monograph publishers to accumulate capital to finance the automation of their labor intensive operations.
- Negative impacts of the Thor Power Tool Co. decision which changed the valuation of inventory.
- Aggravated need to make a short term profit since back inventory could no longer be maintained because of the Thor decision.
- Genuine inflation in the price of serials from rising costs of paper, printing, proofing, postage, and personnel.
- Price discrimination with U.S. libraries being charged more than their foreign equivalents.
- Price gouging on the part of several large European serials publishers.[4]
- Falling value of the U.S. dollar against major foreign currencies.
- Competition for the market with other formats, including online databases and CD-ROM products.
- Profit-minded price tags on new products, such as CD-ROM databases, laser disks, and educational videocassettes.
- Privitization of government services and publications, with one out of every four previously free government publications eliminated.[5]
- Decreasing access and increasing costs of depository materials including changing format of some materials, such as census information.

It is as if Madame DeFarge herself were knitting up the prices. These factors have combined to make it the worst of times for trying to meet user needs with traditional materials budgets.

Because of these pernicious drains on buying power, what appears to be steady-state funding over the last few years must be reckoned as retrenchment. In "Beyond Retrenchment: The Reallocation of a Library Materials Budget," Stella Bentley and David Farrell demonstrate a 130% increase in serials costs and a 42.5% increase in monograph costs. Combined with a 30% increase in binding costs, the total increase amounts to 73.9% for the period 75/76 to 81/82. Bringing similar figures up to date for 1985/86 shows the following increases in Table 1.[6] During that same period of time, overall materials budgets have grown only slightly.

Percentages provided from University administrations for inflation in materials budgets have ranged in the 7-10% category, while real price increases have been much higher, from 10-30%. The result of these diverging numbers is that both steady-state and mildly growing budgets become, in reality, retrenchment rations. Under these conditions, the three "Rs" of education become in the 1980s "Reduction, Reallocation, and Retrenchment" as library materials budget managers engage in cutting, squeezing, and trimming procedures.[7]

DIVISION OF LIBRARY RESOURCES

Libraries have never been, nor can they ever be, free. They are expensive to create and maintain, and, as their mission becomes increasingly tied to sophisticated automated systems and new formats, their price is escalating. Since libraries cannot be free, the

TABLE 1. Percentage Increase in Materials Expenditures

Total Expenditures	75/76 ($)	81/82 ($)	Increase (%)	85/86 ($)	Increase (%)
Serials	50,884,028	117,046,121	130.0	180,514,571	254.7
Monographs	75,065,242	106,960,987	42.5	144,181,198	92.0
Binding	11,325,198	14,717,225	30.0	20,916,910	84.6
Totals	137,274,468	238,732,333	73.9	383,432,676	179.3

question then becomes who will pay for them, how the appropriated monies will be divided, and which services will be offered from what funds. Libraries are a sacred and integral part of American civilization; their missions are inextricably tied to the fostering and preservation of democracy.[8] Yet, their services are, in fact, targeted at a relatively small percentage of the population. In the case of academic libraries, the services are traditionally restricted to a cleanly-defined population.

Libraries have always been faced with the problem of dividing their resources. In the best and worst times of the 1980s, funding difficulties have been acerbated by decreasing budgets and increasing costs of modern services and materials. For instance, the availability of computerized database services for education and research has added a new variable into an already complex equation for dividing a research library's budget. Library budget managers have responded variously. Since the expenses of an online search are easily measurable, the total cost of what has been perceived as a new service has been passed on to the user in some cases. Other libraries have partially underwritten the costs of the searches to various extents. In certain instances, online searching has been at no charge to the user. Monies to support online searching are raided from already strained operating budgets.[9,10]

CHOICES UNDER RETRENCHMENT

The choices under retrenchment and steady-state seem as painful as the guillotine of the French Revolution. Cutting new programs and abjuring new formats must be weighed against winding down into mediocrity in existing collection development programs. Continuing serials subscriptions and buying current imprints become the bread of the collection while newly-instituted formats and newly-coveted services are cataloged as butter and jam.

Both the proponents of new services and the opponents of mediocrity have compelling theses. In a letter to the *Chronicle of Higher Education*, Herbert White lends his authoritative voice to the arguments in favor of funding new programs such as online services from the materials budget.

. . . The fascination with sheer volume not only has become impossibly expensive but, even more important, has kept academic librarians from evaluating and implementing user-services that are often in place in government, corporate, and even some public libraries and information centers.

My only quarrel with the conclusion as reported is that the article uses the concepts "user needs" and "user wants" interchangeably. It is precisely the slavish response to what users have asked for that has created the dinosaurs academic librarians are now trying to feed.

The identification of user needs requires a never-ending dialogue between equal professionals that may have to begin with the identification of service possibilities of which the academic user is not even aware. This is particularly true because the advent of computerized bibliographic networking and document delivery has created many new options for us.[11]

White seeks a balance between dinosaur collections and evolving technologies.

The President of the University of Missouri in defense of budget cuts underscores the prospects of embarrassing mediocrity. Faced with the need to reallocate $12 million in operating funds over the next three years, President James C. Olson said: "The University has coped with ten years of inadequate funding by making cuts across the board. . . . It becomes clear that a continuation of that policy was a prescription for mediocrity." Among the programs Olson recommended eliminating was the School of Library and Information Science.[12]

Careful attention must be paid to projecting the length and severity of anticipated cuts. Library administrators must keep themselves well informed about national financial trends and their impacts on materials costs for the local library. For public institutions, state economic forecasts and the actions and intentions of state governments need to be carefully monitored to determine how long periods of retrenchment may last. University politics must also be considered. The place of the library in the priorities of its parent funding institution needs to be assessed. All of this information can be used to select an appropriate response. A strategy of moderate cuts to all programs seems more acceptable for cuts of short duration, i.e., one to five years, than for those extending into longer time frames. If the long range economic forecast is bleak, then library administrators must reassess levels of support and reconfigure menus of services accordingly.

PHILOSOPHY OF FUNDING ONLINE SEARCHING

In "Funding Online Searching from the Materials Budget," the authors have argued that the information provided by an online search satisfies legitimate educational and research needs and should be funded with monies from the print materials budget.[13] This act should not be seen as a final resolution to the problem but rather as a transition until libraries can establish the efficacy of this expenditure, justify it to their funding agencies, and acquire permanent funding designated for this use.

The philosophy behind funding online searching from the materials budget is a sound one. Historically, libraries have spent millions of dollars to buy print materials. The conjunction of selection and acquisition is that materials monies are inevitably spent, to a greater or lesser extent, on a "probable need" principle. Librarians have studied their patterns of buying through multiple measures of statistical analyses; the result remains that many purchases of books are based on a professional hypothesis on the part of the librarian. Given a penchant for statistics, librarians know that a very small percentage of the books bought serve the major portion of user needs. Naturally, some decisions to purchase are more precise than others. When a professor requests supplementary reserve room reading materials for a large lecture course, the probability is high that the print materials will at least have the appearance of being used.

Approval plans, which allow libraries to establish a pattern of needs, provide a more codified type of planning. The tremendous savings approval plans offer in lowering the costs of selection and acquisition without apparently degrading the quality of selection make them attractive to institutions already under budgetary strain. Still, the literature on approval plans, including a recent comparative study on the responses of two science and technology specialty vendors and two general vendors to the same profile, suggests that vendor selection is crucial.[14] To a certain degree under an approval plan, the vendor's professional judgment, rather than the local librarian's, builds the collection.

Collection development and management involve careful studies of the strengths and weaknesses of the collection as it complements the curriculum and the research activities of the institution. Still, no matter how carefully constructed the procedure, the collection manager is always attempting to anticipate the needs of the user.

Lack of use in a collection is rationalized by the idea that the material may be used in the future. If this future use does not materialize in the short term, then the materials may be used for research purposes at some far removed occasion. As a consequence, storage facilities are constructed to house materials of possible historical interest, and librarians agonize over their archival functions.

The knowledge and experience that librarians have brought to the process of selection has resulted in collections that fulfill user demands. However, librarians must accept the fact that many materials purchases are infrequently, if ever, used. The summation of this perplex of selection and acquisition is that the "probable need" principle dominates materials monies spending. An element of contingency persists in collection building.

Yet, collections are used, and in amazingly diverse manners. An in-progress study, funded by the Council on Library Resources, has been measuring collection use at two large science and technology oriented universities and two small religious liberal arts colleges. One of the first and most striking conclusions emerging is that use of the collections is more diverse and innovative than would have been predicted. Beyond the citations laboriously copied from the card catalog and the major periodical indexes, students reach out to all kinds of materials to construct their term papers. Videocassettes, movies, TV programs, radio shows, popular magazines, billboards, phonograph records and their covers, software programs, lectures, letters, interviews, online databases, and conversations with boyfriends have all appeared as citations on student papers. While compilation of the results is still incomplete, academic and public libraries would clearly be justified in greatly expanding types of materials collected.[15]

Further, libraries have always spent a large portion of their budgets in processing and analyzing materials to make them accessible. In a talk to the Annual OCLC Northwest Directors Meeting, Fred Kilgour estimated that over 25% of library budgets were expended in the acquisitions and cataloging of materials.[16] The costs of materials selection, acquisition, cataloging, and processing have always been considered essentials. Research libraries have always analyzed the contents of their collections and provided access to them. Only recently with the advent of Robinson-style libraries have a few public librarians accepted collecting without analyzing as a mission.

Spending monies for access to materials is a traditional, in fact essential, library practice. Large supplements to the materials budget cannot be accommodated without at least equal funds for acquisitions and cataloging costs. More and more frequently, libraries have recognized the extent of these added costs and begun to request them in budget justifications and grant proposals.

Thus, access and materials are both aspects of the user's relationship to the library. The relative amounts of money spent on access and materials, while technically divided in the library's budget, are not separable. Monies taken from the service budget impact on the amount of money available for the materials budget. The natural outgrowth of the realization that comparable amounts of money must be spent on access leads to an acceptance of online access as an interim materials expenditure.

Similarly, the impact of new formats on existing support services is also both dramatic and widespread. The installation of a compact disk area in a research library becomes a revolution with implications for various other services. Increasing photocopy activity places a heavier burden on the shelving unit. Interlibrary loan is jolted out of complacency by the large number of requests for materials not available in the local library. A research library seeking cost recovery in interlibrary loan must rigorously monitor costs or it will find its budget quickly in the red.

MATERIALS BUDGET ALLOCATIONS UNDER RETRENCHMENT: AN EXAMPLE

The effects of declining and steady-state budgets on library collections and services seem disembodied when discussed in the abstract. In order to understand hard times a little more clearly, the case of a single research library's problems in adjusting to a state budget reduction is presented.

The state economy was suffering from a shortfall in revenues from natural resources income. Institutions had been asked to plan for a 10% reduction in expenditures. The 10% figure coincided with that portion of a materials budget which might legitimately be allocated to online searching.[17] It would seem a convenient solution to a difficult problem simply to cut subsidized searching and to let other programs continue unscathed. However, the research library had endorsed spending a portion of its materials budget on subsidizing online search for both philosophical and practical reasons. The practical concern was meeting the needs of newly-franchised users from a somewhat small and definitely biased collection. The clientele had grown from that of a small science and technology military school to that of a major multipurpose university in less than two decades.

In better times, the example research library's budget was divided as shown in Figure 1. Three percent of the budget was set aside to support online services. Fifty-two percent was allocated for serials, 12% for approval plan monographs, 4% for sci/tech selection, 4% for humanities selection, 5% for social sciences selection, 1% for government documents (depository items not included), 1% for reference, and 2% for special collection. The problem of cutting such a budget was that all areas were in need of further development, and each considered itself to be the veritable staff of life for the library's collection.

Certainly, a discussion among the interested parties would bring forth a number of concrete suggestions for cutting this budget. The heads of reference and online searching would suggest reducing the approval plan. Their common allegations would be that the main fare received on the approval plan consists of picture books, coffee table offerings, and popular trash. If these allegations were true, then cutting the approval plan would be a viable option.

The library's bibliographers would have some priorities for cuts themselves. For their purposes, monies spent on videocassettes, laser disks of films, and software seem to be fattening butter and jam, not the everyday necessity of an academic collection. Ten videocas-

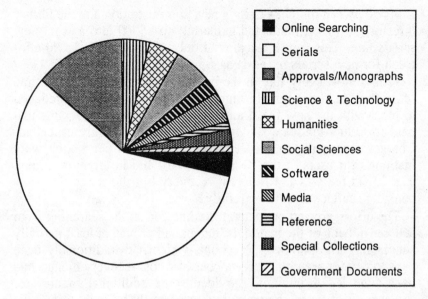

FIGURE 1. Library Budget

settes of *The Day the Universe Changed* for $2250, and even the moderately priced $50 for each laser disk of *Star Wars, The Empire Strikes Back*, and *The Return of the Jedi* would not seem to be the absolute bread of a research collection. Nine copies of *DBASE III* at $3542 and five copies of *Lotus 1-2-3* at $1125 would also appear a little superficial. Perhaps, these items might be purchased by and stored in a university-funded media center. The bibliographers would also allege that monies spent on special collections purchase only rare and expensive materials little used in basic instruction and research.

The wrangling continues, acerbated by the fact that serials inflation had put an additional enormous burden on the already strained budget by necessitating an extra allocation of $200,000. To give the participants in the struggle for materials budget dollars their due, no one had the audacity to suggest that current serials take the brunt of the budget cutbacks for this science and technology oriented library. Wholesale cutting of serials was still a spectre of the future, but new serials did fall under the guillotine, being reduced to zero.

A visit between the University's new administration and the library director, however, mandated gathering up $5000 into a scant new serials line. This figure constituted only 10% of the $51,000 allocated for new serials in the 1984-85 budget.

With almost every line in the budget asked to take a cut, online searching could not remain untouched. It, too, had to be reduced to meet with the new fiscal austerity. Avante-garde programs that paid for many graduate student searches were abruptly cancelled. Charges amounting to a cost recovery of $5.00 per search were instituted for users of the BRS After Dark and Information Index. The $5.00 fee was not full cost recovery but did make the users consider search strategies carefully.

The efforts to find permanent funding for online searching from sources outside of the materials budget had proven at least partially successful. The photocopy account, which had traditionally been used to pay for searching anyway because cost recovery monies had been funneled through it, provided some additional monies for searches. Profits for photocopying could easily be spent to provide needed user information. During FY 1985-86, some monies were appropriated for this purpose, allowing $20,000 to go towards the inflationary prices of serials.

Nascent efforts towards gaining funding from outside donors had also proved fruitful. The generosity of an alumni family had provided the library with a new Infotrac installation. Although keeping the system up to date will eventually become a materials budget expense, the initial installation and sets of databases in engineering, business, and science allowed the library to offer sophisticated new online searching services without massive expenditures from the library's budget.

The success of these two forms of alternative finance for online services made the library even more determined to continue online searching services in some way. A reduced figure of $33,000 was set aside to continue the commitment to online searching as a valuable part of the library materials budget. Figure 2 illustrates the relative fundings of online searching in the periods discussed.

The newly revised budget for the hard times of 1986 allocated $33,000 for online searching—only a little over 1% of the materials budget, only one-third of the allocation in pre-cut years. Serials allocation was up to 72%, with approval monographs down to 8%, science selected materials at 2%, humanities selected monographs at 2%, social science selected monographs at 2%, software at 1%, media at 2%, reference at 1%, special collections at 1%, government documents at 2%, and new serials barely holding at .1% in Figure 3. None of the parties to the decision was pleased, but the

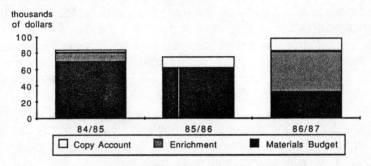

FIGURE 2. Funding Sources for Online Searches

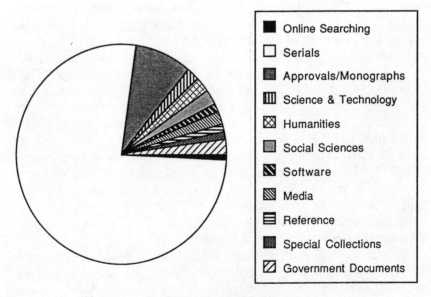

FIGURE 3. Revised Budget

hard fought compromise seemed superior to the demise of any one worthwhile program.

CONCLUSIONS

A budgetary crisis forced movement beyond the interim in the research library example. Additional funding for online searching was found in other parts of the budget — a little money from the photocopy account, a little money from a generous donor. With those contributions and with a strong philosophical determination that funding searching from the materials budget is a legitimate practice, a diminished level of funding has been maintained in spite of budgetary cutbacks.

The final solution for the problems of avoiding mediocrity in traditional collection areas while adding excellence in newly emerging technologies must once more gain inspiration from Dickens. Library materials budget managers may not cause the "general start" in university administration budget hearings that Oliver Twist caused when he said to Master Limbkins, "Please sir, I want some more."[18] But library administrators must persist in their requests for more materials money. The starvation of our materials budgets is as deadly to the intellects the library seeks to nourish as the denial of sufficient rations was to the orphans of the workhouse.

Democracy itself is nourished by freedom of information. The economics of privitization and other policies on information make this concern both compelling and pressing. Knowledge must be available to all the people in order to avoid an aristocracy of intellect which has the power to destroy civilization.[19] "Let them eat cake," Marie Antoinette's fabled retort to the cries of the French people for bread, was the product of the distance between the people and the power. Such examples compel librarians to provide equal access to all users of collections. This commitment necessitates the continued funding of online searching and the introduction of other innovative services in libraries.

Collection staples of scholarly journals and books may feed the body, but the less tangible online search satisfies the longing for more information. The fast imposed under austerity budgeting has a deadening effect on research and intellectual enterprise. The library must be able to provide a feast to delight the senses and inspire the mind to new and creative enterprises.

REFERENCES

1. Charles Dickens, *Tale of Two Cities*, Dodd, Mead & Co., New York, 1942, p. 3.

2. Ronald G. Leach, "Library Materials Price Update," *Library Issues*, V.8, No.2 (November 1987).

3. *FAX Letter*, V.4, No.1 (Jan/Feb 1988), p.1.

4. Stuart F. Grinnel, "The 6 Percent Effect." *Library Issues*, V.8, No.4 (March 1988).

5. American Library Association, *Less Access to Less Information by and about the U.S. Government: A 1981-1987 Chronology*, Chicago, 1987.

6. *ARL Statistics 1985-86*, Association of Research Libraries, Washington, DC, 1987.

7. John F. Harvey and Peter Spyers-Duran, "The Effect of Inflation on Academic Libraries" in *Austerity Management in Academic Libraries*, Scarecrow Press, Metuchen, NJ, 1984, p.36.

8. "Ramp Opens Doors," *Corvallis Gazette-Times* 111 (Wednesday, April 20, 1988), p.A4. Mayor Charles Vars' remarks at the ribbon cutting for a handicapped access ramp to Corvallis Public Library confirmed this relationship. The mayor said: "The library is clearly the most beloved institution in the community . . . We can't have democracy if we don't have an open society in which information is available to all."

9. Suzetta Burrows and August Lahocco, "Fees for Automated Reference Services in Academic Health Science Libraries: No Free Lunches," *Medical Reference Services Quarterly*, 2:1-15 (Summer 1983).

10. Carolyn G. Weaver, "Free Online Reference and Fee-based Online Services: Allies, not Antagonists," *Reference Librarian*, 5/6:111-18 (Fall/Winter 1982).

11. Herbert S. White, Letter to the Editor, *Chronicle of Higher Education*, February 17, 1988.

12. Paul Desruilsseaux, "Missouri Campus Bitterly Divided over How to 'Reallocate' Funds," in *Organization Theory: Cases and Applications*, ed. by Richard L. Daft and Kristen M. Dahlen, West Publishing Co., St. Paul, MN, 1984, pp. 221-25.

13. Jay Martin Poole and Gloriana St. Clair, "Funding Online Services From the Materials Budget," *College & Research Libraries*, V.47, No.3 (May 1986), pp. 225-237.

14. Gloriana St. Clair and Jane Treadwell, "Science and Technology Approval Plans Compared," Under revision for *LRTS*.

15. Gloriana St. Clair and Rose Mary Magrill, "Undergraduate Use of a University Collection," Research in progress.

16. Fred Kilgour, "The Electronic Book: Electronic Information Delivery Online System (EIDOS) Project," presented at the Annual OCLC Northwest Directors Meeting, Vancouver, WA, December 8, 1987.

17. Glyn T. Evans, "Collection Management Information Systems," Acquisitions Round Table of Texas Library Association, April 15, 1985.

18. Charles Dickens, *Oliver Twist*, Folio Society, London, 1984, p.12.

19. Jacob Bronowski, *The Ascent of Man*, Little, Boston, 1973, p.435.

Caught in the Squeeze: Limited Reference Budgets and CD-ROM Products in the State-Assisted University Setting

Rebecca Sturm

SUMMARY. Reference departments in academic libraries, especially those in state-assisted colleges and universities, are currently in a dilemma. They are eager to make use of the opportunities for enhanced and expanded service that CD-ROM technology offers. They are also finding it difficult, if not impossible, to locate the necessary funds within the small or no-growth budgets they receive from the parent institution, especially given the still-increasing cost and proliferation of more "traditional" reference sources. This difficulty can be placed within the broader context of the problems inherent in public higher education and its relationship to state funding and allocations. Although no one solution will be appropriate for local consideration, options for short-term funding include the following: funds direct from the library director, the provost (or other chief academic officer), the Friends group, special interest groups or grants, as well as multiple scenarios for reallocation of internal funds. These will be discussed both pro and con as well as the crucial and necessary issue of securing permanent funding for CD-ROM services. Our best hope for the future may be for higher education to seek cooperation instead of competition with education (K-12) when pursuing state funding.

The conflict that began in reference some years ago with the deadly combination of inflation and increasing material prices vs.

Rebecca Sturm is Head of Public Services and Reference Librarian at Steely Library, Northern Kentucky University, Highland Heights, KY 41076.

stagnant budgets has now intensified. For we not only have the past problems, but they are accompanied by the increasing availability of new and attractive, but costly optical products, especially in the form of CD-ROM. This crisis seems to be unusually tense for academic libraries in state-assisted colleges and universities: reference librarians see the feasibility of such formats for users, yet the state-controlled funds for higher education are failing to keep pace with even our current "traditional" needs. The recent professional literature contains articles on the pros and cons of CD-ROM services[1] as well as on the speed with which mere retention of the status quo can quickly liquidate the acquisitions budget in a reference department.[2] While both discussions are relevant and important, what seems to be missing for the practicing reference administrator is *how* to afford these new services. Beltran[3] appropriately states that we really don't have a choice whether or not to take advantage of automated information systems. They will be increasingly necessary for us if we are to fulfill our mission to our institutions, i.e., to provide access to relevant information in a timely fashion.

What I will try to avoid here is a general discussion of online products for reference and their funding,[4] especially the heavily-contested fees for online searching controversy. Acknowledging the growing acceptance for CD-ROM reference services among librarians, I'll focus on some scenarios for funding such information sources locally. These should not be construed as solutions to a complex problem — stagnant reference materials budgets and growing informational sources — but as some options to consider for dealing with this particular tip of the iceberg.

THE NECESSITY OF CD-ROM PRODUCTS

Although this has been argued more eloquently elsewhere, there are myriad appeals for CD-ROM products for both the informational specialist (reference librarian) and the information seeker (faculty, staff, student or the public). The "seeker" is drawn to its convenience: multiple years in one source; improved searching ease — especially to our increasingly computer-literate clientele; and perhaps above all, the ability to print off citations or other information, ready for future use. For the reference librarian, the advantages are also many: enthusiastic acceptance by users; convenient "packaging" (especially when micro, printer, etc. are all functioning well!); savings on already limited shelving space; relative ease of retrieval; increasing choice of available titles in CD-ROM format; and a balance between some titles that are available both in print and online.

The real argument for these services lies with our obligation to provide reasonably up-to-date information to users and our inability to conduct the appropriate number of online searches that would be required; in this respect, CD-ROM fulfills a very real need. The major obstacle to their widespread use in state-assisted college and university libraries is the exorbitant cost: both to subscribe to the service itself and to provide the microcomputer-run workstation (including printer) for each. If costs were $300-$600 instead of often ten times that (subscriptions plus workstations), we would not be discussing whether or not to purchase/lease CD-ROM services, but rather the problem of where to place all of those workstations! The problems of one user per station, quarterly updates and lack of standards among search commands would be relatively minor ones.

HIGHER EDUCATION AND STATE FUNDING

Perhaps a look at the funding problems for public higher education will help put the difficulties of academic reference budgets into some perspective. It is a fascinating, though bleak picture. Historically, state legislatures, which in turn determine funding for their institutions of higher learning, met biennially and determined their budgets in the same fashion. But between 1941 and 1986, the number meeting annually had risen from 4 to 43.[5] The business of running a state had increased in complexity and required additional commitments in time from legislators, though twenty states still prepare biennial budgets.[6]

Preparing a budget for a state on a biennial basis has some very obvious flaws, particularly because it must be based on projections that very often don't work out: how much tax revenue can be furnished, economic growth and development in general for the state for the next several years, and finally, the state's anticipated share of funds from various federal programs. Add to this the general uncertainty with the national economy, and the state biennial budget looks more and more like crystal-ball gazing or wishful thinking and less like careful financial planning for the state's numerous crucial programs and goals.

State colleges and universities, or higher education, are further hampered by several factors. One is that "higher education" in most states is separated from "education" (which is grades K-12) in all levels of legislative discussion (and hence the rhetoric for public consumption) as well as for actual funding. This is tragic, because it splits education, which should be viewed on a continuum, into two factions — elementary/secondary and higher — which are forced to compete with each other for public sympathy, support, and funding.[7] And in this competition, higher education often loses for several reasons: natural sympathy lies with education for children (K-12), and there is also an almost inborn suspicion on the part of the average state taxplayer towards higher education. We've unconsciously nurtured this through the mystique of university life, only to have it backfire on us now when we're in keen competition for already limited funds. A popular misconception is that higher education mismanages the money it already has. This belief persists despite the cuts colleges and universities have suffered in recent years and the creative methods they have employed to try to continue to meet changing expectations. The public also believes, and many legislators as well, that higher education can seek funding elsewhere but education (K-12) can't.[8] Yet most state colleges and universities depend just as heavily on state funds to run their institutions. Higher education in many states is truly at the mercy of the current governor and his/her view of its needs.[9]

Another hazard for state-assisted higher education is any sort of formula funding, which puts each university and college in competition with the other as well as the younger institutions vying with the older, more established universities. The problem here is that younger schools may be doing a good job and attracting new pools of students, yet in years of little or no budget increases, they are hard pressed to divert funds within the institution for other purposes; older universities can have more success in reallocating funds internally. Also, if the state provides incentive programs requiring any type of matching funds, larger schools tend to be in a position to participate and the "rich get richer" syndrome shifts into action.[10]

IMPLICATIONS FOR ACADEMIC LIBRARIES

The gist of all of this is the essential truth of the trickle-down effect for state-supplied budgets: the state scrambles for money for its budget, higher education struggles for its piece of the pie, a given institution competes for its portion, the library pushes for its share and finally, the reference department battles for its allotment, often in competition with other legitimate needs for services to the public. (And the funds the state assigned to higher education were too small to start with!) Let's look now at the competition for funds for materials just within the concerns of reference.

REFERENCE BUDGET CONFLICTS AND CONSTRAINTS

Separate from rivalry between various general aspects of the reference budget is the competition solely in its materials portion. To begin with, these budgets are the same or slightly larger each year, but with some inflationary effects still in force, retain only the same or even decreased purchasing power. There are the ever-rising costs for reference monographs and continuing titles as well as the tremendous expansion of new titles available in print sources alone. There are the decisions to make between print and online sources, a philosophical discussion too complex to enter into here, but one that must be faced by every reference department.

There are also the ever-increasing variety and disparity within the population our reference collections must serve. Faculty, staff and students as three groups have altered and blurred to include older adults returning to college, older adults who were never college students, people pursuing career changes, people seeking "retooling" from redundant industries, increasing numbers of high school students needing library instruction for school assignments and the ever-present "general public." *Where* library services, especially library instruction, are offered is even changing, due to higher education's increased desire to meet potential students in neutral or even job-linked locations. Other offerings in the public services domain impact on available funds for reference materials and services—these may include increased pressures for specialized photocopying services, additional end-user searching capabilities and, especially as online public catalogs and other library automation proliferates, more SDI (such as the copying and delivery of actual articles and documents to the library user). Finally, the emergence of attractive CD-ROM services begins to come forward as another contender for reference monies. How are we to find the funds to provide for CD-ROM products?

SOME OPTIONS FOR INITIAL FUNDING OF CD-ROM SERVICES (AND THEIR PITFALLS)

In examining some ways to provide for the initial CD-ROM experience in an academic reference setting, I will also be playing devil's advocate, i.e., showing the counterbalance for each suggestion, lest this come off as a pat and simplistic approach to a complicated issue. What I hope is that one or two of the following will be worth considering for your local situation and will aid in temporarily procuring a CD-ROM product while plans can be laid for the permanent funding for such information sources. Also, it is recommended that the trial CD-ROM title be one that is as general as possible (such as InfoTrac/Academic version or ERIC) to appeal to a wide range of users. The larger the percentage of your service population that use this source and like it, the stronger the arguments you can gather for its retention and introduction into the formal budgetary process, especially if simple evaluation forms are posted at the CD-ROM workstation.

Selected Scenarios

1. Request funding from the library director. The need to locate $4,000 + for a one-year CD-ROM service warrants special tactics. The director, with knowledge of the entire library's budget, may well be willing and able to locate the necessary funds, perhaps by funding the request from several budgetary areas. And because the

CD-ROM workstation will get the attention and use of many library users, somehow it will seem more like money spent for the library as a whole, rather than just for the reference area. The appropriateness of asking the director will have to be evaluated for your own library environment.

2. Ask the provost or chief academic officer at the institution for funds for a CD-ROM service for a year's trial. This individual often has a discretionary fund and may be willing to assist the library with the venture into a new informational format. This will depend greatly on the library director's relationship with that office, the reputation of the reference department, the size of that discretionary account and the other pending requests against that fund.

3. Ask the Friends group or other support organization for the academic library for such funding. Your library may not have this organization, but they would be useful for funding a service that holds wide appeal for its technology alone, even if the subject matter is not of immediate interest.

4. Seek donations from individuals or from area businesses. Many nonprofit organizations keep extensive "wish books" from which potential donors may select—people especially seem to like knowing that they have helped provide a library with a particular item, something concrete and identifiable. Of course, before approaching anyone outside the institution, you must be certain that this is a permissible option and if so, how to best proceed. The foundation for the university (if one exists) should be helpful in this endeavor and may even be able to locate some funds in its own organization for such a purpose.

5. Grants may be possible, though it may take some creativity to turn up the appropriate source for provision of CD-ROM services. Local or state funding may be available (public or private), but the time spent in grant location and writing must be weighed against the possibility of funding. If your institution has a grants office, they should be able to provide guidance as to whether this option is worth your while.

6. Seek partial funding from a particular group—the department or college of education for an ERIC CD-ROM service, for example. Again, a lot will depend on their current budget for other library materials, their interest in new informational formats, their current

relationship with the library/reference department or the existence of other funds available within their department or college budget for such a request.

7. Lease software and hardware whenever possible — this would help reduce upfront costs and allow time for equipment to become more compatible as well as for prices for CD-ROM workstations to drop. It might also allow for funds to be used from an equipment account, an account for "rentals," "subscriptions," or "leases," from some aspect of the online budget (if it is a "healthy" one), or from some other existing budget line. Of course, your own budget may have restrictions built into it which prevent this from becoming a possibility.

8. Obtain consortia prices if possible. If your library is not formally a member of such a group, see what libraries in your area are interested in some group orders for group (reduced) prices. This will depend on the number and type of libraries in your immediate geographic area, your relationship with such libraries, the possibility of the strength of your massed order, and the interest of the CD-ROM publisher.

9. Buy cooperatively with other libraries. Users don't like this and neither do we as librarians (we all prefer everything at our fingertips!), but perhaps you can order one CD-ROM service and a nearby library order another compatible title. Variables will depend on the proximity of other libraries, your ability to cooperate and share resource availability as well as the actual materials, and the inclination/ability of your users to travel to these other libraries.

10. Become a test site. This should provide for a free placement or at least some reduction in price. Unfortunately, this will only be possible with new products, which may be more specialized or esoteric than your service population requires; it also does not help you in funding the often more desirable general titles available in CD-ROM format right now.

11. Do more reviewing of print sources. Assuming that the reference department will keep a complimentary copy for each review written, this may be a method to assist in trying to keep up with the basic print titles, while freeing some money for something new, such as CD-ROM. However, given current pricing, money recovered from print sources will have to involve lots of reviewing (or at

least the reviewing of expensive titles) to provide any amount worth applying to CD-ROM purchase or lease.

12. Be more selective with reference titles in print format. Reference librarians will have to (if it's not already been done) scrutinize their titles very carefully, retaining only titles with multiple purposes or with heavy potential use, for a more "tailor-made" collection. Library faculty will have to be more ruthless as well as more cooperative than when acquisitions money flowed more freely — each of us in a reference department will have to give up several "old friends" if another source will provide for similar or better use, is less expensive or fulfills multiple objectives. Your department may already have fine-tuned its collection when reference budgets dropped earlier. If not, this may be a good reason to not only refine the collection (fewer titles, but each more heavily used), but to work to free up additional funds for other purposes, such as CD-ROM products.

13. Rotate renewals of print titles by year. Related to the above suggestion, this would allow for the reallocation of reference monies by decisions to renew titles on a less frequent schedule: renew title w every x years, renew title y every z years, etc. If this is already being implemented in your library, this is not helpful for funding CD-ROM and it must also be balanced carefully against damage to the collection's usefulness or relevancy to our reference users. Another consideration is whether or not your ordering process is automated; built-in variations for ordering frequencies would then be possible, but could be overwhelming if attempted on a strictly manual basis.

More Controversial Scenarios

14. Fund print and nonprint (CD-ROM) in some clearly defined proportion. CD-ROM users like this new format and will use it while many excellent print sources sit on the shelves despite their potential value and great cost. Deciding on what proportion will be difficult and must be balanced against the same variables weighed in suggestions 12 and 13, for example.

15. Alter/implement fee structures elsewhere in the library to generate funds for CD-ROM. This could involve the charge back

for online database searches, interlibrary loan charges (for copied pages, for each interaction, etc.), for overdue fines, for lost materials/processing fees, or for a "borrower's" card (for borrowing privileges extended to other than your service clientele, such as the local non-university affiliated individual). This will obviously require careful deliberation with other members of the library staff, but may be a way to legitimately finance an informational source accessible to all of your users, especially if some of your fees are out of date and need to be reexamined anyway. Of prime consideration here is which collected fees return ultimately to the library budget; some may go instead into general university accounts, and if so, will not directly assist you in the location of new monies.

FITTING CD-ROM FUNDING INTO THE PERMANENT BUDGET

As with any recurring library expense, CD-ROM services must find a niche in the normal budgeting process; funds for it cannot be located ad hoc each year. The decisions on how and where to permanently fund these informational sources should involve more than just reference personnel, for we are dealing with SUBSCRIPTIONS (CD-ROM titles), EQUIPMENT or LEASES (the workstation) and SUPPLIES (paper, printer ribbons, etc.). Complete justifications for placement of these items may be made within the reference budget as well as outside of reference. Consequently, the entire library budget may need to be reexamined to locate the best area of the budget to support these new expenses. More than just reference personnel must be convinced of the usefulness of CD-ROM for our library users and a trial period of such sources (as described earlier) should be beneficial in that respect.

Concurrent to location of permanent funding for CD-ROM, which might ultimately involve seeking monies outside of the existing budget, is a reexamination, especially for state-assisted academic libraries, of our local commitment to archival/preservation goals. As always, our responsibility to the future must be weighed against our duty to provide adequate informational services to our present users. For many of us, preservation of the historic record may not be supported as heavily as it was in the past, primarily due to our limited budgets for materials, the explosion of informational sources and our expanding service populations. Local decisions will have to be painfully made, again as a unified library staff, as to the focus of our collections. Hopefully, the ability to select cooperatively and share those collections (enhanced by OCLC and other networking systems) by direct loan or through interlibrary loan, will make these collection development decisions a bit easier to make.

CD-ROM, like online databases and other reference sources of current and convenient information, must be made available to our users, despite limited budgets. Like microfilm and microfiche years ago, this is another new informational format that must be funded. It is our responsibility as information professionals to creatively seek the methods by which they can be provided for our users. Again, Beltran appropriately urges each of us to action in locating the necessary funds for this new informational source:

> What we must *not* do is allow officers and agencies outside the library to define our responsibility in terms of the past alone. Nor must we fail ourselves or the public with narrow, self-imposed budget categories. We must not use those budget categories as excuses for inaction.[11]

HOPE FOR THE FUTURE?

What *can* we hope for with regard to reference budgets in the future? Realistically, not drops in book, subscription or service costs or even fatter budgets from our state legislatures anytime soon. But reference librarians, by their inclination and professional training, are well-equipped to handle the funding problem CD-ROM presents. We work daily as creative problem solvers, whether for ourselves or for our users, and as such should be able to effectively approach *how* we are to permanently provide CD-ROM and other new informational services for our users. I have every confidence that in these extraordinary times of decreasing funds and increasing formats, reference faculty, in accord with their non-reference colleagues, can make the decisions and take the actions that are required to continue fulfilling our mission as information providers in an academic setting.

My biggest hope for the future is that higher education and education (K-12) can forget their old quarrels and begin to *cooperate* in their pursuit of state funds and public support instead of being in *competition* for the same. As Abrams[12] convincingly illustrates in his article, education seen as a whole has much more to gain than it does by remaining split into two warring factions, forcing the public to choose between them. If academic libraries, and in turn, reference departments, *ever* hope to receive the kind of financial support they require and desire, working for a unified and cooperative education lobby may be the only way to achieve that dream. The desire for CD-ROM services with their large price tags, in conjunction with other pressing university needs, may be the push we need in higher education to brush off our negotiating skills and think about approaching elementary and secondary education as our friends and allies.

REFERENCES

1. Some examples are: Ann Bristow Beltran, "Funding Computer-Assisted Reference in Academic Research Libraries," *Journal of Academic Librarianship*, 13(March 1987): 4-7. W. Fisher, D. Ingebretsen, T. Portilla and M. Waters, "Reference Sources and Services: Four Current Issues," *Reference Services Review*, 15(Summer 1987): 33-36. Virginia Moreland, "Online Searching in Times of Retrenchment: An Informal Survey of Regional Academic Libraries," ED 276 458: 145-157. Sandra Sinsel Leach, "Optical Disk—The Electronic Library Arrives," *The Reference Librarian*, 15 (Fall 1986): 251-268. Mary Boulanger, "Online Services at the Reference Desk: New Technologies vs. Old Problems," *The Reference Librarian*, 15(Fall 1986): 269-275.

2. Two examples: Nancy R. Posel, "Reference Books Costs: 'Pricing Us Out of the Market,'" *American Libraries*, 16(July/August 1985): 506-507. Heather S. Miller, "Keeping the Lid On: Approaches to the Control of Costs in Reference Book Purchasing in an Academic Library," *The Reference Librarian*, 15(Fall 1986): 281-302.

3. Beltran, p.7.

4. For this, see: Beltran; and Jay M. Poole and Gloriana St. Clair, "Funding Online Services From the Materials Budget," *College and Research Libraries*, 47(May 1986): 225-229; and Sheila Dowd, John H. Whaley, Jr., and Marcia Pankake, "Reactions to 'Funding Online Services From the Materials Budget,'" *College and Research Libraries*, 47(May 1986): 230-237.

5. *The Book of the States: 1986-87 edition*. Lexington: The Council of State Governments, 1986, p.76. (See also p.76-81 for additional information on state legislatures.)

6. *The Book of the States*, p.220-222.

7. For an excellent treatment of this fierce competition: Douglas M. Abrams, "Political Competition and Cooperation Between Public and Higher Education Agencies of State Government," *Journal of Education Finance*, 12(Winter 1987): 369-390.

8. If you doubt that this rivalry exists, you have only to read accounts in your local newspaper of state politics (and especially in the newspaper from your state capital) when the budget is being hammered out. In most states, the war between education and higher education is very real and bitter.

9. L. Edward Purcell, ed. and Thad L. Beyle, ed., "The Governors and Higher Education," *State Government*, 58(Summer 1985): 52p.

10. Scott Jaschie, "Somehow, Higher-Education Budget Officers Must Reconcile Politics, Reality," *Chronicle of Higher Education*, 33(June 24, 1987): 17,22.

11. Beltran, p.7.

12. Abrams.

Elasticity and Journal Pricing

Mark Bebensee
Bruce Strauch
Katina Strauch

SUMMARY. Over the last ten years, academic libraries have begun to spend nearly half of their annual budgets on journals. This figure has risen from an earlier 28% share at the same time that total library budgets have quadrupled. What is the cause of such a trend? This article deals with the economic concepts of elasticity and inelasticity of demand as applied to academic journal prices and explains how a strong demand for a product will cause nearly the same quantity to be purchased despite increases in price. Having recognized this, journal publishers are able to increase their total revenue by raising prices and betting correctly that the lessening in demand will be slight. Having defined the issues, the authors suggest econometric studies as a means of dealing with them.

INTRODUCTION

One of the biggest budgetary problems facing librarians today is the rising cost of subscriptions to scholarly and professional journals, especially those which are scientific and technical.[1] Over the last ten years, the average price of a one-year subscription to a journal has risen, in total, by 190%, or 19% per year.[2]

In cases where a library's total acquisition budget has increased less rapidly than these subscription prices, a library is faced with the dilemma of either reducing the number of journal subscriptions it purchases or spending fewer dollars on books in order to be able to

---

Mark Bebensee is Associate Professor and Bruce Strauch is Associate Professor, Department of Business Administration, The Citadel, Charleston, SC 29409. Katina Strauch is Head, Collection Development, College of Charleston Library, Charleston, SC 29424.

219

afford the same number of journal subscriptions as before. Indeed, figures for academic library acquisition expenditures for periodicals, as reported in the *Bowker Annual*, show an increase in the estimated percent of total acquisition from 28.2% (1975/76) to 44.54 (1987).[3]

In trying to understand the behavior of journal publishers, the economic concept of elasticity of demand becomes very important. What follows is an explanation of this concept and how it applies to the problem of rising journal subscription prices.

THE LAW OF DEMAND

In order to understand the concept of elasticity, one must first understand the so-called "law of demand." The law of demand simply says that as the price of a product *rises*, consumers will tend to purchase *less* of it; and as the price of a product *falls*, consumers will tend to purchase *more* of it, other things being equal. This "law" is commonly illustrated by a *demand curve* like the one pictured in Figure 1. When we plot the price of a journal subscription on the vertical axis and the quantity of subscriptions which

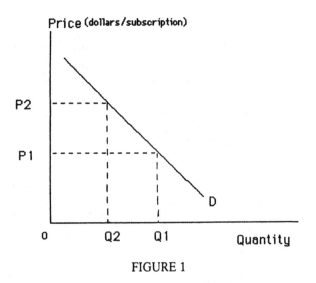

FIGURE 1

libraries will be willing and able to purchase on the horizontal axis, the resulting demand curve (or demand schedule, as it is sometimes called) shows that the relationship between price and quantity is inverse. In other words, price increases (such as from P1 to P2) cause fewer subscriptions to be demanded or purchased (shown by the movement from Q1 to Q2), and price decreases (P2 to P1) cause more subscriptions to be demanded (Q2 to Q1).

ELASTICITY

The concept of elasticity goes beyond the directional relationship embodied in the law of demand. Elasticity is a measure of *how responsive* quantity demanded is to a change in price. In other words, the law of demand tells us that if publishers increase subscription prices, then the number of subscriptions demanded will decrease. However, elasticity is a different but related concept. Elasticity concerns the *size* of that decrease in number of subscriptions demanded. Will a given price increase cause the number of subscriptions to decrease by a small amount or a large amount? More specifically, will the size of that subscription decrease be larger or smaller than the size of the price increase which caused it, in percentage terms? The two demand curves in Figure 2 illustrate this point. In each case, if the price of a subscription rises from P1 to P2, the number of subscriptions demanded decreases — this is the law of demand. The *sizes* of the decreases, however, are quite different. A demand curve such as the one labeled DA is not very responsive to the price increase. On the other hand, DB is extremely responsive to the price increase.

We can therefore conclude that the demand curve pictured in the right diagram (DB) is *more elastic* than the demand curve pictured on the left (DA).[4]

As mentioned above, the concept of elasticity is made more specific by considering the size of the price change in percentage terms relative to the size of the quantity change it produces, also in percentage terms. When the percentage change in quantity is *larger* than the percentage change in price which caused it, demand is said to be *elastic*. If the percentage change in quantity is *smaller* than the percentage change in price which caused it, demand is said to be

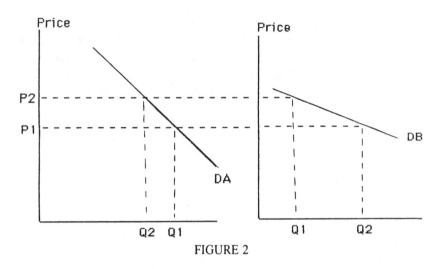

FIGURE 2

inelastic. In cases where the two percentage changes are equal, demand is said to be *unitary elastic*.

JOURNAL PRICING

At this point, the reader no doubt wonders why any of this matters! With the groundwork laid, we are now ready to look at the application of elasticity to the problem of rising journal prices. The primary way in which the concept of elasticity is used is to predict how a seller's *total revenue* will change when the price of a product is increased or decreased. Total revenue is the total number of dollars a seller receives from selling a certain amount of a product at a particular price. It is computed by multiplying the number of units sold by the selling price per unit. For example, if a publisher charges $100 per year for subscriptions to a particular journal, and if that publisher currently sells 40 subscriptions per year, then the total revenue generated by sales of that journal would be 40 times $100, or $4000 per year.

Total revenue, then, is the product of price times quantity. But the law of demand tells us that these two factors are inversely related—if price is increased, quantity demanded will fall; if price is decreased, quantity demanded will rise. If these two factors always move in opposite directions, then what will happen to their *product* when one of the factors (i.e., price) is changed? For example, suppose the publisher mentioned above decides to increase the price of subscriptions to his journal from $100 per year to $125 per year. The law of demand tells us that the number of subscriptions he can sell will decrease. What will happen to his total revenue, computed by price times quantity? Will it move in the direction of the price change (increase), or will it move in the direction of the quantity change (decrease)?

The answer is that the direction of the total revenue change will depend upon the elasticity of the demand for that journal. If that demand is *elastic*, then the quantity change is the relatively larger of the two changes (recall the definition of "elastic" given above), and total revenue will therefore follow that larger change and *decrease*.

On the other hand, if demand for that journal is *inelastic* then the price change is the stronger of the two changes, and total revenue will follow that larger change and will *increase*. In order to more clearly understand how this works, consider Equation [1] below:

$$[1] \; P\,(\uparrow) \times Q\,(\downarrow) = TR\,(\uparrow?\downarrow?)$$

As the arrows indicate, when price (P) rises, quantity demanded (Q) will fall (law of demand again). The price change is putting upward pressure on total revenue (TR), but at the same time the quantity decrease is putting downward pressure on TR. Will TR follow price and go up, or will it follow quantity and go down? The answer is that it depends upon which of the two changes is *stronger*, and strength here is measured in terms of percentage change. The process can be thought of as a "tug-of-war" between price and quantity, with total revenue being pulled in the direction of the stronger "pull." Elasticity is a concept which tells us which "pull" is stronger. When demand is *elastic*, that means that *quantity* is the stronger "pull"; when demand is *inelastic*, that means *price* is the stronger "pull."

JOURNAL PUBLISHERS

Journal publishers are assuming that the demand for subscriptions is inelastic. When they raise subscription prices, they know that because of the law of demand, the quantity of subscribers will decrease; but if the demand is inelastic, then that decrease in the number of subscriptions will be smaller in percentage terms than the increase in price, so publishers' total revenue will increase as it follows the larger price change. In other words, publishers will now be taking in a larger amount of dollars, and at the same time they will have to produce a smaller number of copies of the journal. With revenues increasing and costs decreasing, profits obviously have to increase. As long as the demand for journal subscriptions is inelastic, the decision of publishers to increase prices is not only rational, but quite desirable (from their point of view)!

INELASTICITY

Are librarians, then, doomed to face ever-increasing subscription prices as profit-maximizing publishers seek continually to increase profits?

If the total demand for journal subscriptions were indeed inelastic throughout the range of all possible prices, then the answer would be an unfortunate "yes."

Fortunately, however (at least for librarians), there should be a limit to how far publishers can go with this behavior. It is probably true that the demand for subscriptions to most scholarly and professional journals is relatively inelastic. This is because there are few close substitutes for many of these journals, particularly in the minds of the libraries' clientele. When a product has few close substitutes, then its demand will be relatively inelastic because its consumers will feel that the product is necessary regardless of what it costs. The demand is therefore not very responsive to price changes (the definition of "inelastic"). For instance, it would be hard to convince most economists that if the price of a subscription to *The American Economic Review* goes up, then some other journal would serve their purposes just as well!

However, as long as the demand for these journals is not "perfectly" inelastic, then there will be a limit to how far publishers can take their price increases. ("Perfectly" inelastic means that the demand for a product is constant; the quantity demanded does not vary at all, regardless of what price is charged.) It is a consequence of mathematics that many relatively inelastic demands will eventually become elastic when the price gets high enough. An intuitive understanding of this phenomenon can be illustrated using the diagram in Figure 3.

For a price increase of P1 to P2, the resulting change in quantity is small in percentage terms—a change of Q1 to Q2 is a small *percentage* of the total quantity still being purchased (Q2), whereas the price change associated with that quantity change, P1 to P2, is a very large price increase in *percentage* terms.

The percentage change in quantity is therefore smaller than the percentage change in price which caused it, so demand is inelastic. Publishers could increase their total revenue by raising subscription prices. But if the price were increased from P3 to P4 (a small percentage of the new price P4), the resulting quantity decrease (Q3 to Q4) is quite large in percentage terms—the distance (Q3 to Q4) represents a very large percentage of the new quantity Q4. Demand in the price range P3 to P is therefore *elastic*, and when publishers

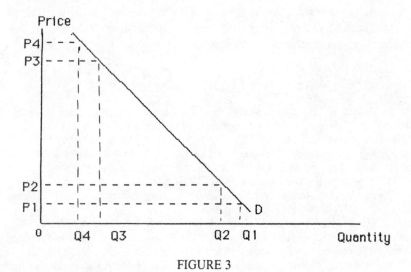

FIGURE 3

raise subscription prices, their total revenue will now fall as it follows the stronger change (i.e., quantity) downward.

CONCLUSION

The conclusion, then, is that subscription rate increases will only increase publishers' total revenue as long as demand for their journals is *inelastic*. Once rising prices put publishers in the *elastic* portion of their demand curve, price increases become counterproductive—total revenue begins to fall rather than rise. If publishers could find the price at which their respective demands change from inelastic to elastic, then they would have found the price at which total revenue would be maximized.[5]

Econometrics is a special branch of mathematics that is used in trying to quantify economic relationships. There is clearly a need for econometric studies which attempt to estimate the demand curves for various types of scholarly and professional journals, along with their corresponding elasticities. Publishers could use this information to help maximize their profits, and libraries could use the same information to have an idea about where prices of particular journals might be expected to level off. And if this research shows some publishers that they have gone too far with subscription price increases, i.e., that they have moved into the elastic portion of their demand curves, then libraries might also expect to see *decreases* in the prices of some journals.

REFERENCES

1. Hamaker, Charles and Astle, Deana, "Recent Pricing Patterns in British Journal Publishing," *Library Acquisitions: Practice and Theory* 8(1984): 225-232; Boissonnas, Christian M. "Pricing and Costs of Monographs and Serials," in *Pricing and Costs of Monographs and Serials, National and International Issues*. Sul L. Lee, Editor, (Supplement #1, *Journal of Library Administration* 8 [1987]), New York: The Haworth Press, 1987, p. 68.

2. *The Bowker Annual of Library & Book Trade Information, 33rd edition, 1988*, (New York: Bowker, 1988), p.426.

3. *The Bowker Annual of Library & Book Trade Information, 23rd edition, 1978*, (New York: Bowker, 1978), p.242; *The Bowker Annual of Library & Book Trade Information, 33rd edition, 1988*, (New York: Bowker, 1988), p.350.

4. Technically speaking, in order to make elasticity comparisons between two

different demand curves, the units in which price and quantity are measured on each graph must be the same.

5. It should be noted that "total revenue" and "total profit" are not synonymous, but since the additional cost of producting a few more copies of any issue is relatively low, profit (i.e., revenue minus cost) is not very different from revenue once fixed costs are covered.

Cancelling Periodicals in the Context of an Unallocated Budget

Dora Biblarz

SUMMARY. The Arizona State University Libraries have evolved, in the short time since becoming a PhD-granting institution, from a faculty selection model of collection shaping to the collection management approach, which includes full-time librarians in charge of policy making and planning, collection analysis and fiscal management. The book budget is not sub-allocated by discipline, which allows a great deal of flexibility. The recent budget crunch felt by ASU, along with other North American libraries, resulted in a review of currently-received periodicals in order to target titles for possible cancellation. One of the consequences of the tighter budget is the increasing popularity of investigating the sub-allocation of book funds. The collection development policy statement contains valuable data that can be used as the basis for analyzing priorities and making sub-allocations.

Arizona State University actually became a PhD-granting institution relatively recently, in 1959, and has had adequate book budgets only in the past dozen years. The growth of the University was not matched with steady, proportional growth in academic support services, so elements such as library staffing were left unattended to until the noise from that "squeaky wheel" became institutionally unbearable.

This means that in the library there were never sufficient personnel to share the workload, especially in the area of collection development. By the late 1970s several attempts had been made to identify problems connected with the execution of collection shaping

---

Dora Biblarz is Associate Dean of Libraries for Collection Development, Arizona State University Libraries, Tempe, AZ 85287.

229

activities: faculty involvement was uneven and unpredictable; they were stretched to the maximum of their abilities and could not devote time on a regular basis to selection of books. Personnel in the library had more or less interest, time, or inclination towards collection development.

The strategy followed by the library administration at that time was to invest heavily in the approval plan in order to receive as many publications as could be purchased with the minimum of human labor expended on selection and ordering.

The consequences were typical: the approval plan did not provide information to predict which titles were coming in; obvious imprints were missed completely (e.g., university presses); if no one monitored receipts carefully, unwanted titles entered the collection. Titles not received automatically right after publication could be missed altogether; by the time their absence was noticed (or pointed out by an angry faculty member), they had gone out of print.

As is also common with approval plans, the profile was drawn up by one or two people in the library who went systematically through the vendor's subject descriptors and identified the subjects needing coverage. There were no data available to indicate the level of library support required by the academic or research programs, priorities, or directions of the University.

The system of assigning collection development responsibilities to subject specialists was already in place, but the actual assignments were based less on expertise or background and more on what was needed and who was available on the existing staff at that time. Subject specialists were given responsibilities by academic department, but no consistent way existed of finding out what the departments needed or wanted from the library.

COLLECTION DEVELOPMENT ORGANIZATION

In the early 1980s, two important steps were taken to strengthen the use of collection management principles. One was the policy of hiring subject specialists to fit the needs of disciplines in which collection development was to be part of the assignment. Subject specialists are defined as librarians with subject expertise and/or degree(s) who were hired to work in a primary department (e.g., reference or cataloging) or be the head of a branch, and also perform duties in five additional areas: collection development, online searching, instruction, specialized reference, and liaison with the academic department(s). The nature of the subject and types of demands made by the particular users are reflected in the amount of time demanded by each part of the assignment; however, until recently, no efforts were made to specify the amount of time each subject specialist should devote to the activity.

The subject specialists are linked to the Collection Development Division via the three full-time coordinators (Science/Engineering, Humanities, and Social Sciences), who train new selectors and oversee their collection shaping activities within the broad areas. They also conduct or supervise special analysis or research projects.

This organizational pattern is fairly common and its advantages and drawbacks are well documented by Bryant[1] and Sohn.[2] The latter clearly articulates the current situation at the ASU Libraries: on one hand, collection management concepts are accepted and can finally be supported by the automated systems; on the other, subject specialists who are responsible for a variety of assignments, are depended upon for the execution of projects which require a great deal of time. When so many demands are placed on them, they can become dissatisfied with their jobs.

The three coordinators are the only full-time librarians devoted to collection management as their primary activity and report to the Associate Dean for Collection Development. Their duties include all eight principal functions of effective collection management described by Cogswell:[3] planning and policy making, collection analysis, materials selection, collection maintenance, fiscal management, user liaison, program evaluation, and resource sharing.

COLLECTION DEVELOPMENT POLICY STATEMENT

The other major step taken in the early 1980s was the launching of a long-term project of collection and program analysis for the purpose of writing a collection development policy statement.

As a fundamental principle, the hypothesis adopted was that academic and research needs can be adequately, if roughly represented by the LC classification system and subject headings. This system was selected because it constitutes a "lingua franca" of the library; a means of comparing needs with actual resources, using the same terminology.

Each subject specialist was instructed in the method of classifying the courses in his/her area of responsibility. The results formed a computer database, capable of being sorted into lists of LC class numbers or ranges, course number, course title, department and selector responsible, and LC subject heading corresponding to class number.[4]

These lists made it possible to see natural ranges indicating logical cutoff points, which formed the basis for the groupings used today. While these ranges are not identical with NCIP conspectus categories, they do fit in to the conspectus and the National Shelflist Count and are thus flexible for use in collection analyses.

The *Collection Development Policy Statement* (CDPS) is now a reality.[5] The Preliminary Edition was published in October, 1987, and regular revisions are planned. This document represents the best efforts of the subject specialists and coordinators to define the strengths and weaknesses of the collection at the time of analysis. It is based on the University of California, Berkeley model[6] and contains narrative policies in the first part. The second part is a listing, in LC class order, of the ranges, locations, levels (using modified NCIP terminology), and language codes. The level of the existing collection is represented in one column, while the one next to it identifies the level of support that should be devoted to that area if the library resources were adequate to meet all current and anticipated (known) curriculum and research needs. The gap between the two levels, e.g., 2-3B, reveals which areas of the collection are in the best shape and which need attention. This gap is therefore critical and it indicates, like a flashing arrow, which areas require further analysis.

The work that went into the preparation of the CDPS had many benefits, such as providing the information for more clearly and sharply defined collection management assignments in the LC class "language." As the research needs of the University are identified in further detail and documented in compatible terminology, the plan is to integrate them into the document more prominently and therefore systematically include research in the analysis of need.

Hiring subject specialists with experience and/or advanced degrees in their subject, as well as reassigning some areas internally brought an important new factor to bear on the collection development program. Approval and blanket order profiles were reviewed and revised; new ones placed, and others eliminated or replaced. An aggressive out-of-print search operation was launched and several subject specialists conducted assessments and generated desiderata lists.

BOOK BUDGET

The unallocated book budget was instituted at the ASU Libraries more than 20 years ago. "Unallocated" means that instead of small sums assigned to individual departments or selectors, the budget has been divided up by format, in categories like approval plans, blanket orders, firm orders, periodical renewals, etc.

Some of the advantages experienced with this system include a high degree of flexibility toward the support of new or expanding programs or areas of emphasis to keep up with a rapidly growing institution; there is flexibility also when personnel change jobs and subjects are left vacant six months or more while the search goes on for a replacement. Another advantage is the ability to avoid the scramble at the end of the year, either to spend out the remaining allocations or to scrape together funds to purchase an unanticipated but greatly needed title. Finally, there is the flexibility to cover multi-disciplinary fields that require attention from many selectors.

As long as there is enough money for people to spend, there are no complaints. As soon as more than 50% of the budget is spent on continuing commitments, the demand quickly outpaces the available funds. As a result of the budget crunch at ASU, faculty requests and orders from the subject specialists easily spent the meager firm order funds early in the academic year 1987/88 and little or nothing was left for satisfying any but the most urgent requests for the remainder of the year.

Some of the disadvantages experienced with the unallocated budget system include the sense of insecurity some selectors feel about their pace and level of expenditure, especially newly hired librarians used to allocations. While the coordinators regularly review the incoming requests and discuss any questions or problems with the selectors, this was felt to be insufficient monitoring in the years of the budget crunch. The fear remains that a few eager selectors with lots of time on their hands will "take over" and place orders for a larger proportion of the available funds than is theoretically "fair." This would mean that the subject specialists who have other, more immediate time commitments, cannot select and order as much as their discipline "rightfully" deserves.

Collection development personnel are challenged to show objective methods of monitoring the activities of selectors under the unallocated system. It is not possible to answer questions about the support each discipline is receiving (in the present or abstract future), all we can do is point to past activity, inasmuch as documentation and management reports exist to record this support after the fact. With an unallocated system it is also more difficult to demonstrate specifically by discipline how current funding is inadequate to keep up with the demand.

Until recently, the Libraries did not have the means to report accurately and promptly the status of more detailed budget breakdowns. The new automated acquisitions system provides the option of tracking expenditures with many sub-categories, making allocation setting and monitoring now possible.

BUDGET CRUNCH

Like many other North American libraries, the ASUL have been feeling the combined effects of inadequate increases from the legislature and higher than anticipated costs for certain materials due to inflation and the devaluation of the dollar. Recent internal organizational changes also had an impact on the way the book budget was reported and expended.

When it became clear in the early fall, 1987, that it would take close to 60% of the available book funds to pay the serials and renewals (i.e., continuing commitments), the discussion of how to deal with the problem began.

The new serials check-in system allows the listing of periodicals and serials by call number. By differentiating between periodicals and serials and between "live" and "dead" titles, it was possible to generate a list of titles eligible for cancellation. Before the list could be produced, it was necessary to complete the project of conversion of all live periodicals into machine readable form. This project was completed by the Acquisitions Department at the end of the calendar year, 1987. In January, the project began.

The periodical review project involved listing all titles in LC call number order; then the call numbers were divided up by assigned ranges and distributed to selectors according to their area of responsibility. Each subject specialist was given two targets: one 5% list and one 10% of the total amount assigned to the subject. Two targets were required since no one knew how much the legislature would appropriate for the 1988/89 book budget and how much would be needed to pay 1989 renewals and still be able to maintain some of the book funds for other types of materials.

Subject specialists were asked to work with their faculty representatives and/or committees to review and comment on the potential titles on each list. The lists they came up with were reviewed by the faculty representative, other faculty members in the department, faculty in other departments, and by the subject specialists and other librarians. Titles that were important to other disciplines were thus discovered and, in some cases, taken off the lists because they were needed for the support of those programs. After much discussion and review during the spring semester, the lists were ready. This project was very visible on the campus: it received quite a bit of publicity and the general outcry of protest against having to cancel any titles was almost unanimous from faculty, students, and administrators.

At the end of the spring semester, the deans decided to pool together funds from all their areas and contribute a "one-time only" sum to the library to help mitigate the impact of the inflation problem. When the legislature determined the allocation for all three Arizona Universities in June, it was clear that there was not a sufficient increase to retain the same level of purchasing power in all areas, compared to last year. When the new Provost/Vice President for Academic Affairs came on board shortly after, he also gave the library some one-time funds to help in this crisis.

CONSEQUENCES

The consequences of a cancellation project such as this have been positive: at ASU, the Faculty Senate approved a resolution commending the Deans for their action at the end of the academic year. There was general support for the library and outrage for the shocking actions of price-gouging publishers who were seen as responsible for the current dilemma.

Nationally, faculty members who are also on editorial boards of scholarly or research journals were encouraged to bring the same questions of ethics to the attention of the boards. Perhaps the outcry served to alert publishers and some may even keep from raising prices above and beyond reasonable inflationary factors.

The consequences for ASU had many positive public relations elements, but for the Libraries the results were mixed (at least from this time perspective): The automated serials check-in system generated its first major list; unfortunately, many prices and call numbers were missing. Selectors were asked to provide lists of suggested titles for each cutting target, but many had to look up the missing information and fill in total costs and target amounts themselves. They complained about the short time frame, as the project could only be done during spring semester so that the faculty had time to approve the titles before they dispersed for the summer. In this way, the lists could be ready right after July 1st for the earliest renewal invoices of the new fiscal year.

This project required a great deal of liaison and each subject specialist handled that according to his/her level of experience and comfort with the assignment. The concentrated commitment of time and energy required for this project also focused attention on the "push-me pull-you" effects of collection management demands versus available time mentioned earlier.

While the pressure has been alleviated, the budget crunch has not disappeared. The titles identified on the 5% list were, for a large majority of the cases, judged to be marginal in support of current academic and research programs. Whenever a title was questioned by anyone for any reason, it was removed from the list. Subject specialists were asked to review this remaining list to see if there were any that should *not* be canceled for any other reasons. The resulting titles may now be canceled and the dollars "saved" may be used to add new titles to the collection.

In the fall the Acquisitions Department will record the cancellations and keep track of the actual invoice amount for each title; that amount will be "credited" to the selector whose area the cancellation falls in so that new titles may be purchased. Since no new periodical titles have been ordered for two years and previous years were conservatively budgeted in this category, this will be a great relief for many disciplines which are falling behind in their ability to keep up with research.

Another consequence of this budget crisis is the increasing support for the concept of sub-allocation by discipline: now the CDPS is available for a new application. This document contains all the elements necessary for determining the academic program and research support currently provided by the library, and actually needed. The gap between current and ideal support can be quantified and used in combination with use and user studies. The assessment of the relevant percentage of the publication base available to support the subject at the desired level is the next step in the sub-allocation process, but harder to determine. These elements address the six procedural rules of fairness identified by Schad as required elements of any allocation process.[7]

The ASU Libraries haven't worked with allocations for so long that we don't have to overcome lots of obstacles, address prejudices or attack assumptions. The value of the CDPS as the philosophical and practical base of the allocation process seems self-evident. Now the challenge is to make the best of it and keep refining the tool. This is a perfect time to bring out a new approach to the subject of allocations; perhaps with a more systematic and objective methodology we can plan more effectively for the building of balanced and well-shaped collections.

REFERENCES

1. Bryant, Bonita, "The Organizational Structure of Collection Development," *Library Resources and Technical Services*, 31:111-22 (April/June 1987).

2. Sohn, Jeanne, "Collection Development Organizational Patterns in ARL Libraries," *Library Resources and Technical Services*, 31:123-33 (April/June 1987).

3. Cogswell, James A., "The Organization of Collection Management Functions in Academic Research Libraries," *The Journal of Academic Librarianship*, 13:268-76 (November 1987).

4. Palais, Elliot, "Use of Course Analysis in Compiling a Collection Development Policy Statement for a University Library," *The Journal of Academic Librarianship*, 13:8-13 (March 1987).

5. *Arizona State University Libraries Collection Development Policy Statement.* (Tempe, AZ: ASU Libraries, 1987.)

6. *Collection Development Policy Statement.* (Berkeley, CA: University of California, General Library, 1980.)

7. Schad, Jasper G., "Fairness in Book Fund Allocation," *College & Research Libraries*, 48:479-86 (November 1987).

Preservation Decision-Making Basics: A University Library Collection Developer's Perspective

Anthony W. Ferguson

SUMMARY. Preservation decisions, whether to fix, film, replace, defer, or weed, are resource allocation decisions. Collection development librarians should be involved because the decision to retain is as important as the decision to purchase. Decisions about what should be preserved in academic libraries should be made by materials selectors, preservation librarians who base their techniques on work done by materials preservation scientists, and the faculty. Not only should brittle or structurally unsound materials identified by library users be preserved but collection development librarians should also incorporate systematic condition evaluations into their collection development/assessment programs. What items merit the expenditure of funds should be based upon a systematic examination of the suitability and cost of conservation treatments or the availability, suitability and cost of variant printings, editions, or formats.

Ultimately, in academic library preservation work, decision making is resource allocation. Decisions about preserving library research materials, whether to take or defer action, are some of the most significant budgetary activities in which collection managers can be involved. If they decide to fix, film or replace an item, they incur human resources costs related to selecting it, checking it out and transporting it to an in-house bindery or filming operation; the

Anthony W. Ferguson is Director of the Library Resources Group, Columbia University, New York, NY 10027.

This paper is based upon a talk, "What to Preserve: A Collection Developer's Perspective," presented at METRO sponsored "Fundamentals of Preservation" workshop, New York City, April 11, 1988.

239

actual fixing or filming costs, whether done internally or sent out to a commercial vendor; the costs associated with changing the bibliographic record if reformatting has been involved; and the costs of either returning the newly-bound item or its film equivalent to the shelf. Developing procedures to govern these processes, training staff members to follow them, and informing users about why these steps are necessary, etc., all have costs associated with them. Even if we defer the fix, film or replace alternatives or even discard the item, costs are still incurred. Preservation, directly or indirectly, can significantly impact the library's budget. However, if the integrity of the collection is to be maintained, if the capital investment which these materials represent is to be protected, these budget needs must ultimately be supported.

In order to maximize the cost effectiveness of these resource allocation decisions, collection managers/developers need to seriously consider three factors: who should be included in the decision-making process, how should candidates for preservation attention be detected, and what factors need to be considered when deciding what merits a preservation resource expenditure.

WHO SHOULD BE INVOLVED?

Up until now most preservation researchers have suggested that library preservation is a tripartite responsibility involving materials selectors, who are supposed to decide what to preserve; scientists, who develop techniques; and conservators, who interpret the available techniques in terms of what is needed.[1] Another participant, however, needs to be added: the faculty. They are important for three reasons. First, although they may not be an academic library's most numerous users, they are the most important users. Most of them use the collection at a greater depth and over a longer span of time than the more numerous students. Second, politically, their support is critical to the long-term growth and development of the library program. And third, the thrust of our preservation effort is to save today's books in behalf of tomorrow's users. Efforts to do something ''for'' others and not involve them in the effort are doomed to failure especially if reformatting is involved. Microfilm captures the intellectual content of an item but it does not contribute to the same sort of research experience that browsing among books and journals engenders. Making reformatting the faculty's decision is an imperative.

A commonly heard comment in libraries is that when librarians lack the requisite subject expertise, the faculty should be involved. Another standard view is that there should be a faculty-librarian partnership but with the faculty as silent partners because they are too busy with their own work to help the library. While this may be partially true, silent partnerships fail when the vocal partner fails to adequately consider the needs of the silent one. In politics the silent majority is occasionally heard from and it usually takes the existing power brokers by surprise. Preservation isn't the place for a silent partner. Columbia University mandates that discussions about basic preservation microfilm principles be discussed with the faculty and that systematic subject sweep preservation programs must have an organized ad hoc faculty advisory group in place for both the planning and operational phases. We have found that in some projects when the faculty are not sufficiently involved, an "us" and "them" relationship develops. The faculty become the "us" and we who have spent considerable sums on preserving their materials became the "them." In other projects, however, we have experienced productive relationships because the selection of materials was the faculty's responsibility and the library provided the technical support to make the project a reality. In this case there developed only an "us" group.[2] Bringing the faculty in on the decision-making process is one of the most significant challenges facing the library.

HOW SHOULD PRESERVATION CANDIDATES BE DETECTED?

Actually, we come across preservation needs at every point in the life of an item in our libraries: At the point of acquisition, when older materials purchased from a vendor are unpacked, or when gifts are reviewed we discover books with structural and brittle paper problems. If these items are overlooked by acquisitions staff they are discovered by our catalog librarians. Once on the shelf, existing problems yet undetected, or ones produced through use are brought to the attention of reference librarians, interlibrary loan officers, and circulation department staff by users. Serials librarians find problems when gathering materials for bindery shipments. All of these serve as sources of preservation work.

But if we allow these ad hoc means of identifying preservation candidates dominate us we will always be running to catch up and will underestimate the volume of the iceberg that lies beneath the tip that we are focusing our efforts upon. There are an additional two approaches to library materials preservation identification that should be employed. The first focuses directly upon preservation activities and the second has preservation as an integral part of a larger collection assessment program.

Typically, in the first approach, library forces interested in preservation conduct a library-wide condition survey to determine what subject areas seem to have the worst damage, deterioration, unstable bindings, or brittle paper problems. Ratios are developed to measure the percent of various subject categories that have these problems. Using this information as a foundation, committees of librarians, advised by users and based upon circulation statistics, ratios employing numbers of students, faculty, or research dollars being spent, etc., set priorities that direct future preservation activities. These priorities are in turn used to develop preservation proposals for funding agencies or to allocate internal supplies, space, and staffing resources. A variation of this model turns the decision-making process upside down. Collections are prioritized based largely upon non-preservation concerns in order to determine what subjects are most important to the library's mission. Condition surveys are then done within these priority collections to identify preservation problems which are then used to develop funding proposals and to make internal resource library allocation decisions.

A second major strategy integrates condition surveys within an overall collection assessment program. It grows out of a belief in two basic principles. First, the goal of the library is to have on its shelves materials that fill the needs of current and projected future users. Second, the decision to retain is as important as the decision to add. In order to follow both principles, the library materials selection officer has to not only be involved in a constant process of assessing patron and collection needs and adding, weeding or pruning unneeded materials, but also not subtracting through poor preservation practices those items that help fulfil users' needs. In the collection assessment process, the selector cannot stop with just finding out if the item needed to support a particular curricular or research requirement is in the collection, they have to go the extra step to find out if it is on the shelf, the condition it is in, and take actions to insure that it continues to serve the function for which it was originally purchased.

Actually, collection assessment methodologies and what have been thought of as pure preservation condition survey techniques are similar and complimentary. Both are interested in compiling statistics about the numbers of materials in subject collections by imprint date, national origin, and checking lists. Both involve direct observation of the collection as a basic methodology. In order to conduct availability and accessibility studies there is a need to go to the shelf and check statistically valid samples of materials in order to simulate the degree to which the patron will find what they need. These same samples can be used to assess the condition of the materials on the shelf. Circulation collection assessment studies designed to identify where more books need to be purchased can also be used to identify candidate areas for book repair sweeps. Periodical use studies can also have added to them checks on the number of unbound serials out in the stacks. At Columbia we have only recently completed a collection assessment techniques seminar for materials selectors. It is our plan that preservation components will be included in all collection assessments conducted by our collection development officers.

Another collection assessment-based approach which has preservation applications is the Conspectus. The Conspectus has until recently been seen as a collection development librarian's tool. Although initially developed as a resource sharing aid, the Conspectus is now going to be used in RLG to record subject collection-level descriptions of preservation actions undertaken by member libraries. Beyond this use, however, the Conspectus can serve as a bridge of common understanding between collection developers and those who have preservation as their focus. For example, the collection-depth indicators suggest that for minimum and basic information level collections, little or no historical support documents are retained. Consequently, expensive conservation or reformatting projects can be ruled out for collections at these levels and the emphasis placed on weeding damaged materials and replacing them with new editions or parallel treatments. Level Four research collections and Level Five comprehensive collections, on the other hand, specify that older materials are retained and this means that by definition, materials should be repaired when possible and affordable, or replaced with a reprint or film. Level Three study and teaching collections are more difficult to make decisions for. In some disciplines older editions are needed and for others, outdated information is unnecessary and in cases like nursing, viewed by many as dangerous.

Conspectus data can also be used as a source of important priority-generating ratios. For example, at Columbia, in order to gain a clearer sense of the relative importance of subject collections, we have examined the proportion of Conspectus lines referring to specific subject categories which have been judged to be Level Four research collections. A recent innovation has been the ARL development of a personal computer-based version of the Conspectus which allows the individual library to attach preservation related information, i.e., preservation priorities, a historical record of projects completed, number of items needing rebinding, etc., to the various Conspectus lines.

Whether preservation-specific methodologies or preservation as an integral part of collection assessment plans are used, unless an organized preservation master plan is developed to direct these efforts, it is easy for a library to begin preserving less important parts of their collections because the needs of these collections match the resources available or because outside funding agencies are willing to pay for the preservation of these collections. It is important for the library to decide what is important for its needs and then focus whatever resources are internally available, can be sought from outside sources, or obtained through cooperative preservation programs to address these needs.

WHAT MERITS PRESERVATION?

Whatever the technique employed to identify materials in need of preservation treatment, the materials selector and the relevant user group still have many other factors to consider before the library's preservation treatment of the material can begin. Wesley L. Boomgaarden from Ohio State University developed a very useful "Preservation Decision Flow Chart" which focuses on the needs, availability, appropriateness, and cost of a variety of preservation options: repair, full conservation of the original, deferred conservation, or replacement with a reprint or microfilm.[3] Those involved in making the preservation decision are given a variety of questions with preservation options suggested:

1. Is it important to retain the brittle item in some format?
2. Is it important to retain the original format?
3. Can the physical object item be treated using conservation techniques?
4. Is the treatment affordable?
5. Is a microform replacement suitable? available?
6. Is xerographic reproduction suitable? available?
7. Is the available replacement affordable?
8. Should treatment be deferred?

To pose and then answer these questions is time-consuming but in the long run necessary if the integrity of the collection is to be maintained.

CONCLUSION

It is popular for modern academic librarians to want to shuck the old image of being collection caretakers. Indeed, our profession has much more to offer. It is also important to recognize, however, that the collections we work with are the result of both our own and our predecessors' acquisitions activities and represent a tremendous investment by our institutions. Librarians come and go. Library buildings are constructed, become too small or outmoded and are replaced or remodeled, but the materials purchased annually live on. More correctly their contents, if not the original format, can live on if collection development librarians recognize the importance of integrating preservation into their overall collection management program. We need to join with our faculty and preservation librarians who in turn base their work on the efforts of materials preservation scientists, to maintain the value of our collections for future generations. We need to integrate collection condition analysis into all collection assessment programs. And we need to develop systematic procedures which evaluate the needs of users, the suitability and cost of conservation options, and availability appropriateness and cost of variant printings, editions, or formats when making preservation decisions.

REFERENCES

1. Swartzburg, Susan G. *Preserving Library Materials: A Manual*. Metuchen, NJ: The Scarecrow Press, 1980. pp. 3-5.

2. Bagnall, Roger S., and Harris, Carolyn L., "Involving Scholars in Preservation Decisions: The Case of the Classicist." *Journal of Academic Librarianship* 13(July 1987): 140-146.

3. *Preservation Microfilming: A Guide for Librarians and Archivists*, edited by Nancy E. Gwinn. Chicago: American Library Association, 1987. p.39.